THE NEW RELIGIONS
OF AFRICA

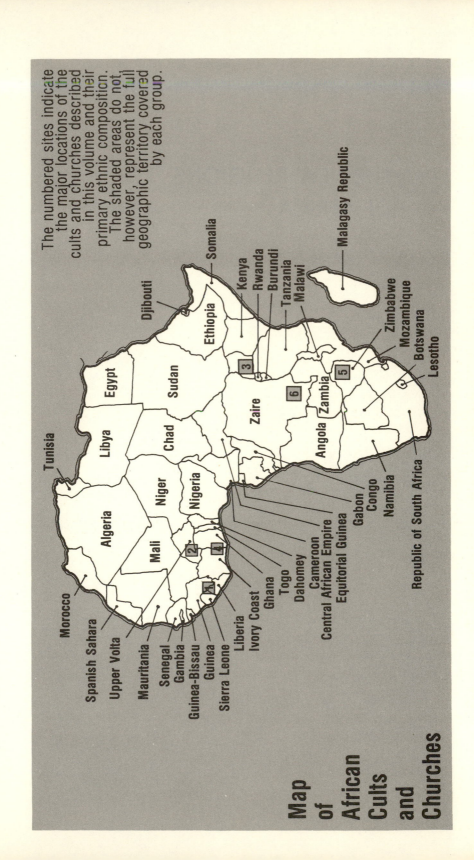

Map
of
African
Cults
and
Churches

The numbered sites indicate the major locations of the cults and churches described in this volume and their primary ethnic composition. The shaded areas do not, however, represent the full geographic territory covered by each group.

Tunisia

Morocco

Spanish Sahara

Upper Volta

Mauritania

Senegal

Gambia

Guinea-Bissau

Guinea

Sierra Leone

Liberia

Ivory Coast

Ghana

Togo

Dahomey

Cameroon

Central African Empire

Equitorial Guinea

Gabon

Congo

Namibia

Republic of South Africa

Morocco

Algeria

Mali

Niger

Libya

Chad

Nigeria

Egypt

Sudan

Ethiopia

Djibouti

Somalia

Kenya

Rwanda

Burundi

Tanzania

Malawi

Zaire

Zambia

Angola

Zimbabwe

Mozambique

Botswana

Lesotho

Malagasy Republic

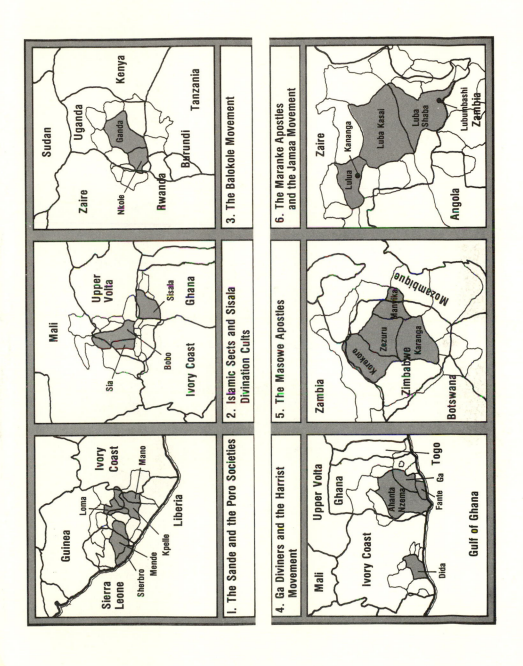

1. The Sande and the Poro Societies

Guinea
Ivory Coast
Mano
Loma
Sierra Leone
Sherbro
Mende
Kpelle
Liberia

2. Islamic Sects and Sisala Divination Cults

Mali
Upper Volta
Sisala
Ghana
Sia
Bobo
Ivory Coast

3. The Balokole Movement

Sudan
Uganda
Kenya
Ganda
Zaire
Nkole
Rwanda
Burundi
Tanzania

4. Ga Diviners and the Harrist Movement

Mali
Upper Volta
Ghana
Ivory Coast
Ahanta
Nzema
Fante
Ga
Togo
Dida
Gulf of Ghana

5. The Masowe Apostles

Zambia
Korekore
Zezuru
Manyika
Mozambique
Zimbabwe
Karanga
Botswana

6. The Maranke Apostles and the Jamaa Movement

Zaire
Lulua
Kananga
Luba Kasai
Luba Shaba
Lubumbashi
Zambia
Angola

MODERN SOCIOLOGY:
A Series of Monographs, Treatises, and Texts

Edited by
GERALD M. PLATT

THE
NEW RELIGIONS
OF AFRICA

Bennetta Jules-Rosette, *editor*

University of California, San Diego

Ablex Publishing Corporation
Norwood, New Jersey 07648

Copyright © 1979 by Ablex Publishing Corporation.

Printed in the United States of America.

Library of Congress Cataloging in Publication Data
Main entry under title:

The New religions of Africa.

   (Modern sociology)
   Bibliography: p.
   Includes index.
   1. Africa—Religion—Addresses, essays, lectures.
2. Cults—Africa—Addresses, essays, lectures.
I. Jules-Rosette, Bennetta. II. Series.
BL2400.N48   301.5′8   78-16925
ISBN 0-89391-014-7

ABLEX Publishing Corporation
355 Chestnut Street
Norwood, New Jersey 07648

*To the Founders and Leaders
of Africa's New Churches*

Contents

About the Contributors

BERYL L. BELLMAN, Assistant Professor of Sociology and Communications at the University of California, San Diego, is the author of *Village of Curers and Assassins: On the Production of Fala Kpelle Cosmological Categories* (Mouton, 1975) and co-author with Dr. Jules-Rosette of *A Paradigm for Looking: Cross-Cultural Research with Visual Media* (Ablex, 1977). His articles include: "Ethnohermeneutics" and "The Sociolinguistics of Ritual Performance." He received his Ph.D. from the University of California, Irvine. Dr. Bellman first worked in Africa between 1967–1969 and has since returned several times for shorter periods. He is currently completing a long-term study and monograph on Poro society initiation and informal education in Liberia.

PAUL S. BREIDENBACH received his Ph.D. in cultural anthropology from Northwestern University. He is currently Associate Professor of Anthropology at Loyola University of Chicago. He has conducted fieldwork on ritual communication in the Twelve Apostles Church of Ghana since 1970. He has written "*Sunsum Edumwa:* The Spiritual Work, Forms of Symbolic Action and Communication in a Ghanaian Healing Movement;" "Color Symbolism and Ideology in a Ghanaian Healing Movement," *Africa*; and "Spatial Juxtapositions and Belief Orientations in a Ghanaian Healing Church," *The Journal of Religion in Africa*. Dr. Breidenbach and his wife Martha also have made an ethnographic film of the *edumwa* ritual and are currently conducting research on Ghanaian popular theater and opera forms.

JOHANNES FABIAN received his Ph.D. in Anthropology from the University of Chicago. He did fieldwork in Zaire on the Jamaa movement in 1966–1967 and on conceptions of work and popular culture in 1972–1974. He has written *Jamaa: A Charismatic Movement in Katanga* (Northwestern, 1968) and numerous articles. He has taught at Northwestern University and at the National University of Zaire (Lubumbashi) as the director of the Social Science Division and is currently Associate Professor of Anthropology at Westleyan University.

JAMES W. FERNANDEZ is Professor of Anthropology at Princeton University. His research interests are cultural change, religion, and cognitive behavior. He has conducted fieldwork in Gabon, Cameroon, and Rio Muni (1958–1960), Natal (1965), Togo, Dahomey, and Ghana (1966), and Northern Spain (1971, 1972, 1976, 1978).

BENNETTA JULES-ROSETTE, Associate Professor of Sociology at the University of California, San Diego, received her Ph.D. in Sociology from Harvard University. Her publications include: *African Apostles: Ritual and Conversion in the Church of John Maranke; A Paradigm for Looking: Cross-Cultural Research with Visual Media*, co-authored with Beryl Bellman (Ablex, 1977); "The Conversion Experience," *Journal of Religion in Africa* (1976); and "Marrapodi: An Independent Religious Community in Transition," *African Studies Review* (1975). Since 1969, she has made several field trips to southwestern Zaire and Zambia to study contemporary African religious movements and the cultural transformations reflected in contemporary urban art forms in central and southern Africa.

CLIVE KILEFF is Assistant Professor of Sociology and Anthropology at the University of Tennessee, Chattanooga. He received his Ph.D. from Rice University (Behavioral Science) in 1970. His publications include: *Urban Man in Africa*, edited with Wade Pendleton (Mambo, 1970); "Rebirth of a Grandfather Spirit: Shumba in Two Worlds," *Human Organization* (1975).

MARGARET KILEFF has completed her graduate studies in psychology at the University of Tennessee, Chattanooga. She received her B.A. from the University of Houston in 1966 and did graduate work in behavioral science at Rice University from 1967–1970. Her publications include: *Shona Customs: Essays by African Writers*, edited with Clive Kileff. She conducted fieldwork on the Masowe Apostles in Rhodesia in 1972–1973.

MARION KILSON, Director of Research at the Radcliffe Institute, has done fieldwork in Sierra Leone (1960, 1972) and Ghana (1964–1965, 1968). Her publications include: *Kpele Lala: Ga Religious Songs and Symbols* (Harvard, 1971); *African Urban Kinsmen: The Ga of Central Accra* (St. Martin's, 1974); and *Royal Antelope and Spider: West African Mende Tales* (Langdon, 1976). She has taught in the Boston area at both Simmons College and Newton College in the Department of Sociology.

CAROL P. MacCORMACK received her Ph.D. in Anthropology from Bryn Mawr College. She has taught at Franklin and Marshall College and is presently Assistant Lecturer in Social Anthropology, University of Cambridge and a Fellow of New Hall. She conducted fieldwork in the Mende and Sherbro ethnic areas of Sierra Leone in 1969–1970, 1971, 1974, and 1976. Among her publications are: "Mende and Sherbro Women in High Office, *Canadian Journal of African Studies* (1972); "Madam Yoko: Ruler of the Kpa·Mende Confederacy," in Rosaldo and Lamphere, eds., *Women in Culture and Society* (Stanford, 1974); "Wono: Institutionalized Dependency in Sherbro Descent Groups," in Miers and Kopytoff, eds., *African Slavery: Historical and Anthropological Perspectives* (Wisconsin, 1976). She is one of the foremost authorities on women's secret societies in Sierra Leone.

EUGENE L. MENDONSA is presently Assistant Professor of Anthropology at the University of California, Los Angeles. He received his Ph.D. in Anthropology from Cambridge University. He has conducted field research among the Sisala of Northern Ghana. His publications include: "Characteristics of Sisala Diviners," in Bharati, Agananda, ed., *The Realm of Extra-Human Agents and Audiences*, Vol. 96, *World Anthropology* (Mouton, 1975); "The Journey of the Soul in Sisala Cosmology," *Journal of Religion in Africa* (1975); "Elders, Office-Holders and Ancestors Among the Sisala of Northern Ghana," *Africa* (1976).

LUCY QUIMBY received her Ph.D. from the University of Wisconsin. She has been Assistant Professor of History at the City College, City University of New York. She carried out fieldwork in Upper Volta in 1969–1970. Her major publications include: "History as Identity: The Jaaxunke and the Sounding of Tuuba," *Institute of African Studies Bulletin* (1975); "Symbols and Society in Muslim Society," review article, *African Studies Review* (1975).

CATHERINE ROBINS is a lecturer in Sociology at the University of Nairobi, and conducted fieldwork on the Balokole movement in Uganda in 1970–1972. She has taught at the California State University at Northridge and the University of Zambia, where she was Senior Lecturer in Sociology from 1975–1976. She received her Ph.D. in Sociology from Columbia University.

SHEILA S. WALKER, presently Assistant Professor in the Division of Higher Education, University of California, Berkeley, has a Ph.D. in Anthropology from the University of Chicago and an interdisciplinary background in the social sciences and religious studies. Her field research and doctoral dissertation on the Harrist Church in Ivory Coast focused on the church's role in the modernization process. Her other publications include: *Ceremonial Spirit Possession in Africa and Afro-America* (Brill, 1972); "Abomey Tapestries," *Essence* (1974); "Black English: Expression of the Afro-American Experience," *Black World* (1971), and numerous journal and magazine articles on panAfrican cultural transformations both in Africa and in the New World.

Foreword

James W. Fernandez

Princeton University

An observation from Sir Thomas Browne's *Religio Medici* comes to mind as an apt prologue to this illuminating book. He wrote "we carry with us the wonders we seek without us: there is all Africa and her prodigies in us." Though this was written at a time when Africa was, as it long continues to be, a mysterious projective screen for certain preoccupations of the European imagination, it may be applied to this collection of essays for a variety of reasons. First, there has indeed been a prodigious growth and spread of religious movements in Africa. Present conservative estimates place membership in the diverse types of contemporary religious groups at well over ten million. There may be as many as ten thousand different movements. Numbers alone command our attention.

The reference is apt in a second sense. To an important degree, spiritual and physical healing is a central theme of African religious movements. Most scholars of African religion have noted this, and some have felt it appropriate to refer to these movements primarily as "healing institutes." The Western concept of the "church" in Africa misses this important commitment. This book does not ignore this aspect and shows us how women's roles in healing give them a central position and special influence in church activity.

There is a third resonance in the epigraph. It raises the question of what is "without" us in our studies and what is within. We are brought to ask whether our own preoccupying images are being imposed on the African materials: our own sense of male-female relations, for example, filtering our understanding of the dynamics of religious movements in the colonial situation. We are well warned about such misinterpretations in these pages. There is the other side of the same question. Is what we have before us so entirely "without us" that we can find no relevance "within?" The reader, I think, will find these African responses to malaise and contradiction alive with universal themes in the human situation.

There are, as we know, either weak and temporizing or strong responses to human malaise. Religious movements are, generally, among the strong. They are revelatory, though they may not be necessarily revolutionary in the political sense—determined to seek redistribution in the material goods and powers of this world. They are strong responses, because in their attempts at lasting healing, they seek basic transformations in world view: symbolic transformations of experience. They thus bring us to reflect upon the roots of human conviviality—the word, I think, captures the core experiences of religious movements—and upon the nature of secure foundations for human faiths, human hopes and, above all, human charities. These strong and creative responses maintained over significant periods of time reveal to us with special clarity those ultimate conditions of existence which weaker responses obscure or which are simply ignored amidst the materialism of the daily round.

In the end, the human conviviality within and between this world and the next that religious movements seek to restore and maintain is imperfectly realized in any society and its lack is always a motivation for movement. But religious movements, as we know them in the social sciences, respond to a particular set of circumstances: the forceful expansion of dynamic self-confident societies into contact with more settled cultures. Africa, in the last hundred years, has, as elsewhere in the nonWestern world, been a particular arena of that expansion and unsettling "colonizing" contact. The consequence of this expansive contact has, characteristically, been a decentering in these recipient cultures, an undermining of their own realities and world views: a sense of peripherality. Such changes bring men and women to a disspiriting sense of not-living-well in their circumstances. Visions of a better life occur and religious movements arise to "set things right" and to restore confidence and a sense of the center.

One emphasizes men and women, because the malaise produced by decentering is likely to be most acutely felt in this most crucial of social bonds, that bond in which a satisfactory *modus vivendi* is most desirable. Colonial expansion and conquest and the more recent and rapid industrialization has had profound effect upon that bond, as anyone who has lived in African villages and towns in recent decades can attest to. It is a malaise compounded of status denied to men and of male feelings of increasing peripherality together with new possibilities offered to women of centering themselves. A great virtue of this collection of essays is that it looks directly at the creative response in African religious movements—the attempt at the recentering of both men and women to this malaise. The response is not always female emancipation as it is understood in the West, and it is often mainly symbolic, but the consequence, whether the new relations are complementary or egalitarian, is greater conviviality.

The responses in religious movements to malaise and decentering are multidimensional, as the editor's epilogue makes clear. They range from efforts to return to a romanticized conviviality of an idealized past to efforts to construct a new world of an imagined and convivial future. But in all movements there is tension as regards the locus of conviviality, tension between the arcadian wish, as Bennetta Jules-Rosette puts it, and the millennial hope.

There is also a tension to be found in the very study of these movements. There is the appreciation of the new world brought into being by these movements, on the one hand, and the student's commitment to the methods and objective sense of reality characteristic of social science on the other. Jules-Rosette herself, in her volume, *African Apostles*, has given us an intensely interesting exploration of that tension—the tension bound up in the method of participant observation itself. Something of her work there carries over into her editorship of this book.

It ought to be said that this is very much a tension of the modern world, where religious convictions and religious communions exist side by side with a powerful scientific positivism and its fruits. That may be another reason why *Religio Medici* came to mind. For that book represents an early attempt by a man of medical science to relate that positivist, practical procedure to a religious world view. Although scholars of religion must acutely feel that tension, it is as surely present in modern religious movements themselves, even though in them that tension may be embedded in symbolic statements and their negotiation of stereotypic gender-evoked roles and symbolic epressions. I doubt that there is any reader who does not carry something of that tension within him and who will not be informed by its hoped-for resolution on a continent that has much to tell us about where we have come from and who we are.

Princeton University
May, 1978

Preface

Over the past decade, a resurgence of field research and scholarly writings on African cults and churches has taken place. This development has accompanied the rise of new African nations in which the relevance of tradition and the position of religion with respect to a changing political order are being reevaluated. The contemporary religious movements can no longer be regarded as colonial reaction formations. The complexities of the ritual process and the changing aspirations of church members must be examined in depth before any such functional conclusions could be drawn. These aspirations in African religions involve the search for a balance between tradition (or return to an idyllic tradition) and progress. I refer to the former as "the arcadian wish," the necessity of preserving valuable aspects of the past in a contemporary religious movement. It is through the creative tension between this arcadian wish and the impetus to transformation and reform that the new groups are developing responses to the challenges of African urban living.

The position of priestesses and priests in the doctrine and hierarchy of the groups is regarded as an indicator of the type of organizational change. In some cases, women move from situations of relative autonomy in separate religio-political organizations like the West African secret societies to situations of more surveillance and overt submission in the newer churches. However, the churches operate as voluntary associations, credit organizations, and pressure groups through which men and women members assert themselves independently. These diverse activities associated with the new religions emerge in the context of the urbanization process. Through examining ceremonial interaction, performers' conceptions of the complementarity of their participation emerge. As a result, this volume begins with an analysis of the relationship between cult and church drawn from the ethnographic studies. It then moves on to discuss the effect of the urbanization process on the rise of the "church" as a form of social organization, particularly as it affects the relationships between women and men. A recurrent theme throughout the book is the process of symbolic innovation accompanying church organization and the psychological impact of new ritual and symbolic changes.

Most of the scholars connected with this collection have had sustained informal intellectual contact over the past several years. While their work in no way represents a distinctive "school" of thought, they have been influenced by the interpretive tradition in the social sciences spanning interactionist sociology, symbolic anthropology, and the more recent biographical and autobiographical methods as approaches to religious experience. It is an underlying assertion of each paper that the structural study of ritual and symbol is not comilete without some consideration of both the levels of personal experience and the larger social context in which the religious groups operate.

ACKNOWLEDGMENTS

Portions of the following chapter have appeared elsewhere: Chapter Four, Ritual Portrait of a Ga Medium, by Marion Kilson, is condensed from *The Journal of African Studies* 2, 3 (Fall, 1975): 395–418, and is reprinted with permission.

The following persons have been instrumental in assembling this volume and manuscript preparation: Edythe Weinberg, Colleen Carpenter, and Michele Mossholder. Thanks are also extended to the elders and leaders of the groups studied for their cooperation in spreading the news of Africa's new religions to an international community.

BENNETTA JULES-ROSETTE
La Jolla, California

THE NEW RELIGIONS
OF AFRICA

Symbols of Power and Change: An Introduction to New Perspectives on Contemporary African Religion

Bennetta Jules-Rosette

African religion is one of the most active and protean aspects of cultural transformation today. Much of the recent first–hand research has not yet been assembled in collections that provide a general overview of religious developments on the African continent. Many authors (Barrett, 1968; Lewis, 1971; Monfouga-Nicolas, 1972; Murphree, 1971) have noted the predominance of women in African cult movements. This major influence has its origin in the complementary cults of traditional Africa in which women were both titular heads and actual instigators. This volume will examine the complementarity between men and women in contemporary African cults and churches. It will, therefore, necessarily analyze both the social organization and political structure of these churches and the status of women within them. These research aims will be treated as complementary: one is indispensable without the other.

In this volume, it is stressed that the study of women is not divorced from general ethnography or from the overall study of contemporary social movements, and that the changing roles of women are manifested in, and motivate the activities in, regionally critical religious cults and movements. While there is no unified theoretical paradigm imposed upon each of these essays, they all employ original field research and a data-driven model for the development of theories of symbolism and collective behavior. These essays delineate critical expressive cultural changes in Africa's emerging nations. Consequently, they reflect a certain phase of contemporary postcolonial research. While their conclusions are not definitive, these articles demonstrate a move away from the analysis of African religions and belief systems as synchronic wholes and a recognition of the direct impact of contemporary cults and churches upon some of the other rapidly changing institutional structures of present-day Africa.

1

This collection is grounded in primary field research by scholars of contemporary African religion. It deals with the phenomenon of African religion in a changing social context.[1] While the topics are diverse, each study presents a theoretical and ethnographic overview of the symbolism, ritual, and belief systems of a given group. The primary focus of the volume is the emergence of new African religions in a rapidly changing cultural environment. A second and equally salient theme is the increasing importance of women's religious activities as a source of cultural redefinition and change. The secret societies, cults, and churches represent a continuum from customary religious organizations to those with more recent structures and externally influenced beliefs. Much of the literature on African religion ignores this continuous development. Customary religions are treated as regionally and culturally insulated, while newer groups are analyzed primarily as social or protopolitical movements and as examples of "acculturation."[2] This dichotomy is too narrow to account for the diversity of the contemporary religious situation across the African continent, for it ignores the link between "traditional" social and ontological interpretations and the newly emerging religions of Africa.[3] This process of mutual influence has been particularly evident across the continent from the nineteenth century to the present. Customary and recent religions coexist in African urban areas and, increasingly, in the rural milieu. In this sense, the traditional religions have become new, adapting to changing social situations. Some have taken the form of voluntary organizations, as suggested in MacCormack's article in this volume. Others have assumed organizational structures resembling those of churches while retaining essentially the same customary beliefs, as exemplified in the discussion of Harrist syncretisms. In yet other cases, traditional religious associations have been transplanted within both mission and indigenous churches, as exemplified in my own and the Kileffs' work (cf. Barrett, 1968, pp. 49–50).

At the opposite end of the continuum are those churches arising within world religions. Two such groups are dealt with in this volume: the Jamaa

[1]In emphasizing the continuity between preexisting African religions and those owing more to external contact, I use the word "traditionalism" in the special sense of the conscious reassertion of cultural patterns claimed as ancestral or precontact. This category includes examples of perpetuative nativism (Linton, 1943) as well as cases ordinarily glossed as "survivals of tradition." I use "customary" to mean preexisting forms as described historically by the analyst or as compared by members with existing changes. The distinction emphasizes that tradition is an intentional construct.

[2]See the classic descriptions of Evans–Pritchard (1956), Lantenari (1963), Barrett (1968), and others. Another view is to discover "essential" qualities of African religion across cultures (Mbiti, 1970). This approach is often too generalized to facilitate a detailed investigation of syncretism. However, note the syncretic use of an essentialist approach by Tempels (1962, 1969, and Chapter 9).

[3]See Lantenari (1963) and Young (1965). However, some Africanists have dealt quite explicitly with this continuity. Herskovits (1948a) noted that within a given area of cultural focus (e.g., religion or the plastic arts), specific "reinterpretations" tended to combine new content with existing patterns. His studies of African religion in the New World (1937, 1948b) documented a number of such combinations. The orientation of these combinations differs markedly from one group to another.

movement within the Zairean Catholic Church, discussed by Johannes Fabian, and the development of varieties of Islamic practice in West Africa, approached in Quimby's discussion of ritual innovation. In this context, Fabian emphasizes the key importance of understanding the complexity of male–female relations in a separatist group that combines diverse symbolic perspectives. He reminds us that in areas that have experienced colonial domination, it is not surprising to find that male domination and female submission *symbolize* major themes in daily social and political activities. This volume describes the symbolic ties and the transplants that have occurred between traditional cults and newer churches, using the changing role of women as a significant indicator of innovation and as a symbolic reflection of larger concerns in the societies that the authors describe.

THE SYMBOLIC ASPECTS OF SEX DIFFERENTIATION IN THE GROUPS

The scope of studies included here spans the entire continent. They allow us to examine how religion influences orientations to the customary and the contemporary. There is a striking similarity in the case study materials drawn from contrasting settings. A typical reaction in both the traditionalist cults and the contemporary churches is a rejection, albeit ambivalent at times, of foreign influences. In the Christian-based churches, this rejection takes the form of mistrust towards missionaries and other purveyors of external doctrines. According to this belief, the "truth" can only be revealed by an African prophet or messiah, or directly to the new members themselves.

The symbolic spheres of men's and women's activities are clearly demarcated in both older cults and contemporary religions. This demarcation, in some cases, has resulted in a virtual separation of sex-typed activities and a secretiveness among members of each sex with regard to the social distribution of knowledge and symbolic representations of power. This demarcation is emphasized in the essays by Bellman, MacCormack, and Kilson. As a result, these activities may be used as indicators of continuity and change in the societies to which they refer. Both traditional West African spirit mediums and the syncretic cults and churches share this strict symbolic and actual separation of the sexes. In some cases, this separation allows women to wield ceremonial and political power through religious channels. This status differentiation grounded in the new religions recurs as an aspect of many cults and churches.

Social relationships crosscut these symbolic differences. This process is evident in Kilson's description of the Ga medium. While the female medium assists male priests in the performance of Ga calendrical rites, her authority exceeds that of the male priest only because it is believed to come from the spirits. The multifaceted relationship between male and female authority appears in other traditional contexts, for example in the separation of ritual and political authority in the Poro/Sande.[4] Although Poro priests are allowed to participate in some Sande rituals, the domain of their interaction with priestesses is clearly marked, ranging from total exclusion to parallel participation. Disease, even death, are said to be the due of those who transgress the limits regardless of their sacred or secular power in other domains.

Mendonsa finds a similar male/female dichotomy in Sisala culture. He notes that women have high positions as diviners even though they do not hold other official positions in Sisala society. The divination sequence among the Sisala is believed to have an objective potency of its own that prevents women from usurping authority from the male elders through the divinatory act alone.

Walker and Breidenbach discuss related divisions of power in the syncretic Harrist cult. While this church has been widely studied in terms of its history and social organization, the very essential complementarity of male/female priesthood has rarely been described (Haliburton, 1971). Harris was viewed as the male focus of charismatic authority and as a miracle worker. The women with whom he associated shared in his powers as wives and spiritual consorts. Their symbolic power ensued from his, and they were viewed as his protegees. The idiom of familial symbolism (cf. Jules–Rosette, 1976b) was cleverly used in extending and legitimating their authority and in passing it on hereditarily, resulting in a division between female spiritual authority and historical supremacy and male political control.

There are several results of female expressive control in religion (cf. Parsons, 1967, pp. 192–219). In one sense, the woman is freed from the burdens of decision-making to attend to higher concerns. However, this very freedom is the source of both her power and her powerlessness. The nurturant activities of women (Fortes, 1966) become the symbolic rubric through which they express themselves in faithhealing and mediumship. At the same time, they are often at a loss to express prophetic inspirations, though the effective channeling of women's power appears in the Harrist church and its more syncretic offshoots. It is also predominant in the Christian-based Apostolic groups of central and southern Africa, two of which are discussed in this volume.

It follows that no simple equation can be made between tradition and the symbolic power of women. However, Fabian's denial of a direct correlation between social change and women's "emancipation" in contemporary cults and churches must also be underscored. In fact, the complexities of the contemporary situation often lead to traditionalistic and revitalistic responses in which women reassume the trappings of conventional roles with more force than before in a symbolic effort to reconstitute a lost sense of community. Robins similarly emphasizes that even when women's emancipation is a potential goal of a religious movement, its broader social and political impact is mixed, as it was in the East African Revival movement.

---

[4]Cf. Erchak's (1974, pp. 344-345) reply to Fulton on the status of Kpelle women, whom he claims have equal and complementary roles to those of men through their participation in the Sande.

I. M. Lewis (1971, pp. 85–92) argues that traditional African religion contains symbolic and strategic vehicles employed by women who cannot otherwise achieve their ends. Through using possession and exorcism as tactics, women, such as those of the Somalian *Sar* possession cults, gain attention and a measure of temporary power in conjugal and community relationships. This power follows largely from passage through affliction. As possessed or afflicted persons, the *Sar* candidates and other cult members receive attention from other women colleagues. As veterans of affliction, they hold the power to cure and initiate others. While there is substance to these interpretations, the fact that both influential and ordinary men participate in similar cults renders the theory advocated by Lewis (1971, p. 77) of sex war carried out on the battlefield of religion somewhat open to question. It is necessary to understand the subjective parameters of possession and the motivations of participants thoroughly before such conclusions can be drawn.

By contrast, Quimby's chapter suggests that efforts to modernize Islamic rites resulted in a decrease of women's freedom of expression and independent income. This is corroborated by Fabian's experience with a Christian–based sect. In both cults and churches, a tendency remains to separate women's power, but no single pattern of dominance or submission is evident. Within the newer indigenous churches across the continent, a woman's power increases after her childbearing period has ended. Daneel (1970, 1971) suggests that Shona custom already contained precedents for an older "neuter" medium figure through whom God (Mwari) spoke, thereby removing all of her sexual characteristics. Gluckman (1956) describes Zulu traditional agricultural rites in which women dressed in male clothing and imitated male familial and work tasks as a symbol of power and potential change. Similar behavioral reversal has been described among the Gogo of Tanzania (Rigby, 1968, 1969) and the Iru of Uganda (Bamunoba & Welbourn, 1965; Berger, 1974). These reversals are occasions for catharsis and symbolic expressions of the tensions of daily existence, and are referred to as commonplace psychological devices in several of the essays throughout this volume. They are also interpreted as ways of stressing and reinforcing the social and symbolic distinctions between women and men.[5] Are these incidents occasions on which women exercise permanent or merely ephemeral power? If women become "ritual men" at the post-menopausal period or at

---

[5]Regarding such behavior reversals, Gluckman states (1956):

> Socially, the lifting of the normal taboos and restraints obviously serves to emphasize them. It is this aspect of the ceremony which most interests me. Zulu ceremony emphasizes the difference between men and women, beyond their biological differences. Women cannot approach cattle; women must be decorous in public; women do not take full part in the national life or national ceremonies; women, when they menstruate, are full of mystical danger. This is part of women's social position, and the customs and beliefs emphasize her distinction and her separateness from men. (p. 115)

some other symbolic phase, the beginnings of institutional powers are present (cf. Martin, 1971, Jules-Rosette, Chapter 7).[6] On the other hand, this type of ceremonial authority is rarely transmitted from one woman to another in the modern cult context.

The customary and emerging power of women rests upon their ceremonial separation. Therefore, the fact that women are sometimes leaders in groups and often constitute a majority of their membership is not an indicator of their level of political participation, especially over the long term. The Legio Maria and related movements in East Africa, as well as the Harrists discussed in this volume by Walker and Breidenbach, illustrate occasions of the ephemeral rise of women to leadership with the support of a cadre of male kin and more passive women adepts. In the Weberian sense (1947, pp. 358–373) the charismatic potential for women is routinized in the group as a whole but not with respect to their specific positions or cultural contributions. The female leaders disappear as rapidly as they surface, succumbing to the slightest failure in their charismatic promise. Gaudencia Aoko's career as a charismatic healer and witchfinder gained her a mass following in Kenya and Northern Tanzania that dwindled when her spiritual gift suddenly disappeared.[7] Alice Lenshina's Lumpa Church of Zambia, whose early political and controversial nature eventually led to its censure, used the model of female chieftainship but was unable to establish an authority structure exclusively or even primarily for women (Taylor & Lehmann, 1961, pp. 248–268). Her closest associates and supporters were men. Recently, as a result of a complex political history, Lenshina renounced allegiance to her own church and established association with a mission-based group.

THE QUESTION OF MEMBERSHIP AS A THEORETICAL ISSUE IN THE STUDY OF AFRICAN RELIGION

Women in African churches are not ultimately powerless nor is their history in the older cults one of unquestionable oppression. Their ceremonial separation, however, seldom connotes political equality. To understand the import of symbolic complementarity as opposed to political equality, even when leadership positions have been obtained, it is necessary to examine African cults and churches from the perspective of membership and participation in them. Such a perspective is discussed by several of the authors in this volume. Bellman analyzes sexually exclusive, parallel, and complementary ritual activities. Dur-

---

[6]This also illustrates the ways in which female status in itself is a managed accomplishment. Cf. Garfinkel (1967), who describes the interactional strategies used in order to "pass" as a female.

[7]For descriptions of the Legio Maria and Aoko's rise, see Barrett (1968) and Perrin–Jassy (1971).

ing certain Poro society rituals, women must remain inside with their windows boarded. Similarly, at the time of initiation, they are excluded from viewing the ceremonies. For other ceremonies in lesser societies, women participate in a parallel fashion: Within the Sande society, discussed in different contexts by Bellman and MacCormack, women hold ceremonies which are complementary to those of men and from which men are excluded. Hence, Bellman presents a theory of illusions and displays that men create for women in Kpelle ceremonial authority and daily life. Certainly, these assumptions about membership are not the only channel to information. MacCormack's paper illustrates the wealth of information that may be collected through examining the public rites of secret societies and learning about their members through historical and interview accounts. This material suggests that the uses and concept of secrecy are modified by reinterpretations of customary social activity in the modern sector.

There is a developing cross-cultural literature that stresses the importance of "ethnographic biography" to providing a narrative and epistemological point of departure for studies (cf. Bowen, 1954; Castaneda, 1968, 1971, 1972, 1974; Jules-Rosette, 1975a, 1976a; Powdermaker, 1966). This type of biography recounts how the ethnographer acquired familiarity with a topic and was able to gain access to particular kinds of knowledge. The substance of African religion carries with it both pragmatic and emotional consequences. Grasping these consequences analytically is not only a matter of the intellectual encounter with an alien but compelling thought form but also a lived experience. As Kilson's essay shows, it is often necessary to suspend one's prior assumptions and modify the analytical stance in order to express the integrity of old and new African religious conventions.

Basic to an analysis of the relationship between the old and the new religions are the accounts that persons give of their process of transition. These accounts are related in recollections of traditional ceremonies and descriptions of conversion experiences. Both Robins' discussion and my own in this volume underscore the range of such conversion experiences among women and their relationship to nurturance, childbirth, and mysticism. These accounts suggest that the new religions retain and enhance the mystical powers of women. They establish special symbolic domains of authority for them by stressing the equal access of women to secrets of religious life and to sainthood. Some of the interview materials collected on this topic reveal an ambiguity in the status of women. In Christian terms, they are assured spiritual equality, yet this equality may only be achieved through the observance of rigid ritual prescriptions and symbolic sexual segregation. Robins is particularly concerned with how an evangelical emphasis on the importance of personal experience in the East African Revival group (Balokole) and a testimony of salvation allowed women to free themselves from conflicts between traditional obligations and changing standards. By examining conversion in relation to the problem of religious membership, these essays present a methodological grounding for the study of symbol and ritual. It is through membership that the multivocal meanings of symbols can be interpreted (cf. Turner, 1967, pp. 20–27).

SYMBOLIC DIFFERENTIATION AND
PERSONAL CHOICE

Once the domain of African religious groups and some of their parameters of leadership have been defined, it is important to consider similarities and differences in symbolic content and the contexts in which culture change is most likely to occur. Is it possible to define the domain occupied by the *great* religious traditions, that is, those religions that predate Western influence? The types of interpretive problems solved by traditional African religion are highly pragmatic. The sensory aspect of traditional symbols in which an object represents its outward form (Turner, 1967, p. 28) allows them to be manipulated in a concrete manner. Turner distinguishes between these concrete features of symbolism and their moral implications. Needless to say, this distinction is often purely analytical rather than empirical. As a belief system alters as a result of external influences or, conversely, as external systems of thought are adapted to new environments, domains of symbolic meaning shift. Concrete and efficacious symbols become expanded. An example emerges in the interpretation of food taboos among the Maranke Vapostori. The food taboos of Leviticus are blended with customary lore. Both the Hebraic and the African customary systems were ways of classifying nature and culture that resulted in logical anomalies and ambiguities (Douglas, 1966, pp. 55–56; 1970, pp. 61–81). The meeting of two contrasting classificatory systems increased the areas of ambiguity that appear in defining the relationship between a human group and nature. The provision against carrion–eating animals and birds is clear in Leviticus. Among the Vapostori creatures that share certain distinctive features with the carrion eaters are added to the list. These include the turkey because of its rarity and its physical resemblance to the vulture, and the duck and goose because of their diet of dead or rotten foods (Tshiluba: *bintu bibole*).

Nevertheless, the selection of these birds is not coincidental. Both are feared in Luba-Lulua traditional custom: the first because of its anomalous appearance and the latter because of its curious webbed feet. The webbed foot of the duck, an intermediary between a water and land creature, is considered particularly dangerous to pregnant women.[8] A direct link exists between the customary taboos and the syncretic interpretations of biblical doctrine.

This pattern of combination is evident in new religious interpretations of the sorcery and witchcraft beliefs emanating from customary practices. Both

---

[8]An association is made between water, water animals, and the child's premature "slipping out." An analogous association is made among the Ndembu of Zambia, who term the ritual designed to cure birth disorders *isoma*, meaning "slipping" (Turner, 1967).

groups of Apostles discussed in the Kileffs' article and my own are well known for witchcraft accusations and trials. Despite an early colonial ordinance forbidding both the use and the accusation of witchcraft in Zimbabwe, the Maranke Vapostori were rarely prosecuted, because their form of witchcraft accusation was considered peculiar to the church (Murphree, 1969, pp. 56, 106). For the Maranke Apostles, witchcraft consists of any malicious intent toward a neighbor or fellow member. The annual Passover or Eucharist commemoration of the Maranke Vapostori is the moment at which witchcraft accusations are made by those confirmed as possessing "prophetic" skills to detect them. Those convicted are required to confess and are prohibited from partaking of the Passover for that year. Nevertheless, the Apostolic definition of witchcraft modifies traditional conceptions by including church transgressions. Accusations serve as a mechanism for maintaining boundaries between the church and the outside world and for enforcing compliance with church regulations. Sorcery and witchcraft are viewed as a single phenomenon, and use of traditional medicines for any purpose is censured. Displayed here is a fear of returning to a former way of life and a reaction formation through its total rejection. Yet, the symbolic expression of this rejection often uses similar elements to the original beliefs in a polar reversal that is intelligible to members and nonmembers alike.[9] Aspects of tradition are retained through their very rejection.

This peculiar ambivalence to tradition arises in different ways in the contemporary cults and churches. To understand this reaction, it is necessary to regard tradition itself as a collection of world views in flux. What appears to the observer to be tradition has been reconstructed as such over the course of recent events.[10] When, for instance, two–century–old African art forms like the Kuba *ndop* (royal figurines) appear today, the present artifacts (depending on the style and the medium of their presentation) are often revitalizations of the earlier forms rather than direct continuations of an ancient tradition.[11] By rejecting traditional medicines, the Apostles, the Harrists, the members of the West African Aladura

[9]Turner (1967, 1969) shows the common use of such polarities *within* customary religion through the symbolic union of polar qualities. When this symbolic reasoning is applied by practitioners to religious change, a new polarization takes place through which new faiths distinguish themselves from the old.

[10]Schwartz (1976, pp. 157–205) emphasizes the importance of this constructive process in Melanesian cargo cults. On visiting the field site, Manus Island, New Guinea, in 1963, he found few traces of the traditional ritual that he had seen ten years earlier. Most of the villagers worshiped in a syncretic Christian church. On his return in 1973, many of the same people had reinstated traditional practices in their daily life. By contrast, their plastic art had moved much more heavily into tourist production. The New Guinea government, meanwhile, promoted a "generalized" Melanesian tradition not belonging to the original island culture.

[11]The *ndop*, or royal figurines of the BaKuba of Zaire (Vansina, 1972, pp. 51–86), and other traditional art motifs, are now used by commercial painters for sale to a non-African public in a process of cultural syncretism that the painters refer to as "modernizing" *(kumoderniser)*. This syncretic process resembles the combination of old and new in religious associations (see Jules-Rosette, 1978a).

(Church of the Lord), and others are refusing to reconstruct tradition as relevant to them in an identical and continuous manner. They are not denying the existence of ancestral and malefic spirits or their ability to affect the waking world. Instead, these spirits, and many of the social obligations required to appease them, are considered subordinate to cult mediumship and Christian or Islamic interpretations of misfortune and its remedies. One interpretation does not unconditionally supersede another. Rather, the cults and churches organize interpretive *priorities* within their doctrines.[12]

In the urban milieu where various assumptions coexist, the strategy of switching from one group to another is accompanied by cognitive shifts that may be extreme. Sundkler (1961) in part describes this process with reference to South African indigenous churches when he asserts:

> The pursuit of health is the gravest concern of the Zulu today. Problems of diagnosis and medical treatment arouse a tremendous interest among them. The reason for this is of course the low standard of health, caused chiefly by malnutrition which prevails among the Zulu today. This causes folk to be constantly on the move from one medical practitioner to another in search of health. (p. 222)

Despite the narrowness of his causal explanation, Sundkler is pointing to one of the pragmatic bases for shifting allegiances between old and new religions and ideological commitments. Doctrines in this instance provide shifting definitions of the situation that serve the immediate objectives and interests of the participants.

If the position of the healer in indigenous churches is examined, this ambivalence toward tradition emerges even more fully. A healer among the Maranke Apostles is known as a doctor *(nganga)* who also preaches. The term *nganga* is also used to describe other folk healers. The same parallel also exists among the Harrists. A distinction is made that the healer performs feats through the power of the Holy Spirit and never uses *buloji* or the power objects of sorcery to obtain results. In interpreting illness, the church *nganga* may use a germ theory, a customary approach to affliction, or the Christian concept of sin, depending on the circumstance, but sin is considered to override all other interpretations. While the biblical interpretation of an event overarches all others and is, therefore, paramount, it is not the only or even the principal interpretation at a given time. Both interpretations are equally personalistic (cf. Horton, 1967, pp. 69–70). However, an overriding doctrine governs which comes first and the sequences of alternatives that may be chosen. While members of the Maranke group are freed from neither the uses nor effects of sorcery, they reinterpret its purview through membership. Joining the group initially reduces their vulnera-

---

[12]Mitchell (1965) describes the process of shifting interpretations of misfortune in some detail. He cites the case of a Nyasa churchman's death in which the diviner changed interpretations to avoid embarrassment. The problem was not that certain interpretations could not be used, but that one interpretation (witchcraft by rival church leaders) was unacceptable in a Christian context, while another (ancestral anger at failed obligations) was still viable.

bility to it by offering members a new repertoire of spiritual probations in a new social arena.

It must be noted that the outcome of syncretic interpretations is considered to be pragmatic and those choices that "work" are opted for in the last analysis. One may then ask under what circumstances an individual or an entire community comes to the limits of an interpretive system. If the conditions for such limitation could be pointed out, our insight into the dynamics of interpretive shifts would increase. Scholars of traditional antisorcery movements (Douglas, 1963; Marwick, 1970) claim that communities tire of an abundance of witchcraft allegations. When all members of a traditional social milieu become objects of suspicion, joining an external cult is one of the ways in which tensions can be alleviated.

The Kabengabenga cult emerging among the Lele of southwestern Zaire from 1910 onward is an example (Douglas, 1963). Initiation into the cult immediately neutralized one's vulnerability to sorcery. It was believed that one who practiced sorcery would die. When such persons and their offspring actually did not die, the cults lost their credibility. Such cults often went underground and resurfaced in different forms. The indigenous churches can be looked upon as manifestations of similar cultural reinterpretations. They introduced new ways of resolving disputes and dealing with community conflicts, in many cases retaining such ceremonies as poison and fire ordeals also characteristic of the sorcery and witch–cleansing movements. Through such ordeals, participants establish concrete causes of death and misfortune while eradicating sorcery, the very root of all conflict in these terms.

There is, however, a major difference between the indigenous spirit churches and the more customary cults: membership in the churches tends to be exclusive and limited, whereas participation in the cults encompasses an entire community. The church conceives of itself as a corporate entity with diffuse aims, while the goals of the cult may be highly specific. The cults retain an organizational structure paralleling that of customary religious practice. In contrast, the churches strive for institutional separation, occasionally in partial imitation of Western models. A larger doctrine and eschatology supersedes their activities as community witch eradicators.

Underlying all of the articles in this volume is the assumption that detailed analysis of the ritual practices and the process of membership in each group discussed is necessary to uncover the basic elements of symbolism in their religious practices. In his discussion of men and women in a Zairean church, Fabian asserts that investigations that omit the dimension of symbolic images and metaphors are incomplete. Turner (1969, p. 14) stresses that symbolism pervades the customary life of the Zambian Ndembu and that much of it is both pragmatic and ceremonial in nature. This is also the case in many African cults and churches. The intent of ritual performances cannot be examined through abstract means in which symbols are removed from their ritual contexts. This methodological perspective recurs in the ethnographic descriptions presented throughout the volume, from MacCormack's discussion of a customary secret society to Fabian's analysis of a Western–influenced separatist church.

REDEFINING THE SACRED AND SECULAR

In the traditional context, a religious ruling structure may supersede all other social and political organizations. While a town chief holds secular powers among the Fala Kpelle, most major conflicts are ultimately referred to the religious ruling structure of the Poro society. When used to describe this aspect of community life, the terms religious or sacred refer to those symbolic powers that are guarded by a separate priesthood. While there is continuous interaction between the religious and the secular domains, the jurisdiction and boundaries of each area are distinct. In towns where the Poro society is absent as an agent of social control, it is often difficult to keep peace and enforce final resolutions to problems. External institutions have influenced shifts and reversals in the relationship between sacred and secular. Alternatively, the impact of modern political systems has required sacred rulers to assume an official status with relationship to juristic authority and national control. Recently, the ancient Kuba chief was, therefore, invested with authority as a local party leader. He retained his religious–political ruling base while simultaneously representing new forms of secular authority. Even within the traditional milieu, the outlets through which custom is expressed and maintained have changed.

In the new religions, a parallel redefinition of sacred and secular is taking place. These sects and churches constitute new home networks, or urban villages for their adherents, as is emphasized in all of the articles in the last two sections of the book. While many new institutional services can be utilized in an urban context, local problems requiring conflict resolution or adjustments between custom and the new environment cannot be legislated from the outside. An example is the process of mate selection in transitional marriage forms. Among the Maranke Apostles, a Shona marriage custom, the virginity examination (ciziwiso) (Holleman, 1952, p. 83), has been revitalized as a female initiation ceremony. This purity examination determines the virginity of young girls between the ages of 10 and 16 and their consequent eligibility for marriage. The importance of virginity as a basis for the exchange of bride wealth has declined in present day Shona society. The church, however, has revived its significance through the mushecho examination. Young women who pass the examination have a free choice of mates, while those who fail must enter into arranged polygynous marriages with church elders. While polygyny is accepted within the church, it becomes a source of stigma for the nonvirgins. There is an ambivalence in the status of those who pass. They are both free to choose mates and are required to remain virgins as a prerequisite of choice. While their success or failure is physically determined by a council of female elders, the young virgins still remain subservient to their fathers who contract the final arrangements for marriage and bride price. Collectively, these young women represent the purity, ritual wealth, and financial resources of the church. Should they marry outsiders, their husbands must become converts. They are the potential parents of future generations of Apostles. The young women are, therefore, structurally instrumental to the church's survival.

In this respect, the syncretic church has taken over many of the duties of the traditional village and kinship unit. Activities that were previously the secular affairs of family life are subsequently built into religious organization. The village mechanisms for regulating endogamy and determining mate selection are no longer operative. In a multiethnic community, there are no assurances of homogeneity or of appropriate background factors such as rank and prestige in the marriage.[13] The marriage decisions pass to new hands under a religious mandate. What holds for marriage is true for other areas of social and political decision-making.

The urban churches such as the Harrist group, the East African Revival, and the Apostolic groups discussed in this volume are voluntary organizations, whereas the religious ruling structures of traditional villages are not. This means that the churches use their public ceremonies as occasions to proselytize and regulate problems among existing adherents. The use of public palavers and confessions to bring secular activities under the control of the religious is a common practice in the newer organizations. The indigenous churches also offer an arena for cases that would otherwise be considered private matters. Personal difficulties are interpreted as within the spectrum of religious doctrine.[14] While it is difficult to specify the point at which a familial difficulty becomes important enough to go to a given church's elders, any disagreement that results in public dispute must be confessed and settled under religious auspices (see Robins, Chapter 10).

It is more difficult for issues internal to secret societies to become public. Nevertheless, when persons outside of one social domain interact with others within it, the organization's priorities may be questioned. Within the indigenous churches, the interaction between sacred and secular content is subtle. The Masowe church discussed by the Kileffs (see Chapter 8; also Kileff, 1973) is now experiencing a leadership crisis precipitated by its founder's recent death. A new leader for the group has not been found, and members have not agreed upon a

---

[13]Compare this with the changing marriage system among the Mossi (Capron & Kohler, 1976). Young men increasingly work for wages outside of the village. However, on their return they are required by the ruling gerontocracy to wait several more years before marriage.

[14]Through making private problems the subject of church deliberations, the individuals' concerns are brought within the doctrinal and political scope of the group. Bittner (1963) characterizes such a process of "preventing energy leaks" of individual commitment as necessary to the maintenance of a radical or charismatic movement.

pattern for leadership succession. The older, officially confirmed members have remained separated from the younger adherents who never had direct contact with the founder. When the younger members attempted to separate themselves and establish a new leadership structure, the elders requested civic officials to intervene. It was hoped that the outside forces would restore the respect of the younger members for religious seniority. The situation ended in compromise. A religious issue was thus placed in a larger social and political context, rather than vice versa.

Within Lusaka, Zambia, the Masowe group provides an excellent example of the blending of the sacred and the secular in a community context. Political matters in their community are referred to the Masowe Vapostori for adjudication. Once a pronouncement has been made by church elders, the matters are referred to administrative and political officials outside of the church. This interdependence parallels that found between the Poro society and the secular ruling structure in certain areas of rural West Africa.

In the newer churches, the religious redefinition of secular activities is essential to maintain the commitments of members in highly insulated religious movements. New orders of experience and events that would have been resolved within the context of traditional social and juristic channels are redefined in religious terms. The old and new religions, as part of a larger society, are viewed with curiosity and, occasionally, with suspicion by outsiders. However, daily life routinely necessitates practical and ideological contact between religious groups in pluralistic and transitional societies. The psychological changes accompanying rapid urbanization are examples of arenas of decision where normally secular (family, work, and personal) decisions may take a religious cast for pragmatic reasons (cf. Hayward, 1977; Jules-Rosette, 1976b).

RELIGION AND SOCIAL CHANGE

Religion is a key part of the total picture of cultural transformation in Africa, but it does not explain, nor is explained by, these changes. The thesis that new indigenous religions have merely arisen as a reaction formation to colonial oppression does not account for enough (cf. Lantenari, 1963; Magubane, 1971). Certainly, the link between colonial oppression and an initial religious reaction is clear and has been proven by scholars (Balandier, 1971, pp. 417–487; Lantenari, 1963, pp. 19–62). This approach assumes that traditional cults and antisorcery movements are also reactions to externally instigated disruptions in African societies. Thus, for example, Zairean antisorcery movements are treated mainly as anti-Western reactions to the economic and social oppression of the colonial regime. The history of Watchtower (Kitawala) in southern Africa exemplifies the political expression of discontent with colonial rule (see Biebuyck, 1957; Shepperson, 1962).

The situation is more complex. It has to do with the types of problems that religious and secular authorities within a given group already handle, and their susceptibility to, and contacts with, external groups. Biebuyck (1957, pp. 7–40) analyzes a case in which adherence to the messiah Bushiri, a Kitawala representative, spread among the Kumu of northeastern Zaire. A similar interest did not develop among the Rega and the Hunde, who already had highly developed secret societies. Many Kumu, on the other hand, were migrants away from their homelands who saw in Kitawala a source of political and economic expression. A new religion is not necessarily opted for as a political outlet. Its presence, therefore, does not signify in itself the frustration of other expressions of power. When a new religion is not adopted, its absence may, however, suggest that adjustments to change have been made within the traditional authority structures. The appeal of new religions can be approached, but not completely explained, in terms of economic variables or ethnicity. Barrett (1968, p. 59) begins with the assumption that indigenous religious movements originate with ethnic homogeneity, and he refers to them as "tribal." As a result, he cannot account for cases in which certain new religions predominate among settler populations like the Americo–Liberians or the Sierra Leone creole, while such groups have less appeal in the rural sector (cf. Fraenkel, 1964). This explanation ignores the contemporary manifestations of old religions in the countryside and in urban areas by imposing the dichotomy between "independent" churches and other society or cult groups to the exclusion of the latter. In West Africa, the broadly multiethnic and multinational distribution of many churches and secret societies is as important to their overall development as their origin within a particular group. All of the chapters of this volume stress the simultaneity of developments in traditional and newer African religions as an aspect of pluralism in contemporary society. In this relationship, there is a complex dialectic between African survivals in the New World and African contemporary and traditional religion. This volume should point the way toward discussion of this process of transformation from a cross-cultural perspective. This approach does not deny historical influence, and it emphasizes that parallel changes of comparable structural importance are taking place.

The conditions under which ethnicity and religion have operated to create protopolitical movements warrant careful study. The history of the Kimbanguist church from the 1920s to the present in Zaire is a case in point.[15] It began as a healing movement with messianic overtones. Kimbangu's followers flocked to his holy village at Nkamba for healing and refuge. While the messianic message included hopes of political and social freedom, it was not until colonial intervention took place that these doctrines began to crystallize. Kimbangu's arrest and the dispersion of the movement only helped to consolidate its ideological stand.

[15]The history and political implications of Kimbanguism are discussed by Andersson (1958), Banda–Mwaka (1970), Chomé (1959), and Young (1965).

A reemergence in the late 1950s with participation from a small but growing sector of intellectuals resulted in the active role that Kimbanguism played in Zairean independence. It was not by virtue of being a religion that Kimbanguism was covertly "political." Rather, the coalition of certain social classes within Kimbanguism combined with the rhetoric of African Christianity to create the seeds of a liberation movement at a particular time. As the movement stabilized, eventually becoming one of the major established churches in Zaire, its political influence became quite different, while specific aspects of the group's doctrine and ideology remained essentially the same.

This case emphasizes that a religious movement goes through several phases as it emerges, and that its relation to a larger political context shifts over time. In discussing religions and secular authority, I have stressed that the definition of an activity in one domain is a culturally negotiated process. African cults and secret associations are engaged in these processes of redefinition just as the newer religions are. The location of an event as part of one domain depends on the membership associations of participants and their access to knowledge in a given case. When the objectives of a movement are to "purify" a society or to rid a community of undesirable tensions, a reaction to external authority may be in order as a part of the overall objectives. While certain movements seem to be direct responses to political and economic changes, others are far more indirect reactions to these conditions.[16]

Ambivalence to external influences appears in many African religious movements, though they may describe themselves as overtly Christian. Imported elements of Christian doctrine are often originally accepted through force, then later rejected by a different use of the same doctrine. The appearance of vernacular scriptures spurs a rise in new religions (cf. Barrett, 1968, pp. 129–131). The vernacular frees both the form and the interpretation of scripture from Western models. The special forms of oratory developed in the indigenous churches preserve traditional oratorical styles, including parables and formal ritual language, while substituting biblical content within these forms (cf. Jules-Rosette, 1975a, pp. 154–183). The churches assert the effectiveness of their adoption of the Bible in reaction to those who have introduced it, claiming that its translation allows them to remove missionary misinterpretations and to change the social situations in which they were produced.

It has been seen that religion is both a precipitant to change and a reaction to external social situations. As a precipitant, the new religions precede changes

---

[16]Fox, de Craemer & Ribeaucourt (1965) discuss the rise of one such politically based movement, the Mulelist uprising in the Zaire. This movement combined Maoist training techniques, a millenaristic political ideology, and magical practices intended to give the members mystical invincibility. Fox et al. consider Mulelism a response to political developments following Zairean independence.

in other cultural domains through innovative combinations of belief and practice. Such innovations can best be seen in terms of a definition of the various symbolic and organizational components of new religious associations. In some cases, social organization and content coincide. The syncretic organizations attempt to take the form of, or revive, former religious associations and beliefs. They are, however, also syncretic in belief structure, combining aspects of conventional symbols with world religions while taking the outward form of a church.

Indigenous churches span a number of doctrinal orientations that are responses to change. They contain messianic, millennial, prophetic, and thaumaturgical elements (cf. Wilson, 1970). Many of the Watchtower groups in southern Africa share a millenarian orientation that combines a belief in the coming of a golden age with the vision of transformed social and political freedoms, of nationhood and change. The relationship of such doctrines to the external society varies. In some cases, they have resulted in the group's active participation in political liberation and in others have led to some degree of retreatism and resistance, as is presently evidenced in the controversy over Watchtower movements in Malawi and Zambia. Millenarian doctrines are apparent in the Apostolic churches (see Kileff & Kileff, Chapter 8, and Jules-Rosette, Chapter 7), but they are subtle and do not provide an exclusive characterization of the groups involved.

A group's orienting doctrines may influence its social organization in several ways. Fernandez (1964) discusses these types of movements in a historical and evolutionary sense, indicating that a movement goes through several phases during its life history. Others (Barrett, 1968, pp. 46–49) list similar processes typologically for classifying the overall characteristics of entire movements. My discussion is not to be confused with these, for I am referring to these processes as elements that may occur, even simultaneously, at various points and that may recur cyclically over the course of a group's development. I propose the following very basic typology for examining the groups that are discussed in this volume.

1. Traditionalism. These doctrines involve decisive traditional or conservative responses to external influence, often more radical and all-encompassing than the original religions and cultural expressions.[17] The return of young people to secret societies and traditional divination is often not a simple continuation of these forms but a wish to revive them in their decline. Previous moral values,

---

[17]Linton (1943, p. 230) defines a nativistic movement as "any conscious, organized attempt on the part of a society's members to revive or perpetuate selected aspects of its culture." Later authors (e.g., Wallace, 1956) have tended to distinguish revitalization from what Linton terms perpetuative nativism. I term perpetuative tendencies "traditionalism" rather than "nativism," so as to stress their orientation to the past rather than their focus on a restricted set of members.

basic interpretations of the world, and conventional conceptions of men and women are reaffirmed. This tendency is not confined to certain groups, but may coexist with radically differing group orientations.[18] The return of the Zezuru of Zimbabwe to reliance on spirit-mediumship as a source for resolving personal problems and as a substitute for political protest illustrates a direct form of nativism, while the inclusion of such traditional elements among others in related Shona indigenous churches is a more indirect type of traditionalism (cf. Fry, 1976, pp. 45–52). The reemergence of the importance of the Poro and other secret societies for younger people in the rural areas also illustrates this type of reaction.

2. Revitalization. In this process, older forms are renewed, whether in response to outside influences or through a group's own internal growth. In the Maranke *mushecho*, the earlier *ciziwiso* rite was modified, but retained its initial purpose of insuring the wife's virginity and value. The new appearance of the rite assured the preservation of aspects of women's traditional roles. In this sense, revitalization is the partial return to the past, in a nostalgic symbolic manner, without the effort to revive an entire traditional institution. This revitalization process is evident in MacCormack's discussion of the adaption of Sande initiation practices to the modern sector and in Kilson's discussion of Ghanaian spirit mediumship as it relates to modern urban life.

3. Syncretism. Cultural and religious admixtures, such as the combination of Christian healing with traditional views of sorcery, illustrate the syncretic process. Any adaptation of a religious practice within a given culture, such as the history of Catholicism in the West, involves some syncretic combination of traditional beliefs with an evolving doctrine. Syncretism is central to the Harrist and Apostolic churches and to many local adaptations of Islam. Walker and Breidenbach's articles discuss these points in their analyses of the evolution of the Harrist religion in West Africa.

4. Messianism. Through this process, a movement centers around a religious leader claiming miraculous powers and skills. The founding prophets of several syncretic groups, including John Masowe and Simon Kimbangu, claimed to be substitutes for, or the equals of, Christ. Women as well as men are attributed with such powers. The discussions of John Maranke and John Masowe and, to a lesser extent, of William Wade Harris in this volume, point to the phenomenon of messianism and to its representation of both male and female political symbols.

[18]Fernandez (1964) emphasizes that a single group may undergo several phases involving different orientations to tradition. I stress here that several of these processes may be present in a single group at one time.

5. *Millenarism*. Millenarism characterizes many contemporary religious groups through defining an ideal end point at which a new world will be established, often implying not only spiritual regeneration but also the acquisition of material goods and authority by group members.[19] However, many groups that possess some millenarian ideas cannot be exclusively labeled millenarian. The Masowe Vapostori have adopted millenarian ideas concerning the necessity for political and religious change as part of a single event. Their awaiting of the Golden Age when Zimbabwe will be free coincides with the advent of heaven on earth. These beliefs do not preclude the presence of revitalistic and messianic elements in Masowe Vapostori doctrine. In this volume, Kileff and Kileff present a background for understanding this type of doctrinal blending. Through the dynamics of doctrine, millenarian dreams may become mixed with an ideal of the past or be expressed by a messianic leader. Millenarian orientations often coincide with an increasingly complex organizational structure, possessing specialized leadership roles.

Hence, progression from one of these five social processes to another within a religious group is not linear. Several processes such as millenarism and messianism or syncretism and revitalization may take place in limited ways at once. These processes mark particular stages in a group's development. The initial or charismatic period may involve a messianic leader upon whose death the group becomes more millenarian or more revitalistic (cf. Fernandez, 1964, pp. 531–549). The configuration of a group changes over time, and a thorough analysis of its themes depends on the historical context in which it appears.

The nonlinear dimension of change also applies to the structure of leadership within the groups and the roles that women as actors play with regard to them. MacCormack, Mendonsa, Walker, and Quimby have highlighted some of the contradictions between the formal status of women in religious groups and their ability in some cases to arise to singular positions of spiritual authority and mediumship. The progression of women is not, as some researchers imply, one from a position of subservience to one of domination in contemporary churches. Instead, these churches often expand upon age–graded and culturally accepted conceptions of spiritual mediumship and ritual rule.

All of the chapters elucidate the importance of these continuities in gender-linked differentiation within a variety of contemporary religious associations. The key social processes outlined here bear upon the critical distinctions between male and female authority and adepthood in the new African religions. The male–female relationships in ceremonial contexts serve as one indicator of the level and extent of cultural transformation embodied in Africa's contemporary cults and churches.

---

[19]See Thrupp (1962) for descriptions of millenarian movements at various periods in history, including the early Watchtower in Malawi.

AN OVERVIEW OF THE IMPACT OF CONTEMPORARY
RELIGIONS IN PRESENT-DAY AFRICA

Africa is the most rapidly urbanizing continent in the world. Despite the long history of colonization, the meeting of past and present is now taking place in new terms. The contemporary religions of Africa express these processes of change through living ritual forms and through a symbolic and intellectual meeting of beliefs. These religions are highly pragmatic.[20] The authors in Part I stress the importance of secret societies and of divination for the resolution of personal and public conflicts. The confession of the Apostolic groups has a similar therapeutic significance. Changes in accepted morality and in the locus of religious and secular authority heighten the importance of the public confession and "speaking out" ceremonies (Jules-Rosette, 1975a, pp. 172–173) as vehicles for psychological adjustment to changing life styles.

There are two sides to the coin. The fact that such adjustment takes place points to problems far more global than the presence of the churches suggests. These problems have some roots in the colonization process and in a variety of adaptations resulting from culture contact. However, these changes are not mere reaction formations. They entail creative cultural combinations of old and new that have influenced the larger social, political, and economic spheres of the societies in which they occur.

Religion allows a combination of the practical and the yet-to-be-realized, of contemporary realities with past and future wishes. The indigenous churches are fertile grounds for the projection of fantasy and its attainment.[21] They provide ways in which an ideal world can be morally and spiritually generated through both projection into the future and preservation of the past. Their balance in preserving the two is of crucial importance, for it is the indigenous churches that offer a common vocabulary, bridging custom and change. Their changing patterns of recruitment and broader impact upon popular imagery and ideals are emerging areas suggested by the studies in the last two sections of this volume.

This volume contributes to a theoretical redefinition of the field of African religion by including traditionally oriented groups, syncretic groups, and Africanization of world religions on equal footing. It demonstrates the importance of these groups for establishing new values and ideals of community. In particular, it stresses the significance of the churches as continuities and modifications of traditional religious authority structures that affect the morality of entire communities. The activities and images of women reflect the most crucial cultural changes taking place in African religious groups.

Many of these changes reveal an ambivalence toward tradition rather than a definitive break with it. In all of the studies, the new never completely supplants

---

[20]Needleman (1973) comments on a similar pragmatic orientation to ritual in Eastern religions in the United States.

[21]Cf. the concept of fantasy developed in Platt and Weinstein (1969, pp. 7–8).

or eradicates the old. The projected influence of symbolic changes in religion upon a larger cultural sphere will provide a salient comparative perspective on change through the contrasts and symbolic continuities that arise in a variety of data drawn from across the continent. Although the data and conclusions represented by these articles are diverse, they all return to the central topic of ceremonial and political authority, particularly as it is represented by shifting relationships between priests and priestesses in contemporary African religion. In urban Africa, religious groups create among the clearest and most remarkable arenas of leadership and unified ideology. Through approaching them as one of the keys to change in a multiethnic postcolonial Africa, it is possible to trace major themes of symbolic transformation as they affect a variety of institutional structures in contemporary Africa.

An ultimate goal of the volume is to make these materials accessible for the cross-cultural analysis of cultural change beyond the geographic and historical context to which the contributions individually refer. The cross-cultural relevance of the contributors' conclusions points to the decisive impact of religion as an instrument of cultural and social innovation in the world at large.

FROM CULT TO CHURCH: RELIGIOUS GROUPS IN CONTEMPORARY AFRICAN SOCIETY

Introduction to Part I

Bennetta Jules-Rosette

The theme of this section is the coexistence of customary religious groups with churches in contemporary Africa and the structural influence of one upon the other. The four essays in this part of the volume deal with these groups. Custom is not synonymous with static (or even historical) types of social organization. These groups are still undergoing change and are redefining themselves in contemporary African society. The West African secret societies emerge as sources of sacred and secular control. Bellman stresses that the distribution of knowledge about and within the secret societies varies a great deal between the sexes, as well as across initiates and nonmembers. He sees this social distribution of knowledge as a key to understanding the impact of the societies on their larger communities.

MacCormack emphasizes the continuing importance of the Sande women's society in Sierra Leone. She states that it has not "dwindled into a wispy relic" since the seventeenth century but, instead, thrives in a new social context. However, the uses of the organization differ in urban and rural areas. In the urban setting, the Sande provides a source of social support, economic sharing, and companionship. Its sacred importance and the specific forms of knowledge that it transmits recede in favor of the group's informal social operations. Recently, the Sande in Sierra Leone has been a source of cultural innovation and reform. Courses in village sanitation and health care have been incorporated into the Sande learning process. In this way, the format of traditional education has been retained with new content.

The Poro–Sande complex represents a case of complementary leadership structures. A few women ceremonially participate in the Poro, but their chief source of power is in the separate Sande association. Even in that case, they are

25

not considered the political leaders of the community, although they hold their own specialized forms of knowledge and positions of power. The Sisala of northern Ghana have this sort of complementarity between men and women built into their cosmological and social systems. While some societies in northern Ghana prohibit women's participation in divination, the Sisala respect and encourage women as diviners. It is accepted that women can perform this revered function, because divination is a mechanical rite. Women diviners are generally past the age of childbearing, and derive cure rather than prestige from joining the divinatory cult. Through the cult they develop spiritual powers of leadership, but are excluded from the political–jural domain. Similar cases of exclusion may be noted in the indigenous churches, where women are endowed with expressive or ceremonial authority in contrast to the male elders who remain in control of the political sphere.

Kilson similarly outlines the importance of women's mediumship among the Ga of Ghana. The medium works alone and under the priest's authority at annual festivals. The knowledge held by the medium is esoteric and governed by principles of secrecy. Kilson uses a biographical approach to stress the centrality of mediumship as a source of ceremonial control for women. While the Ga medium is an awesome figure, she is not a political leader and is subject to the control of priests. She is an older woman who, even outside of her mediumship, retains the conventional association of women with healing, mysticism, and nurturance.

Overall, the first section of this volume introduces the changing state of African religion as a topic and the position of women in African religious groups as a way of looking at the basic social organization of a given group and an index of processes of change and revitalization. All of the discussions in this section stress the mystical power of women through mediumship and ceremonial authority, as opposed to a direct political contribution. Nonetheless, the studies reveal the complexity of the relationship between priests and priestesses and offer a necessary background for looking at larger structural changes in contemporary African religion.[1]

---

[1]The concept of independency widely used in the literature (Barrett, 1968; Barrett, 1971; Sundkler, 1961), assumes that indigenous churches are independent with respect to missions. This mission–centered orientation is in many instances misleading.

1

Sande: The Public Face
of a Secret Society

Carol P. MacCormack

INTRODUCTION

Sande is a women's secret society that initiates girls into womanhood and makes them eligible for marriage. Since social grace, good health, fertility, successful childbirth, and nurturance are not matters to be left to nature but are conditions and events caused by Sande wisdom, rites, and practical expertise, it is an institution that continues to assist women throughout their adult life. It is secret in the sense that it owns knowledge so valuable that it must be guarded against debasement and transmitted only in ritual situations to initiates properly prepared to receive it.

When asked about the origins of Sande, women in Sierra Leone either say that it has always been there or suggest that it might have come from the north. European travelers on the Sherbro shore during the first half of the seventeenth century observed in some detail Sande's organization and its initiation rites. The account which Olfert Dapper published in Amsterdam in 1668 differs in no important detail from Sande organization and initiation today (Dapper in Fyfe, 1964, pp. 39–40). Where Sande was an important, pervasive social institution in the seventeenth century, it has not dwindled to a wispy relic today but thrives in the very heart and soul of contemporary culture. An estimated 95% of the women in the provinces of Sierra Leone are Sande women (Margai, 1948, p. 228). Even women who have migrated into Freetown, Sierra Leone's major urban area, continue in active association with neighborhood Sande chapters, needing the companionship and social support in life-crisis situations that Sande provides (Banton, 1957, p. 185).

Sande spreads as women migrate, following marriage, to live virilocally with their husband's people. New chapters originate whenever a woman who knows the secret wisdom can attract an initiation class of local girls. This women's society is active in all of Sierra Leone, parts of Guinea, and at least the northwest half of Liberia, its distribution related somewhat to the distribution of Mande and Mel languages (Dalby, 1965; Greenberg, 1966). Since Sande is widespread, there may be regional variation in organization, beliefs, and practices.[1] Therefore, unless otherwise specified, this paper refers to the Moyamba District of Sierra Leone, including four Sherbro-speaking and ten Mende-speaking chiefdoms.

ORGANIZATION

Sande is an acephalous system of corporate groups organized by residence rather than by descent. Local chapters maintain their autonomy, and only an informal integration of chapters is achieved by local officials participating in initiation ceremonies in other areas. There is no centralized hierarchical organization to match organization at the local level. Chapters are corporate in that they "own" secret knowledge, ritual objects, and "medicine."[2] They exist in perpetuity. Local founding ancestresses are the source of knowledge, laws, and sanctioning power.[3] In Sande ceremonies, libations are poured to these ancestresses, and food is prepared to "feed" them. New members are "born" into the corporate body through initiation and pass at death into ancestresshood through Sande mortuary rites.[4]

Since an initiate must be sponsored by an older Sande woman, most girls are initiated into their mother's chapter. Initiation entitles a woman to marry, and residence following marriage is usually virilocal; thus, the young initiate soon affiliates with the chapter in her husband's village. Ideally, she returns to her mother's chapter to give birth to children, often under the care of the midwife-official who initiated her. In much of the world, virilocal residence separates women from the solidarity of their own kin, leaving them fragmented and powerless as a group. By contrast, Sande is a focus for lifelong organization and cohesiveness wherever a woman may reside.

[1]Sande is known as Bundu in Temne and Krio. Field research conducted intermittently between 1969 and 1976 has been funded principally by the National Science Foundation and the British Social Science Research Council.

[2]Medicine refers to physical substances with effective pharmacological properties, and to physical substances that link persons to sources of power in the universe.

[3]In Lungi, Moyamba District, Sande women are buried in a great mound in the village. The mound symbolizes the power of women to bless and succor, their power existing in unbroken continuity from the living to the dead.

[4]At death, a woman also joins the ancestors of her natal descent group.

All members of a local chapter congregate for a minimum of two or three days in the initiation grove at the culmination of each initiation season, and sponsoring mothers and officials may remain in the grove for weeks or even months. The Sande women of a village also meet to air common grievances, for sociability, and to dance as a group on festive occasions.

Each local chapter has a head, called *majo* in Mende, and a council composed of 20 to 35 women in high grades. There are five ranked grades within Sande, the lowest being young women who have recently been initiated and the highest composed of an exceptional few who command great knowledge, control Sande ''medicine,'' are effective teachers, and are authoritative leaders in guiding people through life crises. Women do not proceed automatically to higher grades but must ask questions, learn a body of theoretical and practical knowledge, and display adeptness through deeds before they advance to a higher rank.

Some leaders derive their rank from other social and political attributes outside Sande. In the Sherbro country, especially, women grown old in wisdom and authority may become the ranking elder of their aristocratic, cognatic descent group.[5] They allocate use-rights to the group's corporate land, have judicial functions, and, being principal political figures in the area, are rightfully members of the local Sande chapter's council. Such a woman may head the chapter.

The *majo* is ultimately responsible for the quality of such initiate's training for womanhood. She passes on strong, positive definitions of womanhood in the imagery of oral tradition, art, and practical skills. She, or another senior official, is also midwife and adviser on all gynecological matters. Women's fertility is not left to nature, but is a matter brought under the control of explicit cultural rules enforced by Sande women and Sande ancestresses.

RITUAL SPHERES OF MEN AND WOMEN

In the southern and eastern provinces of Sierra Leone there are several sodalities that command secret knowledge and call upon the wisdom of ancestors and other spiritual forces. The fertility of the land and people, their physical and mental health, and the general social order are maintained by the power of these forces to bless or punish.

Poro, the men's secret society, is overtly political, functioning in an institutional fashion at the local level to counterbalance the largely secular power of chiefs (Little, 1965, 1966). However, whereas all members and officials of Sande are women, Poro is not exclusively a male society.[6] A necessary official

[5]Descent groups ranked according to origins: (1) first settlers or conquerors, (2) client groups, (3) former slave groups. See MacCormack (1977a).

[6]D'Azevedo (1973) gives a brief description of a male principal but not male membership in Liberian Sande.

of each Poro chapter must be a woman. Women who inadvertently discover Poro secrets are initiated and brought within its moral sphere as well.

There are other sodalities whose membership is open to anyone regardless of sex, as with Thoma or Njaye (known in Sherbro as Yasse). The local chapters have coheads: a man and a woman. A woman initiated into Thoma cannot be a Sande woman, and a man initiated into Thoma cannot be a Poro man. It is a separate but equal alternative to the single-sex initiation societies. Njaye is concerned with treating randomly occurring crises in peoples' lives, such as a bout of depression, rather than the more predictable puberty, childbirth, and death crises which are accompanied by status transformations. Njaye chapters have coheads, and in some areas (e.g., the Mokobo region of the Upper Kagboro), the woman cohead automatically becomes an ex officio member of Poro. Such a woman usually has the ability to remember names of ancestors to great genealogical depth, calling them for blessings and assistance. Through these crosslinking women, the complementary spheres of men and women are joined on a ritual plane.[7]

A second link is that of the overarching ancestors and ancestresses, often of autochthonous groups, who are called in a variety of ritual contexts.

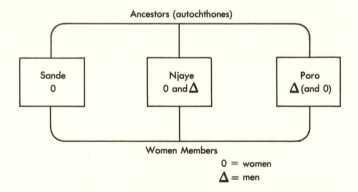

Figure 1.1 Chart of Secret Society Organization among the Sherbro and the Mende of Sierra Leone

In many chiefdoms, the ruling descent group is of recent origin, beginning with a warrior, invited leader, or colonial appointee. Religious authority in the hands of deeply–rooted autochthones counterbalances the political authority of chiefs.

Male chiefs may never be the head of a Poro chapter, but they may sit with the group of advising elders. With Sande the structural situation differs, and women paramount chiefs or their sisters have founded and led Sande chapters.[8]

----

[7]A woman initiated into Poro is regarded as a man and no longer a Sande woman, but she continues to work and live in the social sphere of women.

[8]For example, two women paramount chiefs of Kaiyamba Chiefdom (Hoffer, 1974, pp. 182–183; Ranson, 1968) and the late paramount chief of Gallinas–Perri Chiefdom (Margai, 1948, p. 230).

Thus, women chiefs might use Sande more directly for their political purposes than male chiefs might use Poro. However, should a chief wish to express his power by physical coercion, and if he can convince the ruling officials of his Poro chapter that force is judicious, he will have a band of strong, loyal young Poro men at his command. Sande women are not trained as warriors, and a woman chief, were she desirous of resorting to force, must utilize Poro warriors through a male intermediary. Women chiefs rely on the personal loyalty of their male kin and their husbands to put their cases forward in a favorable light within the Poro council. In some cases, a woman paramount chief will choose a Poro leader as her speaker or important subchief. Women chiefs also take sons, daughters, or grandchildren of secret society officials into their households as wards to help strengthen political alliances (see Hoffer, 1971, 1972, & 1974, for additional political strategies used by women).

Finally, it is important to stress that Poro and Sande do not exist in opposition to each other (as incorrectly suggested by Millett, 1970, pp. 48–49). Each has its particular domain of social control which complements but does not overlap with that of the other. Poro officials see that scarce resources are conserved and that people do not let disputes escalate into fights. Sande officials, for example, treat certain illnesses and enforce moral prohibitions against voyeurism. Each lays down explicit laws of behavior known to the entire community. If a law is breached, the transgressor and his or her kin are equally to blame. The sodalities provide laws and services for the health and well-being of the entire community, not for their group alone. When one secret society begins its initiation season, the others, out of respect, remain quiescent so as not to steal the ceremonial stage.

INITIATION: A RITE OF PASSAGE

For analytical purposes, the female life cycle might be divided into four stages. Girlhood extends from birth to the onset of menstruation. The second stage bounds the brief period between the beginning of physical maturity and marriage, when a female is no longer a girl but not yet a wife who may procreate. The third stage is adulthood following marriage or cohabitation with a man, and the final stage is ancestorhood, following physical death.

In the second stage, a girl, sponsored by a mature Sande woman, leaves the social domain of the village and passes through a screen of palm fronds, entering the Sande "bush." It is a cleared place in the forest or a secluded part of a town, where she is ritually separated from the larger society. The girl's sponsor sees that initiation fees and food are contributed from family and, perhaps, a potential husband.[9] If a family cannot raise the fees from kin or moneylender, a girl may

---

[9]Initiation fees were about 20 pounds sterling in very rural areas of Kagboro Chiefdom in 1976. Bridewealth payments were about 25 pounds sterling.

become the ward of the *majo*, remaining in her care for four or five years, and in the liminal status of an initiate for three or four of those years. Girls from families that are wealthy or influential enough to send them to school may remain in the liminal state for the duration of a Christmas school vacation only. At a pragmatic level of analysis, there are social distinctions made between aristocratic girls who are transformed into women with a minimum of time and toil, while girls from less fortunate families may work for years making farms (a new farm is "made" each year) and extracting palm oil for the chapter's officials.

At a symbolic level of analysis, the liminal period is a timeless, abnormal, sacred period of marginality for all the initiates (see Turner, 1969, & Van Gennep, 1960 for a discussion of liminality). Old clothes and names are left behind. The girls' bodies are covered with a coating of white clay through the entire period of liminality. Every day is turned to night, since the initiates are required to arise, sweep the area, wash themselves, and sing Sande songs after the first cock crows, even if it is three o'clock in the morning.

"Dirt" is ritually washed away in daily cleansing rites. Senior officials stress their responsibility for teaching the cultural rules of cleanliness. Menstrual blood is properly disposed of, bringing that which is potentially polluting or dangerous, at the margin of the body, under cultural control. Cliterodectomy, performed at the beginning of the initiation period, is also described as making women "clean." One might speculate along the lines Douglas has developed that by excising the clitoris, a rudiment of maleness, all sexual ambiguity is removed from the incipient woman. She then fits "purely" and "safely" into the social structure, free from the "impurity" and "danger" of categorical ambiguity.

Any visible initiation scar or body modification is a public sign that the adult has been brought within a moral sphere marked by a social status. The body modification of a Sande women, however, can only be known through intimate contact. The partner with whom she is sharing a sexual relationship is probably a man trained in the moral responsibility of a potential procreator in Poro, the men's initiation society. He will be confident that she is a Sande woman, trained in women's moral and practical responsibilities in procreation.

The pain of cliterodectomy is a metaphor for childbirth, which ideally takes place in the same grove under the expertise of the same *majo*, with the protection of Sande "medicine" and the social support of Sande "sisters." Shared pain and risk of death from infection in initiation helps to bond initiates together into a cohesive group. At the end of the initiation period, they swear an oath on Sande "medicine" never to reveal a fault in another Sande woman.[10]

Pleasures of feasting, singing, games, and dancing are measured with ordeals in the initiation grove, and girls look forward to the time when they may

---

[10]This is the ideal. An occasional dispute between Sande women may go outside their moral community into the Native Administration court. In such cases, Sande "medicine" may be used for swearing an oath to tell the truth in court.

go into Sande. Initiation occurs in the postharvest dry season, and quantities of special food are sent into the "bush" on the girls' behalf. It is a time of fattening, and wood carvings, which are ritual accoutrements to Sande ceremonies, depict females with three rings of flesh at the neck. A woman who is plump enough for the neck to crease is judged healthy, fertile, and beautiful, in contrast to "dry" and barren girls.[11]

The initiation period ends when a "medicine" made by brewing leaves in water is used to ritually wash the initiates, removing the magical protection they enjoyed since entering the initiation grove. In their liminal state under magical protection, they were dangerous to any man who approached them sexually. Following the washing and final rituals of status transformation, all ambiguity about their womanhood is removed. They have become mature women in knowledgeable control of their own sexuality.

It is only after the initiation ceremonies have been completed that the women are eligible for marriage and childbearing.[12] Sande alone may certify women as eligible wives. Before hospitals provided an alternative, it also had a monopoly on delivering their legitimate children. Women seem to have the awareness that as a social group they control production of a scarce resource: offspring for their husbands' descent groups. To withhold that good is to have great power, and a woman can justifiably withhold herself from her husband if his behavior contravenes Sande law. Even more disconcerting, she, often in league with her mother, may threaten to use "medicine" to make him impotent. Rarely, however, will a woman withhold herself from her husband, since it is in her own self-interest to bear children. Children give her an honored status and rewarding roles to play during her fertile years. Later, children give her emotional and economic security in old age. After death, her children will remember her, giving her immortality.

Women organized into corporate groups thus intervene at the focus of social interest in a female's life: the period between first menstruation and onset of procreative sexuality. A bride is not transferred directly from one corporate descent group to another but passes through the intermediary institution of Sande initiation. Fees for initiation are as essential as bride wealth in obtaining a wife. The incipient husband and his kin are expected to help with initiation fees, often contributing the major portion together with bride wealth. Sande initiation is an important public ceremony. First menstruation, marriage, defloration, and birth of a first child are not. The structural point to be noted is that much of what is functionally bride wealth is not part of a reciprocal exchange between descent

---

[11]See Frisch and McArthur (1974) for correlation between body fat and fertile ovulation cycles.

[12]This is the ideal. Some women have had sexual experience and even have had children and marriage with bride wealth before initiation. Although officials disapprove, they keep the doors open to initiation at any time in life. Similarly, some girls enter an initiation class before they begin to menstruate, although ideally they should not.

groups but is used in enriching and maintaining the Sande society in the expectation that it will continue to bring forth a plentiful supply of good wives.

A further point to be reiterated is that when the "natural" events of
menstruation, pregnancy, childbirth, illness, and death come under the organized
control of Sande knowledge, laws, and ritual they are brought decisively within
the domain of culture. A theoretical model in which women are analogous to
nature or outside the domain of culture and society does not apply to this study
(see Ardener, 1972; Mathieu, 1973; MacCormack, 1977b).

INITIATION: A SCHOOL OF INSTRUCTION

When a girl goes through the portal of palm fronds into the forest grove, she is
greeted by the older women singing "My child, come join society." The girls
sing a response of "Yes, mother" (ya in Sherbro means mother or respected
elder woman). The girls greet the elders with a hands-on-knees stooping gesture
showing respect and obeisance.

A girl may enter the grove on her own initiative. For example, a student in
a small rural secondary school was considered by her classmates to be a "girl,"
beneath the respected status of woman because she had not been initiated. At
Christmas vacation she went into the grove and once there, her parents sent the
necessary fees and food to see her through initiation.

The initiation class is hierarchically organized, with the first girl to pass
through the portal being head girl, called kema in Sherbro. She may be the
daughter of a high–ranking Sande official, but is not necessarily so. First to arise
in the morning, she sees that the others arise, sweep, and wash themselves.
During the day, she is the initiator and organizer of activities. She has the
authority of an eldest sibling, or, more to the point, of the head wife in a
polygynous household. The first in a set of siblings, cowives or initiates has more
time to learn, becoming more skilled in practical and social matters than those
who come after.

Ultimately it is the majo and other senior officials who are responsible for
instruction. They stress that girls observe everything: farming, spinning, child-
care, diagnosing illness, compounding and administering medicines, singing,
and dancing. When a girl feels confident enough, she takes up a specific task.
Ridicule and threats are used to spur the inadept and idle. If these fail, the girl is
directed to other tasks rather than being punished. In the evenings initiates and
elders gather about the fire, singing, dancing, talking, and telling stories. The
stories end in a moral or a dilemma which is debated long into the night,
encouraging a more mature exploration of the human condition.

Most of what the household and farming work girls do during initiation is
not new to them. Since they have assisted their mothers from an early age, it is
not new skills but new attitudes toward work that they learn. In childhood they
work in the role of daughter, but in Sande they begin to anticipate the role of wife

in which they will have to work cooperatively with their cowives and husbands' kin. During the initiation period they work on the *majo's* farm. They also cook, wash clothes, and daub mud houses in the manner of a married woman working cooperatively with her cowives. The imagery of death and rebirth is not as prominent in Sande initiation ceremonies as it is in Poro, where boys give up a more carefree childhood in taking on adult tasks.

Women spin; men weave. Men prepare the ground for cultivation; women weed. Sande and Poro are the root of a sharply delineated division of labor based upon sex. It is also the root of a symbolic interdependence between men and women, a force keeping marriages together against the pull of emotional security in the natal descent group.

POLITICAL CONSEQUENCES OF
ORGANIZATION AND AUTONOMY

Because Sande women are organized into effective corporate groups and enjoy female autonomy in all matters pertaining to Sande's sphere of interests, their political position in the larger society is enhanced. Although all members and officials of Sande are women, men, especially male chiefs, would like to control Sande. One incumbent Mende paramount chief stresses the fact that the most powerful local *majo* is one of his wives. Implicit in his statement is the allegation that he controls his wife and, therefore, controls Sande. However, when women go off to the Sande bush, they are physically separated from male control. A male chief who intrudes into the Sande private areas or secret ceremonies is trespassing against ancient Sande law. Whoever trespasses against that law is liable to suffer the divine retribution of physical illness or the concerted secular legal maneuvers of Sande women acting as a political interest group.

The community is dramatically reminded of Sande's sanctioning power when masked female ancestral figures appear in the village at the close of the initiation season. There may be two or three clothed in black helmet-type wooden masks and black raffia capes, completely hiding the figure of the woman inside. By the smooth, glossy black finish of the mask's "skin," its three rings at the neck representing fat on a well-fed woman, and the composure of the features carved on the face of the mask, the ideal of healthy, virtuous, serene womanhood is expressed. But a single mask of a second type also appears in a rough brown finish with white blotches about the face. Part of the cape is stained green, the rest red, a "strong" color, with a great bunch of large snail shells hanging on the cape. The blotchiness and decay of disease is represented on the mask, and the snail shells contain Sande "medicine." Where the black figures dance with controlled gracefulness, the blotched figure strides about shaking a bundle of switches at wrongdoers of either sex and all ages, reminding all who watch the public ceremony of Sande's power to catch and punish transgressors even if they sin in secret.

When one's illness is diagnosed as being caused by disrespect for Sande laws, the offender must go to the officials of the local chapter, publicly confess, pay a fine to the Sande officials, and submit to a cleansing ceremony. Or, Sande women may not wait for divine retribution but may physically carry the offender off to the Sande bush and chastise him.[13] If a paramount chief attempts to interfere in Sande affairs, women may generate pressure to have him declared "unfit to rule." If a commission of inquiry is held, Sande women will testify in court and may be instrumental in his deposition from office.[14]

Sande laws make explicit the respect that should be shown to all women. The laws are carefully observed by both men and women, being reinforced by supernatural sanctions and by pragmatic political action on the part of women locally organized into a hierarchy of offices.[15] Beyond considerations of organization and law, a deep feeling of social solidarity stems from women's activities as producers and reproducers within Sande's moral milieu, enhancing their capacity for concerted political action. In agricultural societies of the type found in southern and eastern Sierra Leone, hoeing, weeding, harvesting, and other tasks are best done in cooperative work groups, and cowives usually welcome a new wife in the household who will share in communal tasks.

Some writers taking a speculative evolutionary view of political development suggest that because women have not shared in the risks of hunting, they are not able to bond into political groups and do not have experience in decision-making. It may even be considered an aberration of human nature for women to hold political office (Tiger, 1969, p. 259). However, we have been a tropical animal for most of our evolutionary history, and among tropical people today women do hunt small and medium-sized game (Goodale, 1971, p. 169). As gatherers, they may make decisions that result in procurement of two or three times as much food, including protein, as men (Lee, 1968, p. 259). In settled agricultural societies as in Sierra Leone, women are important food producers, and the head wife in a complex household has considerable decision-making and executive powers that may lead to high political office (Hoffer, 1974).

In regard to risk-taking and social bonding, females in the hominid line have been experiencing the hazards of childbirth for at least as long as males have been experiencing the risks of hunting large animals. Childbirth is no less a social act than hunting, usually involving at a minimum the woman in labor and the midwife. In Sierra Leone, this risk-taking is embedded in the highly institutionalized Sande society. Vows explicitly expressing a social bond are taken

[13]Residents of Kagboro Chiefdom recall the time Sande women carried Paramount Chief Samuel Africanus Caulker (who ruled from 1919 to 1932) off to the Sande bush for using abusive language to his wives. They kept him there for several days, and he allegedly returned chastised and mellowed.

[14]See the case of the Paramount Chief of Tane Chiefdom, deposed in 1957 for offending Sande and other "native law and custom" (Sierra Leone Government 1957, p. 19).

[15]The Hut Tax War of 1898 was largely coordinated through the Poro society which is organized into informally linked local chapters similar to those of the Sande society (Fyfe, 1962, p. 55ff.; 1964, p. 247; Manna-Kpaka, 1953).

by initiates following the pain of clitorodectomy, a metaphor for the social support in pain in childbirth they will experience later. Qualitatively, this solidarity associated with risk-taking is not different from Poro vows of solidarity sworn on "medicine" before warriors go out. On an everyday level, there is a complementarity and balance in the strain and risk of work activities. Men climb oil palm trees to cut the fruits, or cut and burn the forest to prepare it for planting. Women do the safer but more extended tasks of extracting oil from the palm fruits, hoeing and weeding the crops, and gathering the harvest.

The decisions of Sande officials are no less fundamental to the survival of the population than decisions made by Poro officials, and executive strategies operated by Sande officials can be as overtly political as those made by the Poro. For example, a woman upon reaching maturity does not immediately leave her natal descent group for marriage and residence in her husband's group, but passes through Sande on the way. It is thus possible for some Sande leaders to have influence in arranging their initiates' first marriage. This strategy was developed to a fine art by Madam Yoko, a Mende chief renowned for her womanly grace and political power. Important families vied with each other to have their daughters trained and initiated in the chapter she headed. She selected girls from important descent groups, initiated them into Sande, and, at the urging of some parents, kept some in her household as wards. Later, acting as their marriage guardian, she gave them in marriage to men of prominence, thus making alliances with both families with each girl (Hoffer, 1974, pp. 182–183). By contrast, a male chief, by taking wives in marriages of political alliance, cannot send the women out again in marriage without breaking the first alliance link by divorce. Madam Yoko was thus able to use a political strategy unavailable to her male counterparts.

In the Republic of Sierra Leone women are enfranchised to vote. Politically prominent women who are also influential Sande women can allegedly insure large blocks of votes in national elections for themselves or candidates they favor by requiring Sande women to swear an oath on Sande "medicine" to vote for a specific candidate. This political strategy is not restricted to Sande women and is allegedly practiced in other secret societies as well (Cartwright, 1970, pp. 247–248).

CONCLUSION

There is a complementarity and balance in this ethnic area of Sierra Leone in which women participate fully in economic and political life. Sande laws insure respect for all women, and they gain considerable political experience in the enforcement of those laws. Their organization stems from a deep sense of social solidarity that begins in the initiation experience and continues in a spirit of cooperative assistance throughout life.

2

The Social Organization
of Knowledge in Kpelle Ritual

Beryl L. Bellman

INTRODUCTION

The Fala Kpelle of Liberia communicate many meanings in ritual that are relevant only within the context of a performance.[1] Here, I examine some of the methods Kpelle speakers use to interpret these situated meanings so that they are, for all practical purposes, the same as intended by their producers. The various meanings of the symbols used during a ritual performance are a member's possession. Thus, there is a variety of different interpretations for any medicine object *(sale)* or event. Different categories of members possess particular techniques for reading intentionally produced secret signs.[2] They have access to particular parable interpretations that permit them to communicate specific meanings during the course of a performance which are understandable only by members of their own or some directed-to category. There is, therefore, a member-recognized social distribution of knowledge.

Mannheim (1952) has offered the programmatic advice that a sociology of knowledge is possible by collecting theories of knowledge from all the cross-sections of a society. The sum total of information would provide the world view of the group even though the description differs from any member's personal understanding. However, this approach does not attend to how members intend or understand meanings, either as observers or participants, during the course of

[1]There are five recognized dialects of Kpelle in Liberia (Kakataa, Tototaa, Ghanga, Zotas, and Fala), and at least two have been identified in Guinea.
[2]These signs are taught during initiation rituals of the various secret societies to be discussed. Often, different signs are learned as one is promoted to a particular society's hierarchy. Hence, there are different categories of members within each association.

a ritual or societal activity. My interest is in how symbols are interpreted within the context of a ritual event.

The different interpretive schema that are used to understand the meaning of symbols are reflexive to two criteria. The most basic is sexual differentiation. In virtually every aspect of Kpelle life, ranging from secret society activities to the most mundane interactions, sexual differences are expressed. This is manifested both in the division of labor and in cosmological beliefs. Sexual symbolism is always a part of ritual activities shown either by the exclusion of the opposite sex or by incorporating as part of the rituals specific meanings associated with sexual differentiation. Men and women have different access to the meanings of the same ritual events. However, each group is stratified according to an individual's relationship to those events. The latter is the second reflexive criterion.

There are sets of interpretive schemata for any ritual activity, each associated with the sex of the members. The various schemata belonging to each set are associated with the status of one's membership within the event. In this manner a male of either high or low status has a different understanding of a symbol from that of a female of the corresponding status. High and low status members of the same sex will interpret meanings differently from one another. This is especially evident during rituals that exclude members of the opposite sex. During those activities, the ritual performers are cognizant that the symbols they use are being interpreted differently by members of the opposite sex. Many symbolic forms are designed to take those differences into account. Hence, sexual exclusion does not involve a lack of participation by the opposite sex. Rather, it establishes a kind of participation whereby those excluded are participating by their formal response to the event. When the devil or masquerade figure of the Poro society is in the community, for example, all women must immediately go into their homes, close all doors and windows, and sit in silence. These acts constitute a form of participation, since they follow a set of prescribed behavioral rules for this situation. The very fact that the women are inside their homes provides an atmosphere which is an essential component of that ritual activity.

SECRET SOCIETY MEMBERSHIP AND THE ACQUISITION OF RITUAL KNOWLEDGE

In Sucromu, the principal Poro town of the Vavala chiefdom in Lofa County, Liberia, there are at least ten secret societies. Everyone must belong to either the Poro or Sande if they are to take an effective part in village life.[3] The Poro or *porong* is the men's society. It is composed of three internal societies, each with

---

[3]Before joining, one is called a *sina* and is considered a nonmember in most important discussions. In many communities there are one or more Mandingo (Islamic) families, but because of their non-Poro/Sande membership, they are effectively excluded from most town matters, except those which directly pertain to them.

different grades of membership. The societies are named by the specific devil or *noi sheng* (bush thing) that performs during their rituals. The largest is the *ngamu* society. When boys reach the age of puberty and the time is appropriate for a bush school session, they are captured by the *ngamu* bush thing and taken into the deep forest. There, they live in an age-set community separate from all members of the opposite sex (except for certain females who have specific ritual tasks to perform). While living in this bush school, the boys are considered dead by those in the town. During this period of isolation, they are washed in special medicines, given the community Poro organization's scars on their chest, back, and neck, taught the laws of the town's protective medicines, and instructed in fighting techniques. After a period of time, they are reborn into the community with a new name and adult status. Traditionally, bush school participation lasted four years, but since the Tubman regime, this has been reduced to one and a half years.[4] These initiations occur about once every 15 years. When the session opens the youngest children enter first, together with those boys who later will assume important positions in the society's leadership. The latter group is initiated into the upper grades or levels in the society's hierarchy. Some stay for a shorter period of time and attend some later bush school session for further promotion. The year after the session opens, boys who are attending school enter into the bush. They remain there for the term of their vacation (about three months) and are initiated into the first grade of the society's hierarchy.

The *ngamu* or devil of this society is also known as the *Zo* or priest devil, since it acts as the corporate representative of the Poro society both within the community and during disputes between towns. Whenever two towns enter into a Poro related dispute, the devils of both communities meet and engage in a ritual battle. If one devil is victorious, the losing community capitulates and offers a sacrifice to the winner. If neither devil is victorious, the towns traditionally would enter into combat. Today, while warfare is prohibited by the government, medicine warfare is still practiced. The towns attempt to kill, by poisoning or sympathetic magic, the *Zo* leaders of one another's societies. Each *ngamu* represents the combined medicine powers of each community. Thus, if a town's devil is able to defeat another, the loser recognizes that the metaphysical powers of that community are greater than their own.

In addition to medicine warfare, the devil is responsible for making announcements to the community. These concern a variety of issues ranging from organizing community labor projects to imparting private information to compound elders. Although each town has a chief and several patrilocal compound leaders, they are unable to require the community to engage in collective work. Once the *ngamu* makes a request, however, all members of the Poro must obey. Each town, thus, has two ruling structures: a sacred one represented by the Poro and Sande and a secular one composed of the chiefs, elders, and government officials. The sacred ruling structure is responsible for major disputes, warfare,

---

[4]President William S. Tubman initiated this policy to encourage children to enter the modern schools he established in the interior.

and serious crimes and abuses. The secular structure is mainly concerned with cases of adultery, divorce, minor torts, and the collection of government taxes.

The devils or *ngamu* of each community are basically independent in their power. However, within each area there is a major devil or father. This devil is responsible for assisting in the adjudication of disputes between Poro chapters in an attempt to avoid combat. This devil, while necessarily the most powerful, is recognized as the political head of the area's Poro societies. When there is a meeting of the numerous Poro chapters in the area, this devil acts as the host and offers the final judgment in the collective discussions.

The only exception to the total exclusion of women and nonmembers when a *ngamu* makes an appearance in a community occurs once a year when the ngamu performs a sacrifice and lays a protective vine around the town's boundary. All dwellings that are encircled by the vine must obey the laws of the Poro society and of the secular leadership of the community. Although women are permitted to be out of doors during the ritual, they keep at a great distance and often shield their eyes from the devil's gaze. If they should come too close, it is believed that they will be stricken with illness. If one is pregnant it is feared that the child will assume the physical characteristics of the devil.

Members of the *ngamu* society may join the *ngamu nea* society. This devil is the wife of the *ngamu* and may be seen by women and nonmembers whenever she is in the community.[5] The devil is also called "the dancing devil" since she often performs during major celebrations both within the community and in the clan. Although women are permitted to see the *ngamu nea* outside of her fence, they actually seldom go near the area where the devil is performing. This devil is considered less powerful than her husband, yet is greatly feared, since illegitimate contact with it can result in either illness or paralysis. The *ngamu nea* often accompanies the *ngamu* when he makes an appearance in the town. As both devils walk through the community the *ngamu nea* sings for her husband. The song is composed by a group of musicians who blow specially prepared horns.

The members of the patrilineal caste who are the *Zo* of the *ngamu* society all belong to the *balasilangamu* society. In addition, there are a few others who, in the words of the society's crier, "know themselves." If a nonmember should see this devil, he or she will either die, become blind, or suffer leprosy. The society performs major sacrifices and prepares protective and offensive medicines for the community. It is considered the most powerful and "dangerous" of all the secret associations.

The Sande society is the women's equivalent of the *porong*.[6] All girls join some time after puberty when the appropriate part of the ritual cycle is reached. The girls are taken into a bush school or female age-set community separate from

---

[5] Since the most serious discussions are held behind the Poro fence in the vicinity or presence of a *noi sheng*, no Mandingos can take part in them.

[6] In Kpelle, the Poro is referred to as the *porong*. There are significant cross-cultural differences in the Poro and Sande internal social structure (cf. MacCormack, Chap. 1).

all men for a year and a half. Traditionally, their bush schools lasted for three years, but were reduced for the same reason as the *porong* bush. In the bush village, they are instructed in women's knowledge, the laws of the town's medicines, and given various medicines and poisons. They are scarred along the waist and, before the coming out or rebirth ritual, their clitorises are cut. This, many have described, is the actual meaning of the word "sande." The girls are then initiated into the community with new names and full adult status. Within the Sande is the *Zohii* society which parallels the men's *balasilangamu*. All the Sande *Zo* (priestesses) and especially powerful female elders belong. This body constitutes the ruling grade of the Sande organization. The medicines of the society are considered dangerous for men. Whenever there is a Sande meeting or ritual, most men keep their distance and only approach the women to offer them tribute.

Both the Poro and Sande constitute the sacred ruling structure of the community. They are responsible for the maintenance and control of the town's protective and offensive medicines. Each of those medicines has laws that pertain to it. Some of these include restrictions against violence, rape, murder, and certain abuses. When the laws are broken, the *Zo* of the societies are responsible for the adjudication of the matter. Violations of the laws can "spoil" the medicines unless an appropriate sacrifice is made over them. The two societies alternate in their responsibility for watching over those medicines. This is directly associated with the initiation cycle. Traditionally, the Poro held its initiations for four years. They then controlled the bush for an additional four years, at which time they ritually turned control over to the women. They, in turn, conducted their initiations and bush school for three years. After the initiation period they continued to control the bush for an additional three years before returning control to the men. Today, the Liberian government has placed a one-year restriction on the bush schools. However, the entire cycle is still practiced. When the Sande are in control they are responsible for sacred matters under the authority of the *porong* leadership. This is exemplified in a case I recorded during the last period of Sande control: an old woman had died who was reputed to possess a medicine pot which reputedly gave her the powers of a leopard. At her funeral, her husband and brother argued over to whom the pot should go. It was decided that the pot be buried with the woman. After the burial, both families drank and danced with musicians and kinsmen as part of the postburial ritual. Both men became drunk and returned to the argument. One of the men struck the other in the face. The two were immediately separated, and the fight ended. A short time later, the Sande leadership met and arrested both of them. They were charged with fighting and taken to the Poro *Zo*. The latter heard the palaver under the women's supervision. The husband, who struck first, was found guilty and was fined. As is the case with all fines, the money was divided; however, the largest amount was given to the Sande leadership, since they were responsible for the moral well-being of the community during that period of the cycle.

In the Poro societies, the *Zo* positions are held by members of a patrilineal caste *(Zoman)* who live in either one of two patrilocal compounds. The female *Zo* positions of the Sande are inherited from mother to daughter. Although it is not mandatory, there is preferential marriage between Poro and Sande *Zo*.

There are two societies that are considered outside of the Poro and Sande but have specific functions to perform for them. They are the *Mina* (male) and *Moling* (male and female). The *Mina* protects the community from *wulu nuu* or stick people. Every person is believed to have two spirits, one for the waking world and the other for dreams. Some have animal dream spirits or *polosheng* (behind things), while most experience themselves as human dreamers. In the latter group, there are some persons who belong to a secret dream society *(wulu nuu)* within which they make human sacrifices of children's dream spirits in their patrilineage.[7] In return for the life of the child, they are given power and wealth. The *Mina* is responsible for protecting the community from such evil spirits. However, individuals must seek the aid of an independent *Zo* for personal protection. In order to join the society, men must draw a cup of water from a particular stream in the forest on a starless night. They must walk to the waterside naked and fend off *wulu nuu* who wait for them in the dark on the path back to town. Then they are given a sword to show their membership. The society then runs through town behind a special night devil who blows into a horn *(mina*, hence the name of the society), making a high-pitched, screaming sound. The members run behind the devil, beating their arms against their sides making whipping sounds. During this ritual, all nonmembers must stay inside their houses and sit in silence in the same way as if either the *ngamu* or *balasilangamu* bush things were performing for their respective societies. Hence, the auditory illusion is produced of a witch or *wulu nuu* being beaten in the night. If any member of the *Mina* should trip and fall during this run through town, he is stabbed to death as a *wulu nuu*. In addition to the sacred task already mentioned, the *Mina* is responsible for protecting the outer fence of the Sande bush school when it is in session. The members also carry goods into the outer fence for the girls to use while in the bush village. Thus, the society functions as a young man's warrior society. This is in direct contrast to Welmers' (1949) description of the *Mina* as simply a young men's society organized to impress the women of the community with the powers of men.

The *Moling* society protects the town from ancestral spirits who are seeking revenge on the community and is responsible for protecting the inner fence of the Sande bush school. In order to join the society, male members must first belong to the *Mina*. Many of the respected women elders and *Zo* also belong. The cost of initiation is high so that only respected and successful persons can join. Normally, one joins around middle age.

[7]Once the dream brain (*lii*, literally heart) dies, so does the waking brain.

There are two societies (male and female membership) that are important to the Poro/Sande in that they protect the bush schools and the community from nonhuman dangers. The *Kawli Sale* or *Gbo Gbling* society (Iron Society) protects the community and preserves individual clients from the mammy water dream spirit or *nyai nenu* (literally, water woman). The society operates an oracle called *faa sale* who speaks directly to the society's *Zo* leadership. The oracle tells the spiritual cause of a person's suffering and makes medicines to cure both the physical and metaphysical problem.

As its name implies, the *Gbo* or lightning society protects the community from lightning and can also direct it to a specified target. The society also has a large collection of poisons in its repertoire of medicines that can be used either by the community or individual members.

The *Kale Sale* or Snake Society is recognized as an imported Mano association. Among the Mano, according to Harley's (1941) description, it plays an important internal function in the *porong*.[8] For the Fala Kpelle, it is recognized as being a highly effective protection against both real and spiritual snakes. The society is reputed to be able to cause snakes to attack persons as part of its war medicines *(koi sale)*.

Finally, there is a voluntary association of young boys who join before entering into the *porong* known as the *Gblingbe* society. In this society they practice what initiation and society membership will be like in their later lives.

THE RECOGNITION OF POSITION AND THE DISCOVERY OF INTENTIONALITY

Each of the above secret societies has its own *Zo* and ruling structure. When a new member joins a society, its structure is taught to him in a ritualized manner. The initiate must undergo an ordeal ceremony and attend not only to the ritual acts performed and their sequencing but also to the performers and their intentions.

During initiation, there is a period in which the new member is shown a variety of medicines for curing snake bites and different forms of intestinal difficulties, as well as antidotes for several poisons. He or she is given certain protections and some medicines for offense. The ritual consists of showing numerous leaves to the member after he has first been shown the special head of the medicine *(Ngung sale)*, taken the oath of membership *(kafu)*, and finished eating food prepared as a sacrifice to the society's special spirit. The following

---

[8]Harley describes the *Bakona*, which is the Mano equivalent of the *Kale Sale*. Among the Mano the Snake Society plays a similar role to the Poro as does the *Kawli Sale* (Iron Society) for the Kpelle.

quotation from my field notes (Bellman, 1975) is a description of one such occasion:

> Yakpawolo Xila, the *bakung* or second man of the society, and Mulbahzua, the third man of the society, returned with an assortment of leaves. After giving the society chant, they put their satchel before Mulbah, the *Zo* (shaman–leader) and said that here were some of the society's leaves. If they were to bring in all the leaves, Yakpawolo claimed, they would have to stay in the bush for four days. Mulbah then said that he accepted the leaves, and the two men proceeded to lay them out in neat piles. After all of them were distributed, Mulbah said that each member was to point to one leaf and show its duty. If any should fail, he warned, they would have to bring a bottle of cane juice (raw rum). Each person in the house then proceeded to point to a leaf and tell what it did and how to prepare it. The major or big men of the society such as Yakpawolo, Mulbah, Kaboku, Tokpah, and Kokulah pointed to their leaves last. The more recent members of the society, such as myself, selected their leaves first. (p. 85)

Since only a portion of leaves was present, and the total number of leaves and their uses were known only to those who, according to the *Zo*, "put their whole interest into the medicines," the order whereby the members selected their leaves reflected, in reverse, the hierarchy of the men in the society. In this way, the society's membership structure was communicated. I noted that different varieties of leaves were shown to the various people I was able to witness join the society. This permits the assumption that the very choice of leaves by the elders is an intentional selection.

The seating within the society medicine hut also reflected its membership structure, since the newer members had to sit up front in order not to push aside the elders as they chose their respective medicines. Concomitantly, appropriate paths had to be maintained so that the elders could pass easily through the ranks of the younger members.

Knowledge of the relative positioning of personages during a ritual is also requisite to an understanding of the *ngamu* or bush devil procession of the Poro society. This ritual involves the dance of a masked member wearing a raffia gown who is possessed by a particular kind of bush spirit *(noi sheng)*. The *ngamu* procession is performed at the call of the Poro *Zo* priesthood. Each *Zo* or priest owns a certain medicine which, when placed alongside all other medicines belonging to the other *Zo*, causes a certain member of the society known as *ngamu woo* "singer for the devil" to become possessed and put on the ritualistic paraphernalia. This takes place inside the Poro *korong* or fence. At the appropriate time, a member, called *ngamu nea tua nuu*, "the holder of the staff," leaves the temple or fence and walks in a deliberate path through the town. Just before he leaves, however, various *Zo* walk about town shouting *"belli la boo,"* "close your doors and windows." At that warning, as stated above, all non-members of the Poro immediately enter their own or the nearest house, close the door, shut the windows, blow out all the lanterns, and sit in absolute silence. The holder of the staff then walks about town until he reaches a previously designated point. At that moment, the *ngamu* leaves the temple and follows the same path that the holder of the staff walked before him. At various intervals, he stops at a house and greets those inside. When he reaches the same place as the holder of the staff, he makes an announcement that explains the specific purpose for the ritual procession. His speech is not comprehensible except to a certain member known as the *pene woo* (interpreter), who translates the *ngamu's* song into understandable Kpelle.

The members are able to locate the ritual's situational meanings by attending to the reason for the *ngamu* procession as translated by the "interpreter." They note the significance of the path the *ngamu* took during his tour through town, what he said to those he greeted during that walk, and the location of the place where the public announcement for the reason of the ritual was made. Of major importance is the arrangement of personnel who stand around the *ngamu*. Only those persons who claim power with the medicines and importance in the sacred ruling structure normally approach him, for when the *ngamu* is outside the Poro fence, many special laws are being enforced. Some of these laws are known only to the high ranking members of the Poro priesthood and the few powerful elders in the Poro inner circle. As a result, laws are easily broken without conscious intent. Hence, only those persons who have special reasons to be around the *ngamu* ever approach him. This is important, because what is considered as appropriate business is reflexive to the specific interaction or ritual performance. Consequently, the circle of persons who stand near the "singer" reflects the intentional structure of the occasion, which is interpretable even by those members who are observing rather than actively participating in the event.

SEXUAL RELATIONSHIPS IN
RITUAL ACTIVITY

There are four types of sexual participation in Kpelle ritual activity. First, there is the sexual exclusion that characterizes the activities of the Mina, Poro, Sande, and the internal associations of the latter two societies. Members of the opposite sex practice formal avoidance rituals. The different symbols expressed during those occasions are differently interpreted by each of the sexes. The performers recognize a complementary belief system of the opposite sex, and are actively engaged in producing cues that their opposites use to construct interpretive accounts of these acts. The interpretive meanings that performers have for these symbolic forms and their methods for accomplishing them are not communicated to the opposite sex. The cues that are transmitted are primarily auditory. On occasion, certain objects are constructed or brought to town while the opposite sex is in seclusion. The latter are then told that a spirit or medicine was responsible for the object's appearance, and are reminded of the sounds that were produced for proof of what possibly could have occurred. There are instances of

Mina members carrying a large uprooted tree to town and telling the women that a witch they had beaten had brought it there to demonstrate the strength of the spirit they had defeated. Similarly, in the center of the community is a small women's medicine house which the men believe is able to hold the entire female population of the community at one time. An important feature of this type of ritual activity is the coexistence of complementary belief systems between performers and nonmembers. The latter's interpretive understanding of the ritual is recognized and managed as part of the performance.

The second type of sexual participation is parallel ritual activity that members of the opposite sex perform in conjunction with one another's rituals. This includes many of the rituals performed by the Poro and Sande in support of each other's activities. During the Poro initiation, the members of the Sande and large groups of young women dancers perform separate rituals alongside the initiates and *Zo* of the society. Each Sunday during the Poro initiation period, young boys are captured by an officer of the Poro known as the *kwelba*. The boys are given a palm thatch sash to wear and numerous head ties which are tied on the sash and on their clothing. No woman is allowed to approach the novices after the sash is placed on them. The boys are then marched around the community where different male members of their own or their mother's patrilineage make presentations in their name to the society. That evening, the boys sleep in a special house and are kept from contact with females. The next morning, the women in their compounds dance throughout the town. Meanwhile, the boys are given food and marched once again around the community accompanied by the *Zo* musicians and various officers and *Zo* of the society. Whenever the male *Zo* musicians enter into the area where the women are playing, the women immediately cease their active singing and chant a repetitious background song until the men leave the quarter. The song is sung in harmony with the men's songs, rendering the music into a joint production. Finally, the boys are taken into the bush. The women are forbidden to follow. Instead, they continue to sing and dance in the community. In a short time, the *kwelba* and several of the other members of the society return to town. The *kwelba* rings a bell signifying that the boys have "successfully fought the devil." When the *kwelba* enters, the women cease playing and loudly shout in unison. The *kwelba* and his accompanying members run through the town making the announcement. The women run behind them. After the *kwelba* has gone into each quarter, the women once again form into groups to play and sing. About an hour later, all the other men who accompanied the initiates into the bush return to the town. They carry with them leaves to signify that the boys have finished their scarification. They run through the community, stopping in each quarter where they form into a circle and dance while throwing pieces of the leaves on the houses of the initiates' families. As they enter into the areas where the women are playing, the latter again cease their playing and chant the repetitive beat in accompaniment to the men's songs.

After the men have visited each of the compounds, two large groups of young women perform in the community. Generally, they are uninitiated Sande girls who dance to music made by shakers tied around their ankles. Each of the groups corresponds to one of the moieties that constitute the community. The leaders are important Sande dancers who teach the young girls while they are performing. These groups continue to perform throughout the day. The rituals of the women complement those of the men.

A third type of participation takes place as one sex acts as a formal audience for the other's ritual activities. During these rituals, members of the opposite sex are either visited or visit the area where the performers are conducting their activities. During the course of the performance, they give tribute in the form of kola nuts or small amounts of money to the members. The participation in these activities is far more passive than that of the parallel ritual activity.

The Kpelle practice slash-and-burn rice agriculture, and rotate their farms every seven years. The work of making a rice farm is sexually divided in the following ways. The men first "brush" the forest; this involves clearing a portion of land and cutting away all foliage except large trees. To do this, the men form cooperative work societies or *kuu*, groups of about 20 to 25 men who go to each other's farm to work the area. The workers are divided into three groups: *tuang, sasexe,* and *bulu.* The *tuang* are the strongest and are the leaders of the group. When all the *kuu* have finished their work, a special farm is selected for the ritual promotion of the members. This ritual is called the *tuang e too.* During the ritual, many women from the town come to the farm to witness it. The initiates must work without stopping for the entire day to the beat of several drums. They are washed in special medicines and then work with great fervor until the farm is completed. After the brushing, the men cut the trees in smaller *kuu* groupings. They then burn the area. Next, they must clear the area and burn all portions that were not cleared in the first fire. They then build fences about the farm and construct a kitchen to serve for storing the rice and as a cooking and resting place for the women. The women's work begins immediately after the men clear the area. They form large *kuu* groupings to plant the rice. Their *kuu* is also organized into the *tuang, sasexe,* and *bulu* rankings. Similarly, they conduct the *tuang e too* ritual after all the *kuu* have completed their work. This ritual is more elaborate than the men's and normally draws larger audiences. As with the male ritual, a special farm is chosen. The women work for several hours before the audience arrives. In the midafternoon those who are to be promoted to *sasexe* and *tuang* are taken to a special fenced area. There, they are washed in medicines. Afterwards, they crawl in procession to where the last portion of the farm is to be worked. Those who are promoted to *tuang* wear a belt of cowrie shells and bells which signify their advancement. After they arrive at the main area, they are given a potion of medicine to drink. All those who were formally *tuang* then work the area of the farm to the beat of drums and shakers. As they work, the new *tuang* lie underneath the hoes and let the dirt fall upon their backs, while the leaders of the *tuang* association brush the woman with leaves and shout encouragement. Periodically, the workers stop and dance to the music and then continue. When the last portion has been worked, all the *tuang* build a mound of dirt in a central place. They continue to build the mound and tear it down. Finally, the eldest *tuang* sits upon the mound and refuses to move. Then the husband of the woman who is responsible for the farm makes an offering of kola nuts and money to the initiates. The old woman then leaves the mound, and the *tuang* members disperse the dirt. Rice is sprinkled on the spot and the ritual is complete.

Throughout the performance, the men of the community stand around and comment on the strength of the women, and make offerings of small coins to the *kuu* leaders. They have no special duties to perform for the women except as an encouraging audience. However, if rain seems imminent, those in the audience who are *Zo* are asked to go into the forest and prepare medicines to ward off the storm.

After the planting *kuu*, the women form weeding *kuu*. When the weeding is finished, they then form harvesting *kuu*. The latter are also organized into the *tuang, sasexe,* and *bulu* rankings, but there is no promotion or rituals associated with them.

The fourth kind of sexual participation is mutual ritual activity. This includes the gatherings of the *Moling, Gbo Gbling,* and *Kale Sale* secret societies which have both male and female membership. Although both sexes belong to these associations, the women hold special positions and are active only in certain of the ritual practices. In the *Gbo Gbling* or Iron Society, there are several women who belong and are often present during societal activities. Although they are normally passive during ritual, their presence is often required for certain types of activities since they possess or own special medicines in the society's corpus. As part of the ritual activity of the society, various members become possessed and act as oracles (see below). It is extremely rare for a woman to become possessed, and when one does, she is immediately taken out of the state by the *Zo* of the society. Women accompany the society in its plays or musical performances in the community but normally stand to the rear of the group and do not dance in the immediate proximity of the leadership.

THE AVAILABILITY OF CONTEXTUAL FEATURES TO MEMBERS

The fact that the kinds of contextual properties discussed above are available to members (i.e., are psychologically real or cognitively salient) is demonstrated on those particular occasions when they become a conscious object of a member's concern. This is evident during a ritual that members must undergo whenever they enter into the *Gbo Gbling* secret society medicine hut. Each member must enter the dwelling in a specified manner, ask the question *"ku meni naa?"* "What is happening here?" and then be prepared to answer any one of the following series of questions: "What is the name of the society?" "What is the real name of the society?" "Where did the society come from?" "What is the name of the *Zo*?" "Where did you join?" "What is the head of the medicine?" and "What does it look like?" The answers are actually countersigns, since they cannot be inferred from a simple knowledge of the questions asked. The number of questions that are asked of an incoming member is reflexive to the relative positions of the person asking to the one answering. If the respondent is a new member, he or she may be asked only one or two of the questions; an old member may be asked all or most of them.

One of the most critical features in this catechetical ritual is who is asking the question and what his or her intentions are in doing so. New members ask only those who join after themselves, unless in the course of time they show a special interest in learning the society's medicines and thereby become more powerful than those who were formerly above them. Consequently, the higher a member's rank, the fewer are the persons who can ask him questions. The *Zo* of the society is never asked a question. Only a member of the Poro priesthood may question or reprimand a *Zo*. If a member of the society desires to move up in the personage ranking, he can do so by simply asking questions of those who are above him. If he should decide to do so, however, he must be sure of his knowledge of the medicines, his ability to muster the help of ancestral and special dream spirits, and the support of others with power in the society and the community at large. If an incorrect assessment of another's powers is made, the questioner might be affected by his own medicines. Hence, when a member enters the society hut, all those in the room make their respective evaluations.

THE LOCATION OF MOVEMENT CUES

We have dealt with the intentional structure of thematic components of ritual. The actual movements that make up a performance cannot be taken for granted. Even though the events that constitute a ritual are highly formalized and normative, it nevertheless remains a member's accomplishment to initiate or terminate each theme.

When a person consistently has bad luck or chronic illness, he may petition the *Zo* of the *Gbo Gbling* for a consultation with the special spirit of his medicine, the *faa sale*. The *Zo* calls several members of the society to participate. He chooses one member to sit across from him on a soft mat. The petitioner sits to the side. The *Zo* then rubs a preparation of medicines on the member and brushes a type of whisk broom in front of him. Very shortly, the member becomes still, then begins to violently hit himself on the sides of his head. The *Zo* then gives him a special medicine bell that causes the possessed to relax his body and shake the bell next to his right ear. As he does this, he gives the chant of the society in a high–pitched stuttering voice. The *Zo* is then able to ask him, as the spirit of the medicine, a series of questions about why the petitioner is having his difficulties. Normally, in the course of the divination ritual, other members of the society also become possessed. The *Zo* then decides whether to allow such persons to talk by giving them the medicine bell to hold. If the *Zo* decides against a member speaking, he simply bends that member's arms back behind his head and hits the center of his forehead with the side of his right fist. This immediately brings him out of the trance.

An essential feature of the *Zo's* decision to allow a possessed member to talk is his recognition that the member chose an appropriate time to engage in his trance behavior. The interaction has similar features to those found in a two-party conversation where a previously silent third party enters in. That is, a member enters into his trance by observing the usual sequencing, floor privilege, and turn-taking rules that obtain in natural conversation. Though the member is in a trance, his intrusion into an established ongoing dialogue between the *Zo* and another member (possessed by the same spirit) necessitates his use of an appropriate conversational opening. Hence, he must attend to the topic and to changes and developments that occur in it. The *Zo* gives him the medicine bell to hold and, in so doing, the ability to speak by recognizing that his intrusion signifies that he has something relevant to add to the topic at that moment. The following (Bellman, 1974) is an example of one such intrusion:

Zo: Why is Yakpawolo suffering so? He has been sick for such a long time and has gone to two different Zo for help. He just keeps getting worse.
Possessed Member No. 1: It is because he has a *nyai nenu* ("water woman") behind him.
Zo: What happened?
Possessed Member No. 1: He met this woman in his dream. She came to him and promised that if he loves only her that everybody will listen when he talks, that he will have much money, and his rice will grow good. But he loved someone on this side (in the waking state). The *nyai nenu* is vexed with him. (p. 18)

As Possessed Person No. 1 said the last few words, another member who was sitting next to the patient suddenly threw out his arms, stiffened his body, and began to hit the sides of his head. The *Zo* picked up another medicine bell from the paraphernalia in front of him and handed it to the second member. The latter then relaxed his body and shook the bell next to his ear. He gave the society chant and addressed the *Zo*, while the first possessed member sat quietly shaking his bell next to his right ear.

Possessed Member No. 2: Let me tell you why this man is sick today. The *nyai nenu* told him once in his dream that he should go to the waterside on the Kpaiyea road. There he would find a cowrie shell. That is his medicine. She said that he must take the shell and put it into a safe place.
Zo: Where is that shell now?
Possessed Member No. 2: It is in a suitcase in the attic above the next room.

The second possessed member jumped up and with wild movements went into the next room, climbed the ladder, reached up into the attic, and threw down a suitcase. He then tore through the suitcase, until he found the cowrie shell.

The *Zo's* recognition of the second possessed member was not automatic. It involved his act of handing the medicine bell to the member rather than bringing him out of the trance. The *Zo* recognized that the second member had new and relevant information to contribute as a development of the conversational topic introduced by the first possessed member. In cases where I recorded the *Zo's* refusal to permit another to talk, the newly possessed man either interrupted while the first member was still developing a topic, or he attempted to speak after the *Zo* had already decided on a course of action and was in the process of terminating the consultation.[9]

How is it possible for a member to recognize the formal properties of conversational structure while in trance? When I later asked those who had been possessed what it was like, they expressed no memory of when they talked, what they said, or why they spoke at all. It, nevertheless, remains that their appropriate use of conversational and kinesic cues provided members who were not possessed with procedures for making decisions about those who were in trance, what to do next in the ritual, what it was that those possessed were experiencing, and its relevance to the ongoing interaction. I do not claim that such cues are what possession or member's personal experience of it is all about. Those cues, however, do become problematic concerns of members as they often provide them with conversational topics, problems, troubles, jokes, and abuses. For example, the inappropriate use of conversational cues can be used by members to distinguish a person as being drunk, psychologically incompetent (*ngung se fengee*), or crazy (*ngung boo*). The ability to recognize, use, and interpret such cues appropriately constitutes an important feature of natural language competence. The actual experience of possession may be different but necessitates that the member has that competence.

THE INTERPRETATION OF RITUAL MEANING: SELECTING BETWEEN ALTERNATIVES

Often, the community or individual petitioner can choose between rituals to accomplish the same outcome. Members recognize that although two rituals or two societies can treat the same physical manifestation of troubles, the cure will not be effective unless the spiritual agents causing the problem are warded off. For this reason, powerful *Zo* of societies often join other societies for ritual treatment. This is illustrated in the case of Folpahzoi.

Folpahzoi is a high-ranking member of the Poro *Zo* hierarchy and is con-

[9]The *nyai nenu* and *kakalii* are referred to generally as *nyai nuu* (water people). The *nyai nenu* or "water woman" is also called the *mammy wata*. This infamous spirit is referred to across the forest belt area of West Africa and into Central and East Central Africa.

sidered to be a powerful curer and a dangerous *Zo*. Several years ago, he was cutting nuts from a palm tree. Such trees are often thirty or more feet tall, and climbing them is hazardous. The only tool used for climbing is a raffia belt on which the climber pushes while climbing and cutting the nuts from the tree. On this occasion, a snake crawled on his arm while he was cutting on the tree. He immediately shook it off, causing it to fall to the ground. The snake then, reportedly, came up the tree after him and entered his pant leg. Folpah threw out his leg and lost his footing. He fell from the tree and broke his back. His family carried him to town and called in a bone specialist *(dong nga ke nuu)*.[10] After a period of time, it was decided that his recovery was taking too long. His family sent for Torkalong, the *Zo* of the *Gbo Gbling* society, at Folpah's request.

One of the medicines of that society is the *faa sale* which possesses various members and acts as an oracle. A member falls under the power of the medicine by violently beating his body. The *Zo* then puts a special medicine object in the possessed's right hand which gives him the power to talk. When Folpah consulted the *faa sale*, he was told that the snake was not an ordinary one. It was the physical manifestation of a particular kind of dream spirit called a *nyai nenu* or water woman. The oracle told him that he had been a dream lover to the spirit and violated a promise of sexual fidelity in the waking state. Such promises with *nyai nenu* are made in return for luck and power. Promises of sexual fidelity are said to be easily made, as they are with one's wives, since they are freely broken. When Folpah's water woman discovered that he had many lovers, she tried to kill him by turning into a snake. When the divination concluded, Torkalong, the society *Zo*, prepared a concoction of medicines to ward off the spirit. Folpah recovered after the consultation.

After regaining his ability to walk, Folpahzoi joined the society. To join another's society is to place oneself under his authority. Folpahzoi does not consider Torkalong to be more powerful than himself on all occasions. He does, however, consider him to be superior within a certain domain of social interactions. This situational recognition of relative power is an important feature when members decide on a particular *Zo* or course of curative procedures. Different situations contain various status structures. It is because of this that we will refer to sets of situations with the same or similar structures as "orders of social reality." This terminology, borrowed from Alfred Schutz, shows that each set or order has an internal time structure of its own, and that each is recognized by members to be transcendent to its appearance in any localized occasion of talk.[11]

These orders are recognized by Kpelle speakers and referred to as *meni*.[12]

---

[10]The power of the bone specialist *(dong nga ke nuu)* is inherited from father to son and mother to daughter. The healing powers of this native doctor are recognized and respected by most Western medical personnel in both public and mission hospitals.

[11]In Bellman (1975), I amend Schutz's (1964) analysis of "orders of social reality" by accepting Gurwitsch's (1964) more phenomenological and less psychological position.

[12]I have discussed elsewhere (Bellman, 1975) how members refer to *meni* and treat them as the organizational basis or grounding for all social interactions.

An event may be seen as belonging to any one of a number of kinds of *meni*. Some of these are: *Poro meni, Zo meni, Sande meni, Gbo meni* (lightning society), *Kale Sale meni* (snake society), *kala meni* (family), *kuu meni* (cooperative work group). A Kpelle speaker must locate which *meni* serves as the grounding for a social interaction, since it provides the context for understanding meaning within that occasion. If he should incorrectly assess the presence of a *meni*, he could speak out of turn and thus be seen as violating laws of secrecy. Often, the outcome of a palaver is determined by deciding which *meni* served as the organizational order of social reality for a certain event. What is recognized as an abuse of power, verbal insult, violation of a law of some medicine, or incorrect assumption of a speaking prerogative (floor privileges) is reflexive to the particular *meni* current at the time. Folpahzoi, for example, chose a cure by correctly locating the *meni* that was relevant to his accident. Both the *Kale Sale* (Snake Society) and the *Gbo Gbling* have medicines for snakes. I was able to join both and in the course of my apprenticeship learned that several leaves are shared by both societies. Hence, if one is bitten by or suffers misfortune because of a snake, he can go either to the Snake or *Gbo Gbling* society. That choice is a crucial part of his cure. If one should go to the wrong society, he will not recover even though the same set of leaves may be used in the preparation of a medicine by both societies. The *Gbo Gbling* not only treated Folpahzoi's snake-caused misfortune but also identified and treated the cause. If he had gone to the Snake society, they would have been able to treat the same set of physical symptoms that he manifested but without success, since their cosmological rights to practice medicine in that case were inappropriate.

One of my teachers in the secret societies explained how medicines work in the following way: When one approaches a leaf that is to be used in the preparation of a medicine, he must first speak to it and identify how he came to know the leaf and his right to have it work for him. All medicines must be learned in one of a number of ways. One cannot steal such knowledge. In the case of a society medicine, a member must give the society chant before picking it. The leaf then addressed itself to the picker from the perspective of the chant's *meni*. If the wrong *meni* is addressed, the leaf will not work. Alternatively, a member may decide that he located the ''wrong'' *meni* in the course of a cure. He will then go to another *Zo* for a new interpretation. The choice of curer shifts the *meni*.

RITUAL AS ETHNOTHEATER

I have presented how an understanding of rituals through an explication of the intentional structure of component themes, a description of the methods for accomplishing a performance, and the analysis of the organization of events and their correct sequencing reveal the methodological procedures that members use to locate situational meanings. Ritual as understood in this manner is like improvisational theater. Although following a structure, its meanings are the accomplishments of each performance. Different members (whether participants or observers) understand the symbols and events in various ways. These understandings both constitute and make use of membership. The meaning of any ritual is a situated interpretation of the attending members. The intentional reading required to locate particular intended meanings is a constitutive feature of that membership.

During any ritual performance, there are several categories of members, each possessing different techniques to interpret the significance and meaning of the events. These categories are member-recognized subgroupings within each society and various groupings outside of the society. In the *porong* society, for example, a member's understanding of the *ngamu* ritual described earlier is reflexive to his position in the grade or hierarchical structure of the society, his personal history of participation in the particular issues being addressed, and his membership in one of the several internal or supportive secret societies in the *porong* complex of associations. Nonmembers differently interpret the events according to their potential membership in the society or the various grades within. Hence, a woman member of the Sande understands differently than a boy (*sina*) who belongs to the *Gblingbe*, or a Mandingo (Islamic) resident of the community. Membership, therefore, provides a specific type of validity for the perspective which one holds on a secret society and may provide an important grounds for its analysis.

The different categories of member-participants in a ritual make use of the interpretive techniques relevant to their respective categories to intend specific meanings and iconic messages to others in their own or some directed to group. Others attending the performance who lack those techniques interpret the events in other ways. Since any member can belong to several of the community's societies, his or her full understanding of a ritual event, symbol, or theme may differ from most others participating in the performance. The participant, nevertheless, has access by virtue of his or her multiple societal membership to knowing the categories of members present in the setting. Consequently, it is possible to manipulate, albeit within the restrictive structure of the ritual, the symbols to communicate to certain members and exclude others.

3

The Position of Women in the Sisala Divination Cult

Eugene L. Mendonsa

INTRODUCTION

The Sisala live in the savanna region of northern Ghana. They reside primarily in the Tumu District, but portions live in neighboring Upper Volta. Their villages are widely scattered throughout the rather densely wooded savanna bush which is cleared for subsistence farming. There are two seasons: the rainy, during which most farm work transpires, and the dry, when most ritual activity occurs.

Social organization is based on the principle of patrilineal descent. Residence is patrilocal. The Sisala form a loose-knit association of patriclans that are subdivided into segments, e.g., village, maximal lineage, lineage, compound-yard, house, and individual room. The village is the most important community and political unit, while the lineage is the corporate unit of production, distribution, and consumption.

Isalung speakers are governed by a paramount chief and a series of divisional and village chiefs who were imposed upon them by the colonial government. These chiefs have persisted till the present day alongside the traditional authority figure, the *tinteingtina* (custodian of the earth). In this system of dual governance, the *tinteingtina* performs primarily ritual functions, while the chief handles politicojural matters (Mendonsa, 1975a).

The *tinteingtina* is custodian of the ancestral shrines which are thought to control the fertility of the earth and the fecundity of women. Ancestors are thought to be actively concerned with the maintenance of the moral code by afflicting the living. This forces them to consult a diviner and perform the necessary postdivinatory, expiatory sacrifices.

57

Economically, the Sisala are horticulturalists. They grow guinea-corn, millet, sorghum, maize, yams, and a variety of lesser crops. Men grow the bulk of the crops on farms cleared by the slash-and-burn method. This is hard labor in which women do not participate. Women aid the men with the planting and the harvest, but the majority of farm labor is performed by men. Women are more likely to keep compound gardens or help the men with their gardening. The same crops are grown in these compound gardens, but they are normally planted earlier and are tended so as to give an early harvest, thus carrying the family through the lean period just before the main harvest.

The main tasks of women are in the domestic sphere. They raise the children, keep house, carry firewood and water, and cook. They may also carry the family's farm surplus to market in an effort to get some cash income (see Table 3.1). A Sisala woman is rarely idle. She is seen as an indispensable part of the family. She is, therefore, normally secure in her role. Men rarely divorce women in this polygynous society, where a man must wait several years for a wife. A man must also expend a considerable amount of money in obtaining his wife. Should divorce occur, he cannot reclaim this expenditure.

Table 3.1
Sisala Sexual Division of Labor

Men	Women	Both Sexes
Heavy farm work	Domestic chores:	Sowing and harvesting
Hunting	Child care	Gardening
Crop cultivation	Food preparation	Fishing (mostly men)
Wood carving	Water collection	Weaving
Blacksmithing	Firewood collec-	Sewing
Xylophone playing	tion	Marketing (mostly women)
Drumming	Pottery	Divination (mostly men)
Gunpowder production		
Medicine production		
Gravedigging		

The authority structure of Sisala society is a gerontocracy. Men are the sole occupants in this system. Office holders (*tina*; pl., *tingaa*) succeed to and hold offices by virtue of their male sex and their advanced age within the kinship segment. They are the custodians of the ancestral shrines which are the ultimate social sanction in their system of social control (Mendonsa, 1976a).

Women never hold office. In this respect they are similar to young men who are also outside of the power circle. There is, however, one important difference between women and young men: young men will eventually succeed to these offices; women never can. While it is said that an old woman who has passed the age of childbearing is "like a man," she may only exert influence— she never wields formal authority. Male control is, of course, linked with the patrilocal system of postmarital residence, but it also squares with the fact that, unlike their neighbors, the Fra-Fra, women are not allowed to farm in Sisala-land. There is a formal proscription: "It is wrong for a woman to take up the hoe." Thus, a woman is an alien in her husband's lineage. She does not partici-pate directly in the production process, and is excluded from holding formal politicojural office. Proceeding from these fundamental facts, a complex cultural theory has developed regarding the disparate nature of men and women and their activities. It is not that women are considered "inferior," but that they are sufficiently different so as to prevent their activities from overlapping into the domain of men's tasks.

More than a division of labor, there is a marked male/female dichotomy in Sisala culture. Manhood *(baalung)* is associated with the bush and the activities that the men perform there: hunting and farming. Womanhood *(haalung)* is associated with the village and domestic activities. In the Sisala cosmology, femininity is associated with the Earth *(Tinteing)*, while masculinity is associated with the sky *(wia)*. The Sky-god *(Wia)* is said to have a wife, *Tinteing*, the Earth-goddess.

The Sisala conceive of all phenomena as being dichotomized into male and female counterparts. For example, there are male activities and female activities, and male space and female space. It is therefore interesting to note that, unlike other peoples of northern Ghana such as the Tallensi (Fortes, 1966), the Sisala have women diviners.

Divination is an extremely important aspect of what I call the divinatory process, i.e., the sequence of events beginning with the perception of affliction that leads to a retributive ritual act, usually sacrifice, that is thought to appease the offended ancestor responsible for the affliction. Juniors *(hengmising)*, which includes young men and all women, cannot cure their illnesses without resorting to divination. Junior persons cannot consult a diviner without the aid of a senior male *(nihiang)* nor can they perform the postdivinatory sacrifice without the help of the male headman *(tina)* responsible for them. It is, therefore, paradoxical that although women can be diviners, they cannot consult another diviner on their own behalf nor can they perform a sacrifice upon a shrine.

THE DIVINATION CULT

Each village has a cult of divination in which the members are hierarchically ranked according to the time of initiation. When a diviner is initiated, he or she becomes the most junior member of the cult. The senior diviner *(vukurahiang)* holds that office by virtue of the fact that he is the male member of the cult who has been practicing the craft of divination longest. He may not be, but usually is, the oldest male diviner. Women are not allowed to hold office in the cult. While a male diviner can ascend the hierarchy through the process of aging, women remain jural minors within the cult, just as they do within the context of the larger social system.

A diviner is a member of the cult of the village from which he or she received the divining shrine. Even if the diviner moves to another village, he still remains a member of the initial cult of divination. If such a diviner eventually becomes the senior diviner, the cult members may ask him to return to the village. If he chooses not to, the next in seniority governs in his absence. Normally, however, he travels home when special occasions warrant it.

The *vukurahiang* has the final authority in matters pertaining to the cult. He is thought to have the greatest knowledge by virtue of the fact that he received his shrine first and that he has been practicing the craft longer than other cult members. Because of his age, he is also a respected headman *(tina)* in the community's gerontocracy.

The cult meets from time to time to discuss divinatory matters, to initiate new members, and even to fix rates of payment. Sometimes they place a ban on divination during times of heavy farm labor. Each diviner is normally consulted on an individual basis. Individual diviners have a great deal of latitude and personal freedom to practice divination as they will, but if one breaks the rules, he may be called before the cult to answer to the charges.

Relations between the various village cults are informal. There is no cult organization beyond the village level. However, cult members from nearby villages are frequently invited to initiations as a matter of courtesy. It is thought to make for a livelier celebration.

At the funeral of a diviner, those diviners attending are required to bring their divining rattles. During the funeral, they dance together and sing diviner's songs while shaking their rattles. After the funeral, the *vukurahiang* ritually discards the dead diviner's paraphernalia and "cleanses" the dead diviner's wand and rattle. These artifacts are kept in the house of the *vukurahiang* until the next initiation of a new diviner, whereupon they are inherited by the neophyte.

INITIATION INTO THE DIVINATION CULT

It is believed that one is called to be a diviner through the manifestation of an illness *(nyannyalung)*, especially mental illness *(nyenyerung)*. When one is afflicted in this way, relatives consult a diviner to determine the exact cause of the malady (see Mendonsa, 1973a). This consultation may reveal one of a variety of causes: ancestral anger, the action of the bush fairies, medicine, or the "desire" of a shrine *(vuying)* to be inherited by the afflicted person.

Any personal shrine may be shared between two or more persons. Shrines may be connected, for example, with the blacksmithing cult, the gravedigging cult, the praise-singing cult, the musicians' cult, the hunting cult, or the divination cult. In any lineage *(jechiking)*, there may be several dormant shrines that belonged to a deceased member of the lineage and that did not pass to any living lineage member at the time of the funeral. Such shrines may remain dormant for a number of months or even years (see Table 3.2) until such time as a lineage member manifests an illness that is interpreted to be due to the "desire" of the dormant shrine.

Table 3.2
Length of Time Between Diviner's Death and Shrine Inheritance (%)

Number of years	1	2	3	4	6	8	10	11	14	20	30
Percentage (N=62)	8	39	25	8	3	2	2	2	3	3	2

Once the diviner announces that a divination shrine is afflicting the patient, it is incumbent upon his or her kinsmen to "promise" *(a taniung)* a sacrifice to the shrine. They go before the shrine and "show it a hen," which they promise will be used later in the performance of the initiation of the patient into the cult of divination.

Once this "showing of the hen" is carried out, the relatives of the patient watch him or her for signs of recovery. If the patient recovers, the promised initiation must take place, or it is felt that a relapse may follow. If the patient does not appear to be recovering, they will consult another diviner.

The initiation ceremony is called the *u lani* rite (for a similar process, see Huber, 1965). It takes several months to complete, during which time the initiate learns the norms and techniques involved in his or her new craft. Each initiate is given a diviner's wand *(vukura daang)* but not the remainder of the diviner's paraphernalia at this time. The wand, which the initiate carries everywhere during the initiation period, is capped with white cowries. People often come to consult the initiate briefly on relatively unimportant matters. In this manner, the initiate receives a small income that is used for the purchase of sacrificial animals for the initiation rite. At the same time, he or she learns the norms and techniques involved in being a diviner.

The trial period covers the time from the point of recovery until the *u lani* rite is performed by the cult members. The length of this period is measured by the reproductive capacity of the hen that was initially "shown" to the shrine. After being shown, this hen is set aside to reproduce. Some of her brood are sold, and the profits are used to purchase a female goat. The other offspring are kept to be used in the *u lani* rite. The female goat is then bred, and her first male offspring is also used in the *u lani* rite.

I will describe the initiation rite of a woman diviner who received her divining shrine from her dead father. Shrine inheritance is not, however, a gender-linked trait. Diviners of either sex may receive their shrines patrilineally or matrilaterally.

Hagbane Bakujang had been cured of a mental illness when her family "showed" a hen to the dormant shrine of her deceased father, who had been a diviner. Since his death, the shrine had crumbled into a pile of rubble in one corner of the room. Once it was confirmed that Hagbane was to inherit this shrine, the leader of the cult of divination of her father's village was informed of the "showing" of the hen to the shrine. Once this was done, they waited for the necessary animals to be born. This is also a period of waiting, during which the patient is watched for signs of relapse.

When Hagbane's male goat was fully matured, the *vukurahiang* was informed, and a day was set for the performance of the *u lani* rite. On the appointed day, Hagbane made the journey from her husband's village to her birthplace. All members of the divination cult of her natal village had assembled in Hagbane's father's compound near the divining shrine. No diviners from other villages were invited, although, in some cases, they may be. This depends solely on the relations between the cult members of the respective villages.

The *vukurahiang* took the eldest cock from the brood of chickens. It was placed in a cage. The diviners and Hagbane then spent the night in the courtyard of her father's compound. When the cock crowed in the morning, the *u lani* rite began. All the diviners rose and sang the following song:

> *Jibaley kong do dole do lana* [repeated many times]
> "The cockcrowing is the time we will see."
> *Bungbaka nyung tomong be la do tu ta gan*
> "The he-goat's beard wants to go south and
> *na puna wia ko.*
> see an animal with much hair."

This means that at cockcrow, the diviners test the initiate to see if he or she is worthy to become one of them. If so, "May the divining bag be able see something wonderful."

Once the diviners had replastered the dilapidated shrine, the cock was removed from the cage and sacrificed upon it. This was followed by the other chickens of the brood, then the he-goat. During the sacrifice, the *vukurahiang* called on all the ancestors and shrines of the village to lend their support to the enterprise.

The initiate is required to fast until nearly the end of the rite. At Hagbane's initiation, the cock was cooked separately from the other meat, as is the custom. It was then given to her to eat. No one else is allowed to eat of the cock's flesh, and, in eating it, the initiate must take special care not to break any bones. Various parts of the cock are used to make the first code-objects *(tayangba)* for the initiate's bag. The other animals were cooked together with millet porridge. This was eaten by those attending the ceremony.

The diviners formed the skin-bag from the skin of the he-goat. Some also spent their time making a variety of code-objects to contribute to the initiate's bag. Most of these were formed out of the bits and pieces of the sacrificial animals used in the rite.

When the bag and the code-objects were completed, the *vukurahiang* added a rattle and a new wand. All were leaned against the shrine. The initiate was made to lean against the other side of the shrine and was required to drink a calabash full of a mixture of honey and millet flour. Although difficult, it is thought best if the initiate consumes it all. As Hagbane tried to finish the thick liquid, the diviners rose and began to shake their rattles, saying in chorus:

Drink all, drink all, drink all, drink all.
If you drink all, you will see all.
If you leave part, you will see only parts.

Hagbane could not finish the mixture, as is the case with most initiates, and the remainder was smeared over her body, the new skin-bag, and the shrine.

Meanwhile, the *vukurahiang* had hidden the head of the sacrificed cock. All the diviners gathered near the shrine to watch the initiate "find" the cock's head. Hagbane removed the wand and held it at the top like a diviner. The *vukurahiang* grasped it at the bottom like a client. Together, they moved the wand until Hagbane "found" the hidden head. This is a final test. If the initiate cannot find the cock's head, he or she cannot become a member of the cult.

Once the head was "found," the cult members, together with the newest member, made the rounds of all the lineages of the village. At each one they begged for gifts. As each gift was given, the diviner said: "Ah! Now you have given us a gift and we have deceived you." This visiting announced to the community that Hagbane was now a fully initiated member of the cult. She was later accompanied to her husband's village by the *vukurahiang* of her father's village. There, together with the *vukurahiang* of her husband's village's cult, they made a similar announcement.

Immediately upon the return of the cult members to Hagbane's father's compound, the lineage headman presented the diviners with gifts of millet and money. The amount of each gift was graded according to the diviner's status in the hierarchy of the cult.

The initiation is the same for a male, but an important difference between the male and the female initiate is their subsequent role in the organization of the cult. Both take up the most junior position upon completion of their initiation ritual, but while the male's position changes within the hierarchy as others are initiated, the female remains the most junior diviner throughout her lifetime.

The cult, like the larger social system, is male dominated; however, the woman diviner is free to practice without restrictions being placed upon her because of her sex. She is free, as is a man, to build a reputation. Once a diviner is fully initiated, it is an individual choice whether he or she will actively pursue the calling. Some diviners take a greater interest in their calling than do others. Female and male diviners are thought to be equally accurate, because the real power of divination is said to lie not with the individual but with the ancestors connected with the divining shrine.

THE FORM OF DIVINATION

Clients consult diviners for a variety of reasons, illness being the most common. When an affliction strikes a man or his relative, he goes to the diviner's room and removes the skin-bag with its code-objects from its hook on the wall as a sign that he wants to consult (it is forbidden to greet the diviner before consulting him). The diviner spreads the skin on the floor and sits facing the client. He opens the bag and removes the rattle and the wand. After a ritual cleansing of the objects, he takes up the wand in his right hand and invokes the ancestors. He asks them to come and help the client ''see'' the truth.

Once all of the code-objects have been examined, the diviner places two metal discs before the client. He grasps his wand by the top and the client takes it at the bottom. The client is expected to question the ancestors who are the real power behind the shrine. He asks them about the cause and cure of his affliction. Since the code-objects are placed in groupings (each is a configuration of symbols telling a story), the client eliminates all but one grouping by asking a series of binary (yes or no) questions about each. When he has determined which configuration of symbols is applicable, he continues to ask binary questions about the specific code-objects of the configuration until he determines the ancestor responsible for the illness, the exact shrine that must be sacrificed upon, and the kind of animal required in the sacrifice.

The diviner's performance is passive. He works mechanically, while the client is expected to find the cause and cure of his affliction. He does this by proposing certain possibilities. These are formulated in his own mind and may or may not be voiced. The diviner may, therefore, never know the exact nature of the client's problem. The diviner merely selects one of the discs by touching it with the tip of the wand. He often does not know what this action signifies to his client. Thus, the diviner is the human agent of the ancestors. His role is methodical. He is not expected to be a native psychologist.

Once the client has determined the cause and cure of his affliction, it is incumbent on him to perform the necessary redressive rites. The role of the diviner is finished. When the client has carried out the instructions of the diviner, he has only to wait to see if the affliction lifts. If it does not, he must go back to a diviner, not necessarily the same one, to determine what went wrong. There is no path of thought that allows him to question the validity of divination as a method of communicating with the ancestors or, for that matter, the very existence of the ancestors (see Horton, 1967; Mendonsa, 1973a).

CHARACTERISTICS OF SISALA DIVINERS

It is impossible to distinguish a Sisala diviner by appearance or life-style, since most are farmers (see Table 3.3) and most lead lives that are indistinguishable from those of their fellows. It is only by word of mouth that one comes to know that ''so-and-so'' is a diviner (Mendonsa, 1975b).

Most diviners are male and the modal age of my sample of 62 was between 31 and 40 years of age. All female diviners whom I encountered were old women past the age of menopause. If a young woman is cured of an illness by promising to initiate her into the cult of divination, she usually does not become a practicing diviner until after her childbearing and childrearing years are over.

Most diviners inherit their shrines when they are between the ages of 21 and 30. This shrine inheritance usually takes place two or three years after the

Table 3.3
Occupation (%)

	None/ wife	Farmer	Trader	Hunter	Laborer	Educated
%Nondiviners (N=271)	3	83	1	1	10	2
%Diviners (N=62)	13	82	3	0	0	2

Table 3.4
Sex of Diviners (%)

	No Response	Male	Female
Percentage (N=62)	2	87	11

Table 3.5
Age of Diviners (%)

			Age Group			
20–30	31–40	41–50	51–60	61–70	71–80	81–90
19	34	24	13	2	5	3

Percentage (N=62)

death of the original diviner. Divinatory initiates are most frequently the eldest in the sibling group, and the shrine is most frequently inherited from one's father. Understandably, practicing diviners are quite traditional. They usually have traveled less than their counterparts who are not diviners, and they own a larger number of shrines than the average Sisala male.

Table 3.6
Age at the Time of Divining
Shrine Inheritance (%)

		Age group		
11–20	21–30	31–40	41–50	51–60
10	63	24	0	2

Percentage (N=62)

Since most Sisala males consult a diviner several times each month and the modal number of consultations per diviner per month is nine, one might expect diviners to be harrassed by clients and amassing wealth. This assumption is incorrect. For about one hour of work, a diviner normally receives less than ten pesewas (the daily wage for a laborer is between 100 and 200 pesewas). In fact, the client need not pay the diviner in money at all. Cowrie shells are still acceptable currency for ritual affairs, but they are useless in the marketplace.

Nor is it true that the diviner is under constant pressure from clients. Each village has several diviners to share the load. Any given diviner who desires not to receive clients can feign illness or rise early and go off to the farm. Diviners also refuse to accept clients after the sun sets, except in cases of divination about death. Diviners sometimes refuse to accept clients during peak farming periods. However, there are always enough older diviners left behind in the village at these times to allow consultations to take place.

CONCLUSIONS

The marginal position of women diviners in the cult is a reflection of factors in the larger sociocultural system. First, there exists the cultural concept that the sexes have distinctive qualities, special spatial correlates, and social activities. Second, in the larger society, men are in exclusive control of the political and jural domains. Women are relegated to the domestic domain. The economic tasks of women, coupled with their other domestic chores, keep them much busier than men during an average day. Men's economic roles require periods of intense hard work. Women's economic roles and domestic duties require of them a steady flow of work from day to day. Men have much more time for matters of politics and adjudication. Third, there is an extremely low population density in Sisala–land (approx. 10/sq. mile). This creates an economic situation wherein children are highly valued (Mendonsa, 1976b). Land is easily procured. The limiting factor to economic production is the small labor force rather than a scarcity of land. Therefore, a premium is placed upon the reproductive role of women. They "produce" the workers. They are crucial in the process of generation replacement. Fourth, the patrilocal postmarital residence pattern means that a woman is removed from her natal village at a very early age (see Mendonsa, 1973b, 1976c).

Thus, the position of women in the cult of divination is a reflection of the nonjural nature of women's social roles in the larger social system. Why, then, are they allowed to practice divination at all, given the fact that it is a pivotal institution in the resolution of social conflicts, and that it serves as a crucial mechanism of social control by the leaders of the male-dominated gerontocracy? I think the answer lies in the fact that, unlike diviners in some other parts of Africa, the Sisala diviner is not in a position to manipulate the client. The diviner cannot, because of the form of divination, do more than perform his technique, allowing the client to do the manipulation. Since the client subjectively poses and answers his own questions, the diviner has no way to control his behavior. The mechanical nature of Sisala divination insures an air of objectivity about the institution. Therefore, women diviners are not thought to be in a position where they can usurp the authority and power of men.

4

Ritual Portrait of a Ga Medium

Marion Kilson

INTRODUCTION

A rekindling of interest in ritual symbolism and cosmology as well as in ethnographic biography or autobiography has occurred in the recent anthropological literature.[1] Drawing upon observations, discussions, and tape recordings of ritual events, the ritual portrait of a Ga medium seeks to present a trifocal perspective on a gifted medium's work. Through a description of some ritual performances, I attempt to convey aspects of the quality of the medium's personality, of the orientations of her world, and of the ethnographic experience. (For a discussion of the relationship between ethnographer and information see Kilson, 1971, pp. 3–17.)

The medium, a member of the Ga people of southeastern Ghana, serves a *kpele* god.[2] Ga believe *kpele* to be their ancient religion. The worship of *kpele* gods is the responsibility of true Ga families whose ancestors are believed to have lived at the inland town of Great Accra in the late seventeenth century. Although each true Ga family is responsible for the worship of an individual deity, the

[1] I wish to acknowledge my appreciation for research support from the Charles E. Merrill Trust Fund of Radcliffe College in 1964–1965, the Institute of African Studies of the University of Ghana in 1965, and the Joint Committee on Africa of the American Council of Learned Societies and the Social Science Research Council in 1968. Portions of this article previously appeared in the *Journal of African Studies* (1975), *2*, 395–418, and are reprinted by permission. For sources on ritual symbolism and ethnographic biography, please see: Beidelman (1966), Bowen (1954), Casagrande (1960), Douglas (1966), Golde (1970), Horton (1965), Powdermaker (1966), and Turner (1968).

[2] Publications and aspects of Ga ritual and mediumship include Field (1937), Fitzgerald (1970), and Kilson (1969a, 1969b, 1971a, 1971b, 1973).

performance of ritual is entrusted to a hereditary priest and a medium whom the god is believed to select to serve throughout her life. Under the priest's authority, the members of a *kpele* cult group perform calendrical rites throughout the year, including a weekly ritual on the days of the week sacred to the god, an annual millet feast, and a set of agricultural rites involving the cultivation of millet. Although the medium of a god joins the priest and his assistants in the performance of calendrical rites, she also performs rites independently. If some crisis occurs in a person's life, he may appeal to the medium of his family god to determine through invocation the identity of the offended spirit and, thereby, the cause of the disturbance. Since spirits may descend from the sky to speak through mediums, possessed mediums have greater authority than hereditary priests, though mediums play subordinate roles in most *kpele* calendrical rites.

Here, I record one *kpele* medium's participation in, and explanation of, certain rites. In order to understand these rites, some appreciation of Ga cosmology and Ga intentions in performing ritual is necessary. Underlying Ga ritual is a conception of the ordering of the world based upon a hierarchy of beings comprising a supreme being, spirits, human beings, animals, and plants. The creative power of the supreme being, the source of life in all its forms, differentiates it from all other classes of being. The immortality of spirits, including gods, twin spirits, and ancestral shades distinguish them from all other forms of created life. The rationality of human beings distinguishes them from animals, while the mobility of animals differentiates them from plants. Through ritual, man attempts to manipulate relations between classes of being within this hierarchy.

Although Ga believe that the supreme being controls the universe, they do not believe that mortal men can achieve direct contact with him. Ga believe that relations between the supreme being and mortal men are mediated by the taxonomically intermediate class of spirits, especially gods. Through ritual, men aspire to achieve contact with spiritual beings in order to insure harmonious relations between the worlds of immortal spirits and mortal men. Ga believe that if relations between spirits and men are disordered, some calamity will befall either individuals or groups within Ga society. Through the performance of ritual, harmonious relations between men and spirits are achieved. Occasional rites are performed in response to specific crises in the lives of individuals or of the community to redress disorder in the relations between men and spirits. Certain calendrical rites are system-maintaining rites recurring to maintain harmonious interconnections between gods and men. These beliefs suggest the importance of ritual in Ga life, for without ritual performances the community of mortal men would be destroyed by the angry supreme being or his spiritual agents.

Below, I describe two calendrical rites: a millet feast for a god and a feast to honor ancestral shades. Since each rite deals with relations between men and different categories of spirit, each necessarily illuminates different aspects of the Ga universe.

OLILA'S MEDIUM

Ofankor nestles beneath the Akwapim scarp twelve miles northwest of Accra, the capital of Ghana. If one enters the village along the deeply rutted dirt road wide enough for one truck, the lack of clearly defined streets masks the extent of the village. At the end of the road stands Yoomo Dantserebi's whitewashed, one-story, tin-roofed house, its well-kept neatness conspicuous among the surrounding unpainted, often crumbling houses.

Yoomo Dantserebi, one of the most affluent and respected persons in Ofankor, is the renowned medium of Olila, god of the wind. This exceptional woman is not physically beautiful, though the serenity and warmth of her personality infuse her otherwise unexceptional features: her small eyes and nose are set in a rounded, high-cheekboned, smooth-skinned brown face. Like many older Ga women, her body is bulky with large pendulous breasts, but the supple grace of her movements belies her size and age. She is probably about sixty years old; her tightly curled hair is grizzled, her eyesight is failing slightly, and she complains of aches and pains, but her skin is soft and smooth, and her muscles are firm, tuned by a lifetime of dancing with the gods.

This large, awkwardly shaped but gracefully moving body houses an exceptionally magnanimous and intelligent personality. Yoomo is a devout believer in an ancient tradition that she knows is passing. She values her role as medium and considers herself an exceptional person, though her manner is unassuming. She is soft-spoken in a society in which people often speak harshly. She possesses an inquiring intellect in a culture which does not foster speculative thought, particularly among women. She has the inner security necessary to be magnanimous about the virtues and failings of others. Her humor is gentle and her laughter infectious. She creates the impression of a person at peace with herself and her world.

As she recounts her life, this serenity was hard won. Looking back, she believes that she was always divinely blessed. She says that Olila caught her before she was born, for not only was her mother pregnant with her for seven years, but whenever her mother carried water from the river on her head, she would become possessed in her mother's womb, causing her to fall to the ground. Moreover, her birth was attended by a tumultuous rain storm, always a sign of divine approval to Ga people. Throughout her childhood, the god made her ill. At times, oblivious to her surroundings, she trembled and shook on her mat for weeks. Her sickness drew her into a cherished intimate relationship with her father who recognized her infirmity as a sign of divine favor, and into bitter conflict with her mother who resented the expensive care required by this sickly, sensitive, and shy child. Her slow physical maturation was an additional source of distress to her mother. In her late teens, Yoomo married a farmer in her village. Although she has married twice and conceived many times, all her pregnancies miscarried—a singular affliction in a society that evaluates a woman by her childbearing. She attributes her barrenness to the jealousy of Olila who did not wish her to marry, and who killed her first husband. She is now married to an herbalist in Accra whom she visits occasionally. After Yoomo's first miscarriage, she wandered into the bush three times. Each time she disappeared for several weeks, but she remembers neither what she did nor where she went, for a person has no memory of periods of possession. After her third return to the village in a violent thunderstorm, Yoomo's vocation as a prophet was recognized. In order to avert the negative consequences of unpredictable and then unwelcome prophetic utterances, the god was entreated to permit her to become a medium who only invokes spiritual beings at the request of supplicants. The role of medium enabled Yoomo to resolve the deep personal conflicts engendered by her identification with her father and her barrenness, for mediumship transcends all other social statuses for those who believe that divinity may descend to earth and speak through living persons. Moreover, Yoomo became not merely a medium as many Ga women do but an exceptionally esteemed medium, known throughout the Ga community for her unsurpassed ritual knowledge. With esteem came financial success and, ultimately, the appreciation of her mother whose funerary expenses she alone dutifully paid as she did for her beloved father. Ultimately, through her vocation, Yoomo achieved not only the respect of others but inner serenity.

Yoomo is the medium of Olila whose attributes she described in this way:

> The power which he has on earth is in the wind, he is the wind. His standing place on earth is in the wind, and he is in the sky. You see the sky, the earth, the sea. Olila covers the sky and he holds the power, all the power which exists, all the many people; he holds us, because he covers the face of the supreme being and the sky. He is the wind; he holds all the world; there is nowhere that you can go in the world where you do not find him.

Like other *kpele* gods, Olila's home is in the sky, but he is associated with a natural phenomenon in which he may take form, either on his own volition or through the invocation of his priest or medium.

In Yoomo's house, as in that of every *kpele* medium, is a god's room (*wɔŋtsu*) in which she invokes spiritual beings and stores various ritual objects. The most important ritual object in the room is a pot *(kulo)* of water through which the medium invokes spirits. When the spirits are invoked, they descend from the sky and take form in the pot from which they speak through the medium to other human beings. Behind the curtain shielding Yoomo's god's room from public view is her shrine made of whitewashed cement in three tiers. On the lowest tier is the invocation pot beside which are placed some bottles for libation and some cowries. On a sheepskin beside the pot lies a large white stool on which Yoomo sits when she calls spirits into the pot. On the second tier are placed some brooms used to sweep away mystical pollution from people's bodies, a pair of animal horns representing twin spirits, and a small white stool for visiting spirits. On the highest tier of the shrine, Olila's brown stool rests on fresh leaves called "leaves of peace" *(omanye ba)*; their name reflects the nature of the blessing that men aspire to achieve through harmonious interconnection between spirits and men. Behind the three-tiered shrine are stashed various small containers in which Yoomo stores ritual objects.

I met Yoomo in 1965 and renewed our friendship in 1968. During 1965, our interaction was restricted to the recording and discussion of religious songs. At our first meeting in 1968, Yoomo expressed her wish that the outside world should know about Ga culture as it did about other Ghanaian cultures, and her hope that through me, she might achieve this goal. Although she wanted to make this commitment to work, she had reservations about the trust that she was placing in me by revealing information which should not be disclosed outside the community of ritual specialists; she suggested that the topics we discussed were so esoteric that I should offer a sheep to placate the gods. I think that the sacrifice of the sheep conveyed to her my sincere respect for her work, for she never again explicitly raised the issue of the dangers associated with revealing the undisclosable.

MILLET FEAST FOR OPOKU

In late July, I drove Yoomo to Kwaabenya village to participate in the annual millet feast *(ngmaayeli)* for Opoku, a *kpele* god associated with a nearby hill. Later, when I asked Yoomo why she had gone to Kwaabenya, she said quietly,

The Opoku medium who is dead was my mother who took me to Accra. She made my invocation pot for me; she put my leg into the ocean so that all might see that I had become a medium. Since she is dead, I must perform the annual millet feast for Opoku. Not a year has passed since her death that I have not gone to perform this rite; when the deceased Koole medium was alive, we went together. Now Opoku has caught another person whom I have trained to be his medium. The new medium whom we visited has assumed my responsibilities. That is as it should be; after a medium's death one of the mediums whom she trained should look after things until her god catches a new medium; when the god catches someone, the old medium's student should instruct her teacher's successor. Now the new Opoku medium knows everything, for I have taught her all. If I cannot go to Kwaabenya, I know that she will be able to perform everything appropriately.

Yoomo had arrived in Kwaabenya late on Saturday afternoon. Throughout the night, the mediums and members of Opoku's cult group *(agbaa)* had kept vigil in the house of the deceased medium, for night is the time of divine activity.

Early Sunday morning, while some of the women of the *agbaa* prepared *fotoli*
the millet dish of *kpele* gods and their worshippers, the mediums began to dance;
their dancing continued throughout the day.

When I arrived in Kwaabenya in the midafternoon, three drummers sat
beating *kpele* music under a spreading baobab tree outside the deceased
medium's house. In the cleared dancing area before the drummers, who were
flanked by a crowd of about fifty villagers, danced the possessed Opoku medium
dressed only in a white waist cloth.

When Yoomo came to greet me, she served me a heaping plate of cold
fotoli. After I had eaten, I went outside and sat on the edge of the dancing circle.
As I watched the Opoku medium dance, one of the *agbaa's* women helped her to
don various accoutrements: first the long ritual necklace of black and white
beads, then a ritual broom, a head-tie, and a new cloth for her waist. While the
Opoku medium danced, the god berated the drummers for not listening properly
to his instructions.

Although Opoku medium danced continuously throughout the two hours
that I watched, others danced for shorter periods. These dancers included the
novices whom Yoomo was training: a young girl, the Opoku medium's mother,
and Yoomo herself. When Yoomo began to dance, she insisted that I dance
behind her as novices do when they are learning from their teachers. After I
resumed my seat, Yoomo continued to dance; as she danced, several people
raised their hands over their heads saluting her as an accomplished dancer and
respected medium. Yoomo was close to becoming possessed. At the conclusion
of one dance, she fell involuntarily forward into the crowd and was helped to her
seat; the next time, she moved even more rapidly and vigorously, though she still
did not become possessed. When she resumed her seat after this rapid dance, her
face was contorted and her big toe twitched. When I told Yoomo that I must
leave, she led me into the deceased Opoku medium's room, where she prayed in
a cracked strained voice betokening her state of near possession.

Later, when I discussed the events of this Sunday on Yoomo's vernadah in
Ofankor, I recalled an earlier conversation about the training of a medium.
Yoomo had said:

> If a god catches a person, her family will bring her to a medium to have her
> mouth opened with medicine. I, myself, have the medicine for every cult; I
> have the power to open a person's mouth, but it is not my own power, the
> medicine gives me the power. When you have the medicine that the god
> likes and you use it to open a woman's mouth, the god will speak and
> reveal his name. The god will say "I have married this woman." Then, she
> will begin her training to be the medium for the god who caught her.
>
> Her training begins with a ceremony at which the novice will be
> bathed in the river and given a bracelet *(abakle)* to wear on her right wrist;
> the god will descend from the sky and sit on the bracelet; it is his seat. Then
> the novice's hair will be cut; she may neither cut nor comb her hair again
> until she has completed her training. During a novice's training she may

not have sexual relations with her husband or any other man, lest she be ruined.

After the novice's mouth is opened, she is in the hands of her teacher, her mother, who will teach her everything. She lives with her teacher, and she may not speak to her relatives, she may not eat food prepared by her relatives. If one of her relatives sees her, he may not call her by name, he may refer to her only as "the bird." While the novice lives with her teacher, she will learn to sing, to dance, and to behave appropriately. If a person is quick-witted, she can complete her education within six months, but her release depends upon her family.

When a novice's teacher says that the novice is ready to be released, a ceremony will be arranged. The ceremony is very expensive for the novice's family. They must provide sheep and fowl for sacrifices, drinks for libation, money to pay the teacher for her instruction and to buy the paraphernalia of a medium for the novice. When all is arranged, the novice's hair will be cut to show that she has a new mind, because she has achieved a new status; she has entered a new world. The medium will dress the novice in the accoutrements of a medium; her hair will be braided into five cones to represent the five corners of the world which our *kpele* gods hold; she will be given the black and white bead necklace and bracelets for both wrists; she will be given her broom, her gong, and her walking stick. The trainer will construct an invocation pot for the novice. In the presence of her family, the novice must sit beside the pot and invoke all the gods and ancestral shades; then the novice must dance from eight in the morning until eight in the evening. If the novice accomplishes these tasks successfully, she may go home; she is now a medium. On Friday before the next annual feast for the ancestors, the teacher will bring the new medium to Accra to show all the priests in Accra that a new medium has come.

Recalling this conversation in connection with the events at Kwaabenya, I appreciated that the ties between a medium and her pupils continue after death and are recreated each year through the millet feast of the senior medium's god. Each medium and her students form a family of mother and daughters as the birth-order names given to each successive pupil reflect. This family of mother and daughters, who are united not by ties of physiological kinship but by ties of sociological filiation, continue over time beyond the physiological limits of mortal life.

FEAST FOR THE ANCESTORS

Homowo represents the annual thanksgiving feast of the Ga people in which living and dead family members join together in their ancestral homes to celebrate the harvest of the old year and the commencement of the new year. At this feast, the bonds uniting family members are renewed as the living gather to honor

their deceased relatives. In Accra, *Homowo* is celebrated on a Saturday in late
August. On the day before *Homowo*, the chief of the Asere quarter of Accra
provides a feast for the founding ancestors of the Ga people at the site of Great
Accra on Okai Koi hill. Since the site of Great Accra falls within the territorial
limits of Ofankor, representatives of the Ofankor chief as well as those of the
Asere chief perform this ceremony for the first Ga ancestors. Ga people believe
that after this ceremony at Great Accra, the ancestors accompany the Asere
chief's representatives back to Accra, where they are welcomed by the chiefs and
priests. Children are warned not to go out of the house after dusk on *Homowo*
eve, because "Okai Koi and his kinsmen are coming."

Yoomo, who assists in the Okai Koi hill ceremony each year, invited me to
accompany her to Great Accra. Although we had planned to start before eight in
the morning, our departure was delayed by a number of events: Yoomo arrived in
Ofankor after ten, because she had had to perform a twin ceremony in Accra; the
representatives of the Asere chief insisted on eating a meal before their departure
for Great Accra; the chief of Ofankor demanded that the sacrificial sheep be
shown to him; finally, a short but torrential downpour further delayed our departure. We ultimately left Ofankor shortly after noon.

Before leaving Yoomo's house, the acting Olila priest poured a libation in
Yoomo's god's room to inform Olila of our mission. Following this libation,
Yoomo, the priest, the Asere stool priest, the Asere hornblower, two Asere
representatives, and I set out. We were preceded by the Ofankor chief's men and
by several children who carried stools, pans of food, buckets of water, containers
with sponges, and all the other necessary ceremonial objects. As we left the
village and turned up the hillside toward Great Accra, we found that the path had
been recently cleared by the Ofankor chief's man. As we walked along, Yoomo
sometimes beat the iron gong that she carried. When I asked why she did this,
she replied, "Yes, can't you see that when I strike, all the grass becomes cool,
because something has gone off the road?" After we had walked through increasingly high grass for about twenty minutes, we turned off the main path to the
shrine for Opobi, a *kpele* hunting god.

Opobi's shrine, located in an area deeply shaded by tall trees around which
wind lush vines and creepers, consists of a small circular fence about one foot in
diameter. Arriving at the shrine, we found that the men from Ofankor had built a
fire. Taking a chicken in one hand and a bottle of drink in the other, Yoomo
stepped close to the shrine; she handed these objects to the Olila priest, who
carefully filled Yoomo's coconut libation cup and held the cock while she
prayed. As Yoomo prayed, the Asere horn blew. She began her prayer by
invoking Opobi and proceeded to explain the plans for the day to him. Following
this prayer, Yoomo carefully poured drink from the cup onto the ground three
times. After the priest deftly slit the throat of the cock, Yoomo sprinkled some
blood inside the shrine and threw the dying bird onto the ground near the fire.
Following the cock's sacrifice, the Asere stool priest also libated, and drink was

served to the assembled people. We left several men from Ofankor to roast the chicken, returning to the main path where Yoomo divided the food leaving a portion to be cooked at Opobi's shrine. As we resumed our ascent of Okai Koi hill, Yoomo explained that the cock had been sacrificed to obtain Opobi's permission to proceed on our way. She said. "When one goes to Opobi's brother's place, one must first ask Opobi's permission; if we hadn't asked his permission, he would have sent a swarm of bees to bite us."

As we continued our walk, the men's mood became increasingly festive; they began to sing traditional war songs with delight. Their singing was interrupted only by the occasional beating of Yoomo's gong. About twenty minutes after leaving Opobi's shrine, we turned onto a narrower path leading to our destination. At the end of the path, we found that the bush had been cleared around a large baobab tree, and a fire was burning at the entrance to the clearing. Under the giant tree sat four men from Ofankor. At the base of the tree were bottles from past libations.

As soon as Yoomo arrived in the clearing, she began to prepare for the sacrifice of the sheep. She took a smoldering brand of palm fronds and fumigated a rock under the tree over which the sheep would be slaughtered. Then she formed three circlets of *nyanyara* and three ringlets of sponge which she placed in a large white enamel pan under the tree. The sheep was then brought to her as she stood under the tree. The men gathered behind her. Facing the tree, she raised two bottles in her hands and began to pray intensely with great emotion:

> Grandfathers hail, grandmothers hail, strike may there be peace. Supreme God, Grandmother earth, Grandfather sea, gods of the sea: Oyeni, Ashiakle, Obotu Kwashi; Naa Koole; Grandfather Tsemu; Grandfather Sakumo; Father Lo, I call you Opobi and Oshwila; I call Grandmother Akwa Bosu, Kobla, Omanye and his wife Afieye; Grandfather Dantu. Our ancestors Nikwe Olai, Nii Boi Tono, Nii Okai Koi and his many relatives. We are counting your number. Our many fathers, our many mothers, Ga people's mothers, I call you. Oshi Dede and Oshi Oko, I call you. I call you for success; I call you for millet. What is today? Today is Friday, Ga people's Friday; I do not call for anything evil, I call for Akweshi and the unborn children in Ga Mashi. I call that the corn has come, and we have turned its badness into good; we will hoot at hunger which has eaten us; we will hoot at hunger with a lot of corn. May all the twins eat; may all the children and unborn children eat until the food flows down their chins. And so grandfathers, this is your four-footed animal which we present to you before we start to eat. Today I call you for life for your children. Here is your four-footed animal and upon it a drink.

Yoomo then poured the liquid of libation three times upon the tree before stepping aside for the Asere stool priest to libate.

During the priest's libation, Yoomo went behind the tree searching for leaves to put into the enamel pan with the sponge and *nyanyara* ringlets. After the stool priest's libation, the assembled men began to sing war songs, which they continued to sing until after the slaughtering of the sheep. When the priest had libated three times on the exposed root of the tree, he lifted and lowered the sheep three times before its throat was slit. The blood of the dying animal was sprinkled on the tree, into the enamel pan, and on the horn of the Asere hornblower. After the beast had been carried away to the cooking area, drink was served to the assembled men. As they finished their drinks, each one went to gather some *nyanyara* to make a necklace of the sacred leaf for himself.

Following the communion drink, the participants began to bathe in the powerful purificatory mixture of blood and leaves in the pan. First, Yoomo removed her shirt and bathed her face, arms, and torso in the liquid before sprinkling blood on the old novice with her ritual broom. Then one by one, the men, beginning with the Asere stool priest, followed Yoomo's example. When Yoomo urged me to bathe in the sacrificial blood, I gingerly washed my arms and hands as well.

While the younger men cut up the carcass of the sheep, the older men sat chatting quietly under the giant tree, and Yoomo sat beside me on the edge of the clearing. I asked her how the sheep was to be divided. She said that the rump was for her, because "I sit on the god," the legs and head were for the Asere chief who was responsible for the performance of the ceremony, and the neck was for the stool priest who carried the sheep on his neck or paid for the sheep. Our discussion was interrupted by a great hue and cry from the young men who had discovered that one of the men had stolen two pieces of meat. The meat was retrieved, and the thief was only briefly subdued by the discovery of his indiscretion.

While the young men began to roast the meat, Yoomo and her two novices molded millet flour into small balls. The millet balls were divided, and one pan was given to the young men to cook. The other pan was given to the elderly novice to take to cook at Opobi's shrine. The old woman objected to this arrangement, for she did not want to miss her share of the meat, but she reluctantly followed Yoomo's instructions.

When the *fotoli* was cooked, the Asere stool priest and the acting Olila priest took a shallow pan of *fotoli* to offer to ancestral spirits. The priest began by sprinkling the *fotoli* around the big tree in the clearing, and then departed to offer the food at different locations where Yoomo had sounded her gong after we had left the main path.

While we awaited their return, Yoomo explained that the men were sprinkling *fotoli* at the ancient house sites of the families of Great Accra whose descendants live in modern Accra. Beginning at the edge of the old town, they would sprinkle at the site of the house of the Dzoshi family, at the place where the people of Great Accra drew water, at the house of the *Ayiku* family, at *Krokoto we*, at *Kpakpatse we*, at *Lante Dzan we*, at *Amaatse we*, at *Adabang*, and, finally, at *Oshi we*. She explained that *Krokoto we* was where "they used to beat all the dances and where they stored the drums for the *kpele* dances. *Ayi Anafo* was the first person to beat the *kpele* drum, and he also sang *kpele* songs; and so we sing in a *kpele* song":

> They don't have anyone to sing;
> Ayi Anafo, come to sing.
> They don't have anyone to beat the drum;
> Ayi Anafo, come to beat.

Yoomo further explained that the big tree under which the sheep and libations had been sacrificed was the doorstep of Okai Koi's house:

It was the middle of the town where everyone used to meet. . . . There our grandfather is, creation is there, and God stands there. It is wonderful and you can see that it was there where God commanded, and God came from heaven and said "You go to settle here." The tree where we offer food is not a little tree, it is not simply a tree, but it is the tree which is greater than all Accra and Ashanti. It is God's tree, where he commanded and the sea divided; the things that he gave grew into these trees. God himself made the Ga settle there. That tree is the place where all Ga come from. From that place some people went to Labadi, others went to coastal Accra. We have a *kpele* song about that tree, it says:

> The relatives are scattered;
> We are scattered,
> But we know ourselves.
> The relatives are scattered;
> We know the tree that bore us,
> We know ourselves.

When I asked her what kind of a tree it was, she said that it was a baobab tree. She continued:

The baobab tree does not grow just anywhere. The only place that the baobab grows is where the gods are. The baobab is power; it is the Ga's power and it is God's very powerful tree. And so it is said that a priest's child cannot eat its fruit, for the tree is king among kings. A chief's child cannot eat its fruit, because God's oath is beside it. It does not grow like ordinary trees, but from the power of God himself.

When the priests returned to the clearing, all the men gathered around a heaping bowl of *fotoli* under Okai Koi's tree. They crouched down and dipped their right hands into the common bowl. When the mutton was brought, each man took a piece and stepped aside to eat the meat or to wrap it in a leaf to take home. This communal feast of the male participants concluded the ceremony at Okai Koi hill.

After the cooking utensils were gathered together and the fire put out, we hurried down the hill to Opobi's shrine. There the old novice had finished cooking the *fotoli*. The Asere stool priest and acting Olila priest sprinkled some *fotoli* outside the shrine before Yoomo carefully placed three mounds of *fotoli* inside the shrine. The assembled men consumed the remaining *fotoli* and the roasted chicken. Hastily, we resumed our journey to Ofankor. During our return to the village, Yoomo beat her gong at the same places as she had on our ascent of Okai Koi hill.

When we had entered the village and were approaching Yoomo's house, the Opobi novice became possessed and started to sing. As she entered the house, she sang:

> Opobi, Opobi, Opobi, Opobi,
> I eat the blue shark.
> When they kill a fowl, I do not eat it.
> And when they kill an elephant, also, I do not eat it.
> When Opobi kills a bushcow, also, I do not eat it.
> If you kill any animal, I do not eat it.
> I eat the blue shark.

The Opobi novice continued to sing inside the compound, until the Olila priest brought her a stool. As she sat down on the stool, she became dispossessed and for a few moments looked uncomfortably dazed, but she then resumed her usual demeanor and began her household tasks.

The Asere stool priest and the other Asere representatives said farewell to Yoomo. They wished to hasten to Accra to meet the chiefs and priests whom they thought were already waiting on the limits of Accra to welcome not only the returning celebrants but Okai Koi and his relatives. After the departure of the Asere stool representatives, Yoomo insisted that I eat a meal before taking my leave as the sun was falling behind Okai Koi hill.

FAREWELL

Although Yoomo came to the airport to say goodbye, our real farewell occurred two days before my departure in 1968. We met in Accra to talk of many things: of the interpretation of dance movements, of the shrine in her god's room, of the control of the gods over cosmic processes, of the songs sung at *Homowo*. When we had finished our discussion, Yoomo took my hand in hers and sang:

> The road,
> May your road be good;
> May you go with blessing.
> Darkness is on the road;
> May you turn to the right with white clay,
> May you turn to the left with white clay.

Lo, on Sakumo's road I am going;
Go call God that he may lead you on the road;
May God lead you on the road.
I am going on the road;
Lo, the road is clear.

CONCLUSION

Through the informal description of the Ga ritual performances, I have attempted to illuminate one *kpele* medium's devotion to a vocation founded on a world in which spirits and humans intermingle and in which imperceptible phenomena are often more significant than sensible experiences. Insofar as possible, I have interwoven my observations of ritual events and circumstances with the medium's own words, taped either at the ceremonies or in later conversations. By so doing, I hope to convey aspects of the puzzle-making quality of the ethnographic experience in which observation, verbal inquiry, and reflection interact to produce an increasingly comprehensive image of another world.

II

SYMBOLIC CONCEPTIONS OF MALE AND FEMALE IN LEADERSHIP AND ADEPTHOOD

Introduction to Part II

Bennetta Jules-Rosette

The separation of male and female religious responsibilities is a hallmark of traditional religious and social organization. While Part I illustrates dramatic divisions between men's political and women's ceremonial authority, this section examines processes of symbolic change through which a new balance is achieved. Symbol, metaphor, and ritual are the keys to understanding living religious transformation. Changes in other organizational patterns generally accompany and are frequently determined by shifts in sex-marked symbolism. While "traditional" societies were open to the rise of innovative and charismatic leaders, the newer syncretic cults make such occurrences commonplace rather than exceptional.[1] Egalitarian leadership, along with an implicit criticism of the old order, often accompanies a charismatic change. These changes also revive customary ideas of complementarity and familial obligation as symbolic bases for expressive leadership. The new urban churches offer broader opportunities for women and younger men to gain influence and prestige (cf. Little, 1973), but revitalistic tendencies and the complexities of a movement's sociopolitical organization also contribute to maintaining traditional forms of authority.

The occurrence of symbolic distinctions associated with male and female ceremonial activities extends from conventional conceptions into the usage of the

---

[1]Cf. Evans-Pritchard's (1956) discussion of the revitalistic role of the leopard-skin chief in Nuer society. These traditional arbitrators, whose spiritual skills were customarily called on to settle political feuds, rose as charismatic leaders during the late 1930s, while the British government was engaged in "pacifying" the Nuer. A variety of traditional/charismatic cults also arose in Zaire during the same period, in addition to the well-documented rise of Christian movements (Kimbanguism, Mpadism, and Watch Tower).

indigenous churches. Breidenbach emphasizes the importance of the symbolic polarity surrounding the prophet Harris and his male and female followers in Ghana. The complementarity between ''the man in the bush,'' Harris's successor, John Nackabah, and the movement's progenitrix, Madame Grace Tani, ''the woman on the beach,'' is exemplified by the very symbolic spaces with which they were associated. Walker and Breidenbach both emphasize the symbolic balance between male and female leadership that developed among the Harrist churches of the Ivory Coast and Ghana. Harris's original intention was simply to make Christian converts whom he encouraged to leave traditional medicines. He did not set out to establish a separatist church. When he reached Ghana, he came in contact with Grace Tani, a traditional priestess who subsequently became an ardent convert. As his ''wife'' and major associate, she carried on Harris's work in partnership with John Nackabah. The two became the spiritual inheritors of Harris's mission and were symbolically conceived of as ''brother and sister.'' Their complementary power was used to accomplish the *sunsum edumwa* (perfect work) that became the ideal of membership. In so doing, they placed the more conventional conceptions of male and female authority into a new framework.

Walker suggests that this ideal of bipolar leadership was not developed in other parts of the Harrist movement. Women like Marie Lalou became self-appointed faith healers and female messiahs, rather loosely following Harris' teachings. Lalou built upon the status of a ritual male and religious power by renouncing marriage for herself and her widowed followers. She was able to establish a series of women successors but was not able to change the leadership structure of Harrist groups. Most of the administrative roles held in those groups inspired by Lalou's miracles and teachings still remained in the hands of men.

The organization of the present-day Ivorian Harrist groups is based on a larger principle: the model of small, ethnically homogeneous villages. Because they remain in small villages and utilize existing social networks, Walker suggests that the growth of the Harrist church is not primarily a product of the urbanization process. Harrist doctrines are superimposed upon the existing hierarchy of village elders. Men retain the most central positions of political control, while women perform ceremonially in processions that commemorate Harris's women assistants and adepts. This dichotomy between political and ceremonial authority is found in all of the indigenous churches examined in this volume. It appears to be a social mechanism whereby certain participants are freed from political responsibility in order to achieve spiritual powers. This very freedom, however, delimits their potential leadership activities in the group.

To conclude this section, I look at women as ceremonial leaders in the Maranke church. This group is an indigenous church completely separate from mission control and resembles the Harrist movement in terms of the importance of its own local prophet-founder. Examining the Weberian theme (Weber, 1947) that charismatic leadership can be the source for redefining traditional authority but does not supplant it without new institutional structures, I analyze the spheres of men's and women's authority.[2] Women in the Apostolic group are recognized as healers, midwives, and prophetesses. The healer–midwifery activities are based upon traditional female roles. Only prophecy brings with it the ability to veto men's political decisions on the basis of visionary inspiration. The position of the prophetess is modeled upon that of the traditional Shona medium. She is instructed in the same way that male prophets are and has an indirect role in community decision-making. Women's accounts of conversion among the Maranke Apostles reflect the limitations of their political aspirations in the group. They rarely join with the hope of active participation, and even those who acquire some ''influence'' in decision-making through personal spiritual skills or through marriage to political leaders are never publicly acknowledged in this capacity by official recognition.

Ceremonial leadership relies on control of social interactions. It offers a critical analytic link between the intricacies of ritual activities and symbolism and the overall social organization of African cults and churches. During ritual events, this control is displayed in stylized ways. There is a strong distinction between leadership and adepthood among the Apostles that parallels that described by Breidenbach for the Harrist movement. Women constitute the rank and file members, and even those who are healers are not generally recognized as special charismatic leaders. This distinction crosscuts sex lines. While there is an egalitarian ethos among all members, only those who have experienced a combination of spiritual inspiration and leadership confirmation are eligible to become influential members.

My analysis presents case study and ethnographic data that describe in some detail a theme that characterizes the entire section: the importance of expressive activities and leadership as both crucial aspects of women's traditional religious activities and as vehicles for change. The position of women in all of these groups becomes an essential feature and indicator of the types of symbolic syncretism that take place within them and of the extent to which larger conceptual and social changes are reflected in all ritual and ceremonial activities.

[2]Weber (1947, pp. 358–373) notes the original conception of charismatic authority in clearly defined spiritual powers. It is through the experience and the reputation of such powers that charismatic leadership first arises (cf. Jules-Rosette, 1976b). Weber extends the concept to apply to a broad range of interactional and ceremonial authority. However, when discussing movements of religious revival, the origin of the term in sectarian dynamics is particularly relevant.

5

Women in the Harrist Movement

Sheila S. Walker

On the West Coast of Africa two of the religious movements inspired by Christianity were founded and led by women, the Deima Church of Marie Lalou in Ivory Coast, discussed here, and the Church of the Twelve Apostles in southwestern Ghana, described in the succeeding chapter. They both grew out of the Harrist movement, a movement of mass conversion in the early twentieth century that promoted religious freedom in the area and caused the several original religious groups to spring forth. Grace Thannie, founder of the Church of the Twelve Apostles, was one of Harris's female escorts, while Marie Lalou became active after Harris's departure, and was inspired by a dream to create her cult. She claimed to continue Harris's work and, indeed, her cult reflects his influence. Although Harris's major emphasis was not specifically addressed to issues concerning women, some of the social modifications he urged in the coastal societies worked to improve women's lot, and created a climate in which these two women would develop significant leadership roles in the creation of new institutions. Thus, Harris's movement gave women as well as men a sense of new possibilities and new horizons.

INTRODUCTION

Toward the end of 1913, a religious revolution began in the French West African colony of Ivory Coast. At that time the native Liberian Prophet, William Wade Harris, began his movement of conversion during which, in a period of months, he baptized an estimated 100,000 to 120,000 people, increasing more than a hundredfold the number of Christians in the Ivory Coast. Perceiving himself as a proselytizer rather than as a teacher, he sent his converts to the few existing missionary churches, telling those people who could not be accomodated by the missionaries to worship on their own according to his instructions, until someone came along to teach them the contents of the Bible. Harris deputized disciples to help spread his message to areas he could not reach, and people who came from distant places to hear and be baptized by him taught what they had learned to their fellow villagers on returning home. In addition, other "small prophets," inspired by the message and the state of religious ferment created by the Prophet Harris, sprang up in the colony, preaching messages of their own.

The man who ushered in this new religious epoch was born in about 1865 to traditionally-oriented Grebo parents in Graway in southeast Liberia near the Ivory Coast border. He spent a significant part of his adolescence living with a Grebo Methodist minister, who taught him to read and write both English and Grebo and baptized him a Christian. He subsequently worked as a crewman on British ships plying the West African coast, as did most young Grebo men, and had the opportunity to broaden his experiential base by visiting countries under different types of colonial rule.

Upon returning to Liberia, Harris worked as a lay preacher, a teacher, and a government interpreter. Often at odds with the government, he was implicated in an alleged coup d'état plot and imprisoned. While in prison, Harris, then a middle-aged man, spent much of his time reading the Bible and praying. The Angel Gabriel appeared to him in a vision, telling him that he had been selected by God as His last prophet whose mission it would be to spread the Christian message to those who had not heard or accepted it. Those people who refused to listen and obey, said the Angel, would soon be destroyed by fire.

On his release from prison, Harris began to pursue his divinely ordained mission. Unable to find a receptive audience in Liberia, Harris set off down the coast to seek converts. The new prophet dressed in a style dictated, perhaps, by the vision and probably inspired by descriptions and pictures of biblical garb. He wore a long white gown with black bands crisscrossing his chest, a black scarf around his neck, and a small round white hat. He carried with him a gourd bowl to fill with water to be sanctified for baptism, a tall cane-cross, a gourd rattle to serve as a musical instrument, and an English Bible. He was accompanied on his journey by two similarly attired female followers. The women acted as a chorus. When they entered a village, they would sing, dance, and play the rattles as an accompaniment to the Prophet's message.

One of those who accompanied him was Mrs. Helen Valentine, an educated woman who was probably the widow of P. Keda Valentine, one of the first two native priests to be ordained by the Episcopalian Church several decades earlier. Mrs. Valentine had had visions that convinced her to accompany the Prophet. His other companion was a rural woman with no Western education. Upon their return to Liberia, she bore Harris a son (Haliburton, 1971, p. 141).

Harris and his two followers walked along the West African coast from Liberia to the French colony of Ivory Coast. There, they stopped in each village they came upon, and Harris would preach to people to accept his baptism. The villagers had to agree to cease all practices having to do with their traditional religions in order to receive Harris' baptism. Should they try to revert, they were told, they would be seriously punished by God. Harris's message was essentially that people should worship only one God, the Christian god.

Eventually, Harris' renown increased, and people came from far and near to hear him. Word spread that prosperity reigned in villages that accepted his baptism, that disaster struck those that refused it. Rumors spread of the Prophet's power as manifest in his ability to defy taboos and to perform miracles of various types. Having been relatively successful in Ivory Coast, Harris continued to go from village to village along the coast, until he arrived in the Axim area in the southwest of what was then the British Gold Coast colony. There, he had phenomenal success, converting many thousands of people in a few months.

In the then Gold Coast, Harris acquired a third woman follower, Grace Thannie or Tani. When the Prophet Harris was subsequently expelled from Ivory Coast, Grace Thannie returned to the Gold Coast and tried to carry on his work. Calling herself Madame Harris Grace Tani, she founded the ''Church of William Waddy Harris, and his Twelve Apostles,'' which subsequently was shortened to the Church of the Twelve Apostles (see Breidenbach, Chapter 6). The emphasis in the new church was on healing through faith in God and through the use of sanctified water (Haliburton, 1971, p. 149).

Upon his return to Ivory Coast, Harris continued to preach his message and make converts. In his absence, his renown had become widespread. People flocked to hear him, be baptized, and receive instruction in the new faith. Harris wished to provide further instruction for those who wanted to become Christians. The Catholics were the only missionaries in the country, so the Prophet directed many of his followers to the Catholic Church. However, the missionaries were few in number and could not accommodate all of Harris' converts. Moreover, to the converts, the church was associated with the oppressive colonial regime.

There were Methodist English-speaking clerks from Sierra Leone and the Gold Coast who worked for British interests in Ivory Coast, several of whom Harris deputized as disciples charged with the responsibility of carrying his message to areas that he had no opportunity to visit. They were also to provide further teaching for people whom he had converted. He told both those who could not be accomodated by the Catholic Church and his Methodist disciples to return to their villages and build houses of prayer in which they should worship as he had told them. Many people pursued this path.

In addition to his religious message, Harris urged a number of local reforms. He urged people to follow the Ten Commandments, to work diligently, to observe the Sabbath, and to refrain from excessive alcohol consumption. Two of his social changes referred specifically to the treatment of women. Prior to

Harris' arrival, menstruating women in the coastal ethnic groups in Ivory Coast were required to separate themselves from the rest of village society. They spent this time in special huts built for the purpose, financed by contributions from all village women. Harris abolished this practice. Although women had been considered dangerous to men and offensive to the traditional gods during their monthly period, this was no longer valid in Harris' religious system. He urged people to abandon expensive and elaborate funeral practices, and the mourning ritual for widows was shortened and made less encumbering. They were no longer to shave their heads or mourn for an entire year.

Unlike the missionaries, Harris did not attack the most basic social institution of the society, the polygynous family structure, perpaps because, as an African himself, he understood both the fundamental nature of the institution and the fact that he would have less success converting people if he made monogamy a condition for becoming a Christian. He said that although monogamy was preferable, in a polygynous family all of the wives must be treated equally.

By the last quarter of 1914, the French colonial administration began to feel threatened by the influence that the Liberian Prophet exerted over tens of thousands of their subjects. They repatriated him and his two assistants and attempted to suppress the results of his movement. Rather than encourage the practice of Christianity, which was the purpose for which they had supposedly summoned missionaries from Europe, they destroyed the new houses of prayer and prohibited people from public worship. They persecuted the Methodist clerk-disciples and the new ''small prophets'' who sprang up in Harris' wake. The only religious choice permitted was the Catholic Church with even the Methodist Church ordered closed. However, many people continued to worship clandestinely.

In 1924, Methodist missionaries came to the Ivory Coast to investigate the reasons for which the Protestant British subjects were not allowed to pursue their religion. To their amazement, they found tens of thousands of people who identified themselves as ''Harrist Protestants,'' and who implored them to send the teachers with Bibles whom they had been awaiting since Harris' departure. The missionaries enthusiastically gathered reinforcements and went to Ivory Coast to teach the Harrist Protestants.

The missionaries initially met with overwhelming success as people flocked to their churches. However, certain of their practices began to alienate some of those who had been autonomously worshiping according to the Prophet Harris' teachings for the ten years between his departure and the missionaries' arrival. The missionaries deprived them of their former authority in the new Protestant church structure, required financial contributions from church members to support the church (which reminded members of the head tax imposed by the colonial administration), and made monogamy conditional to Christianity. This alienated many of the church's most influential potential members—the old men whose many wives displayed their wealth and power.

The Protestant missionaries, to legitimize themselves in the eyes of Harris' converts and to establish themselves as his true successors, sent a missionary to Liberia to visit the Prophet. Reverend Pierre Benoit returned with a Will, supposedly dictated to him by the Prophet, saying that all of his converts should join the Methodist Church. This proof that they were, indeed, following in the path established by Harris won the Protestants many converts.

However, some of the Ivorians who were particularly dissatisfied with the Protestant practices were not convinced of the validity of the Will and, having found out that the Prophet was alive, set out to find him to ask him how best to proceed. Three men were selected from the Ebrie village of Abia-Niambo (or Petit Bassam) to go to Liberia. This delegation explained its grievances to the Prophet. They complained particularly about the requirement to contribute money to the church, since Harris had never accepted payment from his converts, and about the missionaries' attack on the polygynous family structure. The Harrists have a copy of a second Will that the Prophet gave to the Ivorian delegation in which he stated that no money was to be required for the administering of religious sacraments. He also expounded at some length on the question of polygyny.

No early accounts or statements by those who heard Harris preach indicate that he either verbally condemned or favored polygyny while he was in Ivory Coast. Since he did not condemn it, one may suppose that his converts assumed that the Prophet expected them to continue the practice. Seeing him with several women followers, they undoubtedly assumed the Prophet himself to be polygynous. Consequently, the missionaries' absolute stand on monogamy as a condition for baptism was seen by the Ivorians as contrary to Harris' wishes.

Together with the Will containing his position on the issues of church finances and polygyny, the Prophet Harris gave the delegation the directives that led to the development of the Harrist Church of the Ivory Coast. The Ivorians told the Prophet that the Protestants were not fulfilling his teachings as they had anticipated and, because of the missionaries' attacks on the social structure, were making it impossible for many people to be Christians. The only possible options were for them to return to their traditional religious practice, an idea that was anathema to the Prophet, or to worship autonomously as they had done before the missionaries came. Harris approved the latter possibility and selected John Ahui, a young member of the delegation, to take upon the task of conversion. As symbols of his mission, Ahui received from Harris a cane-cross and a Bible.

The delegation returned to Ivory Coast with the Prophet Harris' decision. Ahui began traveling, encouraging those people who had been baptized by Harris to continue worshiping as the Prophet had taught them and trying to convert those people who had not heard or heeded his message. Ahui was assisted in this task by several other men from nearby villages who had been baptized by Harris. They continued their work in spite of opposition from and persecution by the colonial administration. However, with the mid-1940s began the nationalist period, during which the Ivorians began to manifest their desire to be free of the French yoke and to control their own destiny. One mode of action for many was to leave the Catholic Church to return to the religion to which they had been converted in 1914. Abandoned churches had a rebirth, and new ones were built in villages all around the lagoons area of the southern coast. With people flocking back to practice the Prophet Harris's teaching, John Ahui and his assistants began to institutionalize the teachings so as to integrate the new aspirants.

The Harrist Church has two fundamental organizational principles. The church structure is based on the traditional social structure with age grade and gender as the major determinants of the division of labor. The liturgy is based on a reenactment of the behavior and gestures of the Prophet Harris and his followers during his brief stay in the country. These two factors determine the role of women in the present-day church. As in the rest of village society, the major decision-makers and functionaries are men. The main figures in the church are the ministers, the apostles, who are the chief administrators, and the elders who act as advisors. Harris had told the delegations to return to their villages and supervise the selection of ministers and apostles. These men were selected from the next to the eldest age grade, the one that furnished the administrators of village activities. Although Harris did not specify the need for a body of elders, traditional social structure dictated that village advisors be given a significant role in the church.

There are other roles within the church. Among the males, there are guardians who keep order in the church during services and bell ringers who ring the bell before services to summon members. Women play the same domestic roles that they fill in the other areas of life, such as washing and ironing the minister's tunic and cleaning the church. Thus, although church membership and attendance is more or less equally balanced between men and women, male roles exceed in number and importance. The major role shared by both is that of choir members, most of whom are young. The choir and its songs are important parts of the church services. The choir leads all singing and plays the instruments, consisting of rattles like the one carried by the Prophet Harris, and, occasionally, an organ. Almost exclusively, the male members play the rattles, and it is usually they who lead the singing.

The one area of prominence for women is in the processions in which church members accompany the chief minister from his home to church and back again after each service. While the procession to church is subdued, with church members walking and singing quietly, the return procession is very animated, with members singing and dancing enthusiastically to the accompaniment of the rattles. Several times as the procession moves down the main street of the village, the ministers who are leading it stop, and women, particularly those who are important members of the choir, dance around them. On religious holidays, these women wear special collars and carry baskets of flower petals to strew. This ceremonial role may be seen to reenact women's status with respect to the

Prophet Harris, recalling how his female followers sang and danced to accompany him when he presented his message to his audience. No early accounts suggest that Harris expected them to play any other religious role in the organization.

The church is presently making some changes in its organizational structure in an attempt to respond to the demands of a rapidly modernizing society. There is an attempt to involve young people by allowing them to have responsible functions in the church. A conference of literate young people was held in 1972 at which many of them discussed possible changes in the church. Of the more than 100 young people at the conference only two were females, and there was no specific discussion about the status of women in the church. The only mention of females came with the suggestion to set up youth groups similar to boy and girl scouts. The discussion about the types of activities that they would perform applied almost exclusively to the boys, however.

In accordance with Harris' pronouncement, polygyny is permitted except for ministers who may have only one wife. Marriage, however, is not a church sacrament, which is, perhaps, in line with Harris' statement that it was permissible to have more than one wife provided that they were not married before an altar. There are those who suggest that many men joined the Harrist church because they can be both Christians and legitimately polygynous.

Various "small prophets" sprang up in different parts of the country for the two decades following Harris' impact, claiming to be his successors. The most successful movement, second to the Harrist Church in population in Ivory Coast, was founded by a woman.

MARIE LALOU AND THE HARRISTS

Marie Lalou was born Dyigba Dawano in 1915 in the Dida village of Gobou near Lakota. Lalou was her married name, and she chose the new name of Marie upon marriage, following Dida custom. She had no children, and one day after four years of marriage, she refused to perform her conjugal duties, saying that she had received such instructions in a dream. Her husband was persistent, but subsequently fell ill and died. As was customary, his brother wanted to take her as a wife. She refused, giving another dream as the reason. When he also died, she was regarded with great suspicion in the village as responsible for both deaths (Holas, 1965, p. 307; Paulme, 1962, p. 17).

As a result, Marie Lalou returned to her natal village and began to preach that God wanted people to cease harming their neighbors through poisoning and witchcraft. She distributed holy water, of which she had been told in a dream and which she found beside her bed on awakening, to all who requested it. It was to protect people with a pure heart from harm. If anyone drank it with the least will in his heart for someone else, she stated, he would surely die. During the months after her return, there were many deaths in the village. Marie was considered responsible for these deaths and had to flee. She went to live with a distant relative, but the same problem occurred again (Paulme, 1962, p. 18).

Considered responsible for all of the misfortune that befell the village, Marie was expelled. She lived in the forest for several months, until a hunter took pity on her and asked the village chief to allow her to return. He did so, and she established a church in about 1942. She had success in healing people with her holy water. When her fame began to spread, her parents wanted her to return to their village and marry again to gain new bridewealth for themselves. Marie insisted that God had forbidden her to be intimate with any man (Paulme, 1962, p. 18).

As her movement grew, the colonial administration became suspicious of her activities, and called her to Abidjan in 1949 to learn more of her intentions. She was reluctant to go to Abidjan, again because of God's warning about intimacy with men, and said that if she went, she would die upon her return. Her followers have a song about this situation:

> I [God] told you not to go near men
> You ride in cars with them
> I will not be with you.

Successful in convincing the administration of the beneficial and nonsubversive nature of her doctrine and movement, Marie Lalou won an influx of new converts (Paulme, 1962, pp. 17–18).

In 1951, shortly after her movement began to grow dramatically, and after her relatives, finally convinced of her gifts, had begun to build her what they intended to be "the prettiest church of all," Marie became ill. Before dying, her last commandments to her followers were to stop poisoning people, stop using "fetishes," and have recourse only to her holy water *(deima)* for healing and protection. She stated that a man's widow should not be tormented and have another husband imposed upon her against her will. She added that men should not force women into the bush to commit unwanted sexual aggression (Paulme, 1962, pp. 18–19).

Before her death, Marie Lalou designated a woman from Grobaridou, the village in which she spent her final years, as her successor. The choice was dictated to her by God in a dream, and she taught the woman, known as Princess Geniss, the songs that had been revealed to her in dreams. The new leader had a husband and several children and had to relinquish her conjugal role in order to assume the new office. Marie Lalou compensated her husband by giving him two new wives, and he and his family continued to reside next to the new prophetess. Princess Geniss visited her congregations in different villages in order to pray for them. She died in 1959 and was succeeded by another woman (Paulme, 1962, pp. 20–22, 48).

Without her approval, another woman claimed to be Marie Lalou's spiritual successor, and set up a separate branch of the movement. Blé Nahi was a Bété woman who had had an unhappy childhood, and, although successively married to two different men, was barren. She was married to her second husband, when she fell ill around 1948. She consulted Marie Lalou, who said that spirit possession or the fact that she was herself a witch was the source of her illness. Her husband, therefore, suspected her of trying to poison him (Paulme, 1962, pp. 23–26).

Returning home after seeing Lalou, Blé Nahi saw a vision of Jesus who told her to sing a song, after which he said that she would no longer be known as Blé Nahi but as Jesus Onoï, meaning "woman in the service of God on earth." She then boarded a bus for her husband's village and upon disembarking saw Jesus again who told her to sing. She sang a song, saying that now that Jesus Onoï had appeared, health and prosperity would reign. Then, walking toward the village, she became unable to move, and heard a voice asking why she was going to her husband's village when she was supposed to cease all relations with men and would be punished if she failed to do so. She told her husband that she would no longer live with him. He then asked her parents to come for her. They encouraged her husband to force her to stay with him, but she refused. Her husband agreed that she should return to her parents, but they refused her. She went to the home of the brother for whose wife her own bridewealth had paid and in whose house she, therefore, should have not only been welcome but also had some authority. The wife would not let her stay, because she said that her sister-in-law was crazy (Paulme, 1962, pp. 25–28).

Rejected in her paternal village, she went to her maternal village, where she was better received. There, she insisted that she would cure sterile, sick, and dying people. While she was there, her paternal relatives summoned her to perform the rites of extreme unction for a dying sister. When she arrived in their village, they told her that if she did not cure the woman by her prayers she would be buried alive with her. She prayed to God for three days to save the woman. The woman recovered. In addition, although she had been childless, the woman found herself pregnant and gave birth to a long desired healthy child. Jesus Onoï's fame grew as she saved numerous other lives by prayer after insisting that they confess their evil acts, including having tried to kill her through witchcraft. Feeling that she had been designated by Jesus to heal people, Jesus Onoï announced that she was Marie Lalou's spiritual successor at the latter's death. Setting up her headquarters in the village of Dahiria, she went from village to village exorcising spirits from the sick, urging people to abandon their traditional religious objects, and preaching a doctrine of work and brotherhood (Paulme, 1962, pp. 27–30).

Unlike Marie Lalou, when Jesus Onoï died in 1958, she was succeeded by two male prophets. One still continues to receive messages from her in dreams and preaches her doctrine in the area around Dahiria. However, although the founder and her successors as heads of the Deima cult have been women, it is men who are the disciples and apostles, who officiate in services, who preach the doctrine, and who direct the construction of new churches. Although women were designated to teach the religion, it is believed that God felt that a woman would not be able to direct it alone, and so gave her male assistance. Whereas Marie Lalou and her women successors had no significant experience outside of their traditional milieu, the male leaders of the church have traveled, speak French, and have moved beyond a traditional life-style (Paulme, 1962, pp. 24, 32–33, 48).

CONCLUSIONS

The women who were the inspired founders of religious movements were extraordinary women in their social context. Both Marie Lalou and Blé Nahi were misfits of a sort, because they did not have any children. Both were suspected of making their husbands ill or of killing them and were, subsequently, accused of witchcraft. They received opposition rather than support from their paternal relatives who were concerned with the loss of bridewealth. They said that they could heal people, and many of their fellow villagers felt that if they could heal, they could also harm. Both, however, eventually proved that their intentions were to use the powers given them by God to accomplish missions beneficial to humanity.

Both women had visions that suggested that their inability to fit into the normal women's social roles of wife and mother was the result of their designation by God for a more important role. The major condition of assuming this new role was to reject entirely the role that the women had been unable to perform in a socially acceptable manner. It is significant that both were concerned that women who were suspected of causing their husband's death cease suffering abuse as widows by having unacceptable husbands and unwelcome sexual advances imposed on them. An important concern of theirs was to cure people, especially women, of sterility, usually considered the result of witchcraft. Lalou's successor, Princess Geniss, did not have to be extraordinary in the same way that Lalou was, in that she was designated to occupy an institutionalized role not inspired directly by God. However, she had to assume the same obligations as Lalou in rejecting the traditional female role in order to accept the spiritual one.

It is significant that it was a vision from God that allowed a woman to begin a new religious movement in which other women were able to become leaders and adherents. Only in the two movements inspired by the Prophet Harris that were begun by women, and in which spiritual visions were important, do women play important roles. In the Church of the Twelve Apostles founded by Grace Tani in the Gold Coast, both males and females could receive visions empowering them to be prophets and prophetesses with the ability to heal people through their spiritual gifts. Although a woman founded the Deima Church and women follow the succession, the most important administrative roles are played by men, because the social organization follows that of the traditional society, and, unlike the Church of the Twelve Apostles, only the spiritual visions of the leaders are significant.

However, in the Deima Church, the personal inspiration of an individual woman provided the basis for new organizational and role possibilities, even if only for a limited number of women. Marie Lalou provided a new organizational principle based upon her own inspiration that was triggered by her role as a social deviant. Her movement allowed certain women to achieve status and power only by legitimizing an alternative behavioral pattern for women who were previously allowed no alternatives.

6

The Woman on the Beach and the Man in the Bush: Leadership and Adepthood in the Twelve Apostles Movement of Ghana*

Paul Breidenbach

> When the man Harris came he changed the whole world.
> He changed all of the people.
> Prophetess Captian of Axim

THE HARRIST MOVEMENT

In the year 1914 a man from Liberia and his two wives departed from Ivory Coast and crossed over the waters of the Tano Lagoon for a brief visit to the small village of Half-Assini in what was then the Gold Coast Colony (Ghana). The eventual result of this visit to the small coastal fishing settlements that dotted the way was the largest indigenous church movement in Ghana, known today, depending on locality, as the Nackabah People, The William Wade Harris Twelve Apostles Church, or the Twelve Apostles Church of Ghana. The man was an African who took on the role of a Christian prophet. His name was William Wade Harris.

At the time of my fieldwork in 1970 and 1971, the small courtyards and communal dwellings used as water healing centers, and referred to by the adherents of the movement as ''gardens,'' were to be found as far north as the Brong-Ahafo region and the urban center of Kumasi in the heart of Ashanti. The

*The research on which this paper is based was funded through a grant from the National Institute of Mental Health (No. 1 FoI MH 49461–01).

Brief sentences and expressions of informants are given in the text without references. Longer passages are footnoted in the text by giving the field tape recording number (R 1, 2, etc.).

coastal area, however, still abounds with the greatest outward evidence of the presence of the upheaval generated in response to Harris. Healing gardens are to be found in nearly every small town and village along the coast from Half-Assini in the west to the coastal capital of Accra in the east.

It is outside the topic and scope of this paper to detail the known events surrounding the encounter between the prophet Harris and the peoples of the Western region (for a more complete picture of these events see Baëta, 1962; Breidenbach, 1973; Haliburton, 1971). Yet, some aspects of this confrontation must be mentioned as they relate to the development of the gender-marked aspects of leadership and adepthood in the current church.

Progressing across the Ivory Coast, with short forays inland, the Liberian performed a simple ritual baptism which the people later called the "sign of the prophet." The people of each village knelt in small groups around the staff which Harris planted in the ground. The prophet, raising the cup and blessing the water, poured the water on their foreheads, tracing a sign of the cross with his thumb, often hitting them with the Bible or placing it on their heads as as a sign of dismissal. During these ministrations, his wives sang and "beat the calabashes" in order to drive out malevolent spirits and to call good ones. Many informants spoke of other dramatic gestures that, like the "baptism," resulted in massive group reactions. He pointed his staff and individuals would fall into convulsive seizures. He held an open Bible before their eyes and people began speaking in "tongues." The populations' general response then was manifested in possession states, trances, and, at the command of their new leader, the apparent rejection of traditional medicines as well as the burning of all paraphernalia associated with former religious practice.

This charismatic man, who neither spoke the language of his "converts" nor remained in any one place for more than a few days, had little time and virtually no machinery to organize people into a church. His success was largely based on inspiration and his facility to encourage people in the direction of radical religious transformation. His efforts did not rest on an elaborate set of doctrinal statements or any form of institutional allegiance. Still, two injunctions were set forth by the prophet that may have been intended to offset the whirlwind nature of his visit and to give his converts some sense of continuity upon his departure. First, he told his new adherents, many of whom followed him down the coast, to go to the few fledgling Methodist or Roman Catholic mission houses in the area to await further instruction in the Book he carried with him. He also designated several of his converts as people "having a good spirit upon them" to continue doing the work that he himself was doing. Significantly, most of these people whom he called "Apostles" (a probable origin of the name Twelve Apostles) had been traditional religious adepts or healers prior to being sealed with the "sign of the prophet."

The first directive backfired due to circumstances beyond the prophet's control. The inadequately staffed mission houses in the Western region were soon swamped with large numbers of Harris converts. At first, the missionaries were amazed in the light of their own meager success in the area of conversions. However, their astonishment soon gave way to consternation when the new "Christians" began to fall into trances, possession seizures, calabash beating, and Bible carrying (carrying the Bibles on their heads) as the prophet had directed them. The new converts were soon informed that such behavior was unacceptable to the Methodist or Catholics, and large groups left or were driven out of the church houses.

The second directive left an alternative for the people. The prophet had singled out for exorcism and "baptism" a few traditional adepts who were formerly *bosomfo* (priests or priestesses).[1] These individuals had worked in alliance with acknowledged spiritual forces or gods *(abosom)* prior to the prophet's advent. They generally applied their skills in manipulating these powers for use in healing. Such religious adepts were both male and female.

> If you go to the beach road Madame Tani is there. If you go to the bush road Papa Nackabah is also there.
> Prophetess Nyameke Ndelah of Kikam

THE CONVERSION OF THE TWO ELDERS

The first group of people Harris contacted were the Nzemas of the far western rain forest. Among the Nzemas, as well as the Ahantas and the Fantes who soon came into the movement in large numbers, traditional methods of healing involved not only empirical remedies such as *edur* (herbs) with medicinal properties, but also processes of what Westerners would call exorcism and possession. The priest-healers in these cultures accounted for both "natural" causes of ill health as well as unseen sources of causality in cases of sickness or even misfortune (concepts that seem interrelated in traditional cosmology). Spiritual influences of the "small gods" and the workings of *Anyen* (witches) were taken as an acknowledged part of reality. These powers were put into creation by *Nyame* (the God of the sky) who also created human beings. Since these forces were an accepted part of the world that human beings inhabit, the powers of the *bosomfo* were not considered "supernatural." Their adepthood rested on the facility that they had for possession by the *bosom* as well as their skill in putting these spirits to work for the benefit of human beings in this world. The adept did this by lessening the dangers inherent in the *bosom's* power or the power of humans who were also capable of causing spiritual harm, witches.

Grace Tani (her name meaning one born of Tano) was such a *bosomfo* (literally, god-person) before Harris arrived. Born in the coastal Nzema fishing

---

[1]This term and all other native terms are Fante. This language is used as a lingua franca in the area of research. All of the Nzema and Ahanta informants cited spoke either English or Fante.

village of Krisan, some 45 miles east of Half-Assini, she had built up a reputation as a famous priestess. In a trance, achieved while dancing in a brass pan which was seen as the dwelling place of the *bosom*, she spoke with the voice of the river god Tano. Achieving this state, she then administered herbs and advice "in order to make childbearing possible or so that women might bring forth safely." The following translated account of her "conversion" by the prophet was rendered by the current leader of the Fante Twelve Apostles, M. Kojo George:

> *Aberwa* [old lady, a term of greatest respect] Tani had a special *edur* [medicine or herbs] that she gave to pregnant women. At that time she was away from the village of Krisan administering this *edur* to a pregnant woman. She had heard of the coming of the man (Harris) but she had made up a point in her mind that if the man comes she would not allow him to convert her and throw away her *bosom*. For, after all, she was using this *bosom* to do her work. But when she was returning from that village, she met Harrisin [pidgin form of Harris' name] near the beach. And Harrisin told her that "it is because of you that I have come." Now Madame Tani's staff was in her hand together with her gong-gong (a small metal bell used to call the *bosom*) and then she couldn't even open her mouth to say that she was not going to allow him to convert her. What she finally did say was this: "If you say that it was I for whom you have come, then purify (baptize) me." So Harrisin put the Bible on her head, and as soon as he put it on her head the *bosom* came, and she threw away all of the *edur* that she had tied around her waist as well as those that were made into trinkets around her hands and legs. So it was in the middle of the road that Harrisin converted *Aberwa* Tani. . . . And he made a white dress for her. (R11)

After the dramatic event described above, the woman followed Harris to the town of Axim some 15 miles down the coast, where Harris took her as one of his wives.[2] She henceforth called herself Madame Harris Grace Tani.[3] She remained at his side throughout the duration of the prophet's stay in the Gold Coast. Harris attempted to take her with him on his return to Ivory Coast. However, according to most of my informants, when they reached the border her kinsmen convinced her to stay with her own people.[4] It appears that Madame Tani did not continue Harris' work for very long. Rather, she eventually "took to traveling, selling palm wine and gin." Some of the elders felt that, as one prophetess put it, "she, being a woman, did not wish to be a leader on her own."

[2]Harris had four wives, including Madame Tani, in 1915. He seems to have married another Nzema woman named Mokwa who was later said to have gone mad (from a conversation with John Aboso Mensah, the grandson of Madame Tani).

[3]In several of her letters found in the Cape Coast Archives, she had the letter writer use the title "Madame Harris Grace Tannie or Tani."

[4]Some of the elders indicated that Madame Tani was called back from Abidjan in Ivory Coast. This seems less likely, not only because more people claimed that she never left the Gold Coast, but because of colonial restrictions on the movement of the Nzemas across the border, which also could account for her return.

But in the light of the very prominent position that she later assumed, it may be more likely that her brief lapse from the Work was due to the dispute with her family over the marriage and the attempt to leave the country with the prophet. But whatever the reason for her temporary withdrawal from Harris' work, she was dramatically brought back into it through events that led her into a kind of partnership with another famous Harris convert, one Kwesi "John" Nackabah.

Nackabah was a Gwira man. He too was a *bosomfo* who had achieved some local fame as a healer and an oracle around his home village of Essowa, located in the bush about eight miles up the Ankobra River. When I visited Essowa, Nackabah's present successor, John Nackabah III, narrated the following story of his conversion. He indicated that after an initial baptism by Harris, Nackabah returned to Essowa and began speaking in "a Liberian language." His kinsmen felt that he had gone mad. They then took him by canoe down river to see Harris once more.

> They then went to the Nzemas and they went to a chief's house in Kikam where Harrisin was staying. So when they got there Harrisin said, "do not be surprised and think he is mad. This man is bringing the work of *Nyame*. So if he is speaking a different language he is not insane. Rather, this is a gift of *Nyame*. He is going to work with it to convert the people." So Harris let him stay with him for a few days. Then Harris said he should be sent back up the river. And Harris said, "I have seen the gift that has been given to me has also been given to you. So look, I am giving you those things that *Nyame* has given to me, the cup, the calabash, the staff, and the Bible." So when Nackabah came back he too did the work and became famous. (R2)[5]

Records of a 1918 court case accusing Nackabah of "fetish" worship attest that Nackabah was continuing a ritual practice modeled on that of Harris, including the "sign of the prophet" and calabash beating.[6] The colonial government's charges of "fetish" worship were dismissed due to lack of evidence, and Nackabah went on with the Work.

Sometime shortly after this court appearance, Madame Tani, who was again residing at Ankobra, became ill. She had undoubtedly met Nackabah at Axim in 1914, and due to the proximity of Essowa, she had become aware of his growing reputation as a healer and preacher acting in the name of Harris. These facts, along with the exhortations of her fellow villagers at Ankobra, led her to call on Nackabah as a healer. He took her back to Essowa, where he cured her of the "mysterious sickness" that had fallen upon her. He then explained that the real reason behind her affliction was the fact that she had been given a power to

---

[5] Among the early letters and proclamations still kept by Nackabah III, I found an updated document called "Testimony of Prophet John Nackabah Founder of the Twelve Apostles Mission Gold Coast." It tended to support Nackabah III's narration of the conversation by Harris.

[6] The trial was held before "his worship" A. G. Ross, District Commissioner (Ghana National Archives, January 9, 1918).

work with "but had now put this power behind her." All of the older people who remember these events agreed that from this time forward, Madame Tani "put the work before her." In the words of an elderly prophetess, "they then began to work together as brother and sister, knowing that they were both doing the same work of Mister Harrisin."

> Yes, she too was the wife of our senior man
> Harrisin so, of course, we had to take her as
> our mother.
> Prophet John Hackman II of Kajibir

THE KINSHIP MODEL: INCIPIENT ORGANIZATION
AROUND THE WOMAN AND THE MAN

Once more, I stress the essential fact that while Harris' person and activities had resulted in a massive upheaval and a movement toward at least outward religious transformation, he had done little to provide the basis for an organizational context supporting the continuation of his "message."[7] The link with his converts was first and foremost his own brief presentation of the ritual symbols, and their manipulation through centrally nonverbal symbolic actions such as his form of baptism and Bible-carrying. In short, Harris preached through symbols and educated through action.

In adhering to the symbolic conventions and constructions of the prophet, his converts ran into the almost inevitable rejection by the missionaries who, in effect, demanded what they themselves could not instantly provide: Western modes of education, literacy, and understandings grounded in a highly formalized doctrinal (and European) model. This to them was "real" Christianity based on what they saw as authentic preaching and education. From this viewpoint, the highly emotive ritual acts of the Harris people constituted simply an aberration and a distortion of "truth" or a new form of "fetish worship." This missionary reaction, for a critical period of time, cut off Harris converts from Western-style preaching and education.

In spite of their blocked access to such structures of cohesion and authority, the inevitable organization and routinization of charismatic events into channels through which they might be shared and redirected, so familiar to students of religious movements, still took shape among the Harris people. This structuring focused around the two outstanding representatives of Harris, Madame Tani and Papa Nackabah. This implies that these two individuals must have had, like the missionaries, a model of organization and leadership from which to work. They

---

[7]The word "message" here stresses the primacy of original messages in the rise of movements. Later adaptations of such primal messages by the first generation of followers cannot be understood apart from the "promise" of the initial religious statement.

did have a model, but this model stands in striking contrast to that of the missionaries. It was derived from notions of family and kinship that were so well known to the two elders that they were taken as "second nature."

The image for organization was primarily grounded in the sophisticated development of the extended family and corporate lineage among the Nzemas, Ahantas, and Fantes. Kinship, in addition to being a mode of reckoning roles, positions, authority and rights within these cultures, constitutes a form of orientational viewpoint or ideology toward the realities of the world. Even anomalies, like the advent of Harris, could be incorporated in terms of this kin-centered view of the world.

Captain Rattray's comment that "descent is matrilineal" and that "this fact is the very basis of Ashanti social organization," also applies to their Fante cousins as well as the Ahanta and Nzema societies (Rattray, 1923, p. 35). Every Fante, for example, is by birth a member of his mother's *abusua* (lineage), which consists of all the descendants of both sexes by a known genealogy of a single common ancestress in the unbroken female line.

The lineage places heavy stress on the blood relatives. Children are identified in their physical constitution with the mother's blood. This identification is often contrasted with the notion that a child receives his spiritual personality or character from the father. The transmission of this "spiritual personality" came through the *exercise of the male's role as authority and disciplinarian*. The members of the *abusua* call each other brothers and sisters. All elders are addressed by the young as mother and father. In the family house, discipline is the prerogative of the oldest living male elder, who is ideally the object of great affection as well as respect.

It is not hard to see how the "partnership" of Madame Tani and Nackabah gradually developed into a dual leadership, based on joint but complementary roles and following principles of sexual distinction as these related to extended kinship organizations within these societies. Repeatedly, prophets and prophetesses of the contemporary movement indicated that the church, like a blood descent group, came from the woman. *Madame Tani*, as they put it, "owned the church." They stressed the idea that *"the woman came first"*: she was converted before Nackabah. I got the distinct impression that most adepts, and members as well, saw the church as a new kind of *abusua* with Madame Tani as *mother*.

In the traditional system, it is clear, however, that what might be called "political" leadership was vested in male elders who directed and made decisions in relation to rights constituted by, and derived from, their relationship to females. Nackabah's relationship to Madame Tani was also conceived of in this manner. It was he who directed Mother Tani back into the Work as though he needed her to make his efforts take on an aura of completeness. He then directed most of his efforts to the maintenance of group solidarity, dealing with fragmentations and factions within the group as a kind of disciplinarian and *father*.

Complementing this mother–father lineage model is an additional principle of growth and transfer of authority based on the concept of *tum*, or power. This power was derived from the contact with Harris and also recognized in the traditional system of religion. Both Tani and Nackabah had been designated by Harris as people who had *tum* because they, after baptism, now had a "proper *sunsum*" (spirit to work with). When applied in converting others (usually through some healing experience), this power to work becomes the "transfer of the spirit." Even this transfer of the spirit, in which the mother and father were equally adept, was cast into the idiom of parent and child relationships, with all prophetesses and prophets becoming the children of the two elders through spiritual filiation or maternity. By the 1940s, a rule had been formulated that women should receive their confirmation of a proper spirit from Madame Tani and the men from Papa Nackabah.[8] This partnership in transferring and confirming the *sunsum* added an element of equality between the sexes that was not as defined in the indigenous *abusua*.

In closing these brief comments on the early organization and leadership, I must mention how my informants looked back to the time when the two *mpayimfo edwuma* (elders of the Work) were alive (Nackabah died in 1947 and Grace Tani in 1958). They continuously extolled this period when the two elders worked together as a kind of "perfect era," or, as they put it, "the time of the *odzi mu edwuma*" (the complete Work). Then, it is said, the two worked together as a "husband and wife" or as a "brother and sister." Then, as in the harmony that is the ideal in the *abusua*, there were no great disputes or litigations over leadership. Everyone was concerned only with the important things, the procreation of more spiritual children to carry on the work.

> It is because of the child that is on your back
> that you have come here to this Twelve Apos-
> tles, isn't it so?
> (A question directed to a female patient
> by Prophetess Mary Gaise of Komenda)

MADAME TANI'S HEALING WORK
AND FEMALE ADEPTHOOD

Up to this point, I have referred to the "Work" but have failed to give the term a more precise meaning beyond implying the continuation of the Harris baptism. To the Twelve Apostles today, however, the term the "Work" *(edwuma)* or

[8]The church's earliest existing bylaws, set down in a meeting at Ankobra (mouth) on November 7, 1944, contain this prescription and a statement of partnership. In capital letters, the bylaws note: "THE FOLLOWING BYE–LAWS HAVE BEEN APPROVED BY PROPHET JOHN NACKABAH AND PROPHETESS GRACE TANI *FOUNDERS* OF THE SAID CHURCH" (my italics).

"spiritual work" *(sunsum edwuma)* is a specific designation for the major ritual event enacted in each garden on every Friday. This ritual embodies the central ideology of the church which is focused around the "bringing into the open" of spiritual influences that are linked to the sources of *Yarba* (sickness). In large part, the "sickness" treated by the ritual is related to the reproductive capacities or disorders of females, misfortunes in trading activities, also a major domain of women, the work of witches, who are generally elderly females, as well as "mental disorders" and family problems, involving males and females alike.

In its basic outline, the ritual of healing is a simple construction that, in essence, recreates the type of occurrences that marked the Harris baptism. Its goal is the inducement of spirit possession. But now, the stylized activities leading up to possession are more routinized. The *edwuma* always takes place in the healing garden courtyard on Friday afternoons, when the sun is at its peak. Patients, mostly females, are lined up in a row in front of a small wooden table by the prophetess. On this table, which is covered in red cloth, a pile of calabash rattles, the Bible, and a cup have been placed. Facing the patients is the staff cross which is leaning on the front edge of the table. The prophetess (or, possibly, a male healer, if one is present) takes the white enamel cup, fills it with water, and raises it to the sky, pointing it in the direction of the sun. She does this in order that the *sunsum* she is working with may "hit" and "bless" the water within. After her arm gives a convulsive jerk, indicating that the *sunsum* is working with her, she pours some of this water into the pans that each of the patients have brought with them and fills the rest of the pan with the common tap water. She then places the basin carefully on each patient's head, placing the patient's hands on the rim in order to hold the pan steady. These pans are the "seat" of the *bosom*, or other *sunsum*, who will come into the garden during the ritual action. It is said by the members of the movement that the action of these spirits can be detected in the whirling and swirling of the water in the pan, when the patient is possessed.

Standing on the opposite side of the table under a shelter made of bamboo and palm leaves are members of the movement, again predominantly females. After a few improvised prayers chanted by the prophetess for the success of the work, this group begins the traditional chants and "Liberian" songs of Harris that invoke the *sunsum*. These chants are accompanied by the "beating" or "ringing" of the calabashes, which at this time are called the "speakers of *Nyame*." If played in a proper fashion, they have the power to call *sunsum* into the garden for interrogation. For a time, the prophetess leads the calabash playing and singing. Then she picks up the staff and begins to point it at the patients; sometimes too, she approaches the patients with a Bible, waving it high over the water pans. She also might swing her calabash around the top of the pan, or perhaps around the exposed stomach of a pregnant patient.

After 45 minutes or so, the patients, who up to this point have been swaying gently back and forth to the beat of the rattles, begin to go into seizures and convulsive jerking, sometimes running about in circles and spilling the water which is quickly replenished by the prophetess or her female assistants. One by one these patients are interrogated. The prophetess speaks directly to the *sunsum* that is upon the patient. The first goal is to identify the spirit, and then to reveal why the spirit is troubling the person, or if the spirit is working with evil people (witches) to cause harm to the patient. Later, it is seen if the spirit will accept some offering or sacrifice in exchange for the good health of the troubled patient. Both mental and physical disorders are cured through this process of bringing out into the open ''evil intentions'' and ''hidden doings.'' The ritual then ends, some three hours after it started, with a communal sharing of water from the well in each garden. This water is called ''Madame Tani's holy water.'' Patients are also bathed at this time, and such ritual baths continue all during the treatment which may consist of several weeks or months of ''water carrying.''

While the brief summary of the ritual given above is drawn from my own observations made in 1970 and 1971, historical accounts indicate that Madame Tani had developed this ''bearing of pans,'' or ''water-carrying'' ritual as early as 1920 and possibly before.[9] The ritual reflects the encounter with Harris in that he too acknowledged spirit possession and was an adept in inducing it. The dominant Harris symbols are utilized in this process as signs of power. The exaltation of the water symbol as the dominant one, to the complete exclusion of herbal remedies, is also patterned on the Harris ''purification'' or baptism as a rejection of traditional medicines.

Other features of the *edwuma* distinctively reflect Madame Tani's orientation prior to her conversion. Examples of this are to be seen in the use of pans as a seat for the *bosom*, and, perhaps more importantly, in the redirection of the possession and purification to the healing of women. Madame Tani's redirection of the Harris ritual is supported by the cultural context in which women see one of the highest fulfillments of life as being embodied in fertility and childbearing. The ritual, while dealing with other disorders, is primarily directed against the ''stumbling blocks'' in the path of plentiful motherhood. Created by a woman, and carried out largely by female adepts, the *sunsum edwuma* is generally directed toward the concerns and needs of women.

The *Sofo* (or prophetess)[10] is today the primary healing adept within the movement. I find it difficult to put into words how tremendously impressed I was with the striking presence, character, bearing, and personal authority manifested by these women who directed the activity in the Twelve Apostles gardens. They seem to command both affection and respectful obedience, not just because they

---

[9]Ghana National Archives, Report of A. Q. Kyiamah to District Commissioner, Sekondi, February 6, 1940. Kyiamah noted: ''Madame Harris Grace Tannie introduced into her movement water carrying. She is a fetish priestess, under the guise of a Christian evangelistic body. She began this work as far back as 1920.''

[10]In other contexts, the word *Sofo* is generally translated as ''priest or priestess.'' The term is still used for native priests and priestesses today. The Twelve Apostles always translate it as ''prophet or prophetess.''

are confirmed with "a spirit to work with" but also because of the wide range of their specialized knowledge and activity. They act as diviners of illness; in many instances they interpret the patients' or their own dreams to effect healing; practically all of them are expert midwives; they bear the major burden of directing the healing rituals, and during the rest of the week, they minister to the physical wants of the patients; throughout all of this activity, they are continuously involved in giving counsel and advice. Some of the prophetesses in smaller garden communities also run their own farm or conduct regular trading activities in local markets.

It now seems appropriate to go into more detail regarding these specialized activities on which the leadership and authority of the prophetess rests. One of the first symbolic actions performed by the prophetess when a new patient is brought into the garden is known to the members as "the raising of the cup." Here, the prophetess demonstrates the "power of seeing" and discerning the spiritual causality behind sickness or misfortune that will lead to the appropriate ritual action or care. With the patient assuming a submissive posture before the prophetess, she fills a cup with water and lifts it to the sky. At this time "messages" come to her that fill in the details surrounding the patient's condition. The following translated "cup lifting" account was given by a noted prophetess who works in a small garden outside the town of Cape Coast. It is typical in that it provides an example of a major type of problem that prophetesses are adept in dealing with:

> Look, a certain woman was brought to me here in the garden. She was pregnant and the time for her to bring forth was long passed. She went to the "hospital" on so many occasions. The doctor there even advised her to go and lay in the room [hospital ward], but her husband sent her here. As soon as I raised the cup a message came that it was her mother who was causing the trouble that had come upon her. Yes, in the night the mother had been removing the child from her stomach and during the day she put the child back into the stomach. The reason why the mother was doing these evil things was because she was *Any n*, a witch. She was a member of a society of witches. And since the year was about to end she had to produce something for their [Christmas] feast. Therefore, she intended to use the child as a goat for the feast. It was because of this that when the time would come for the woman to bring forth the child, and the child would not survive, all the people would say that this was just the woman's own misfortune [i.e., *hoham yarba*, body sickness]. You see, they would not know the real causes (which were *sunsum yarba*, spiritual sickness), that it was the mother who brought this thing about. So as soon as I raised the cup I saw it. (P-4)

In this particular instance, the prophetess summoned the woman's mother to the garden and directly accused her of trying to "eat the soul" of the woman's child. When the mother attempted to leave the garden the prophetess had the woman's husband keep her there. The prophetess then noted that: "I kept the mother in the garden and her son-in-law watched her. The child (woman) brought forth. After three months time I allowed the mother to return to her home town."

As should be evident from the foregoing description of the *edwuma*, the prophetesses take on the roles of directors of all ritual action. They initiate the prayers, bless the water, lead the songs, cajole the spirits to come, and, when the spirits possess the patients, they direct the interrogation. However, throughout this action they are also constantly engaged in giving advice and making predictions about health and sickness. This advice is most often given when they are being directed by the "spirit they work with."

While the healing ritual is the central event of the week and the most dramatic realization of the *sunsum edwuma*, it must be put in the context of the constant and attentive care that the prophetesses give to patients during their entire stay in the garden. In a very real sense, the prophetess, like her prototype Madame Tani, deserves the title "our mother."

> Although Grace Tani was really the moving
> spirit, Nackabah was more prominently in the
> public eye.
> C. G. Baëta (1962, p. 34)

NACKABAH, THE PREACHING SERVICE, AND THE MASTERS

If on Friday, the day of healing, female adepts preside and direct ritual activity in a dominant fashion, the reverse is true on Sundays when the second major ritual of the movement is held. The "Chapel," or "*kyɛpor*," as the members refer to it, is conducted by younger males, who qualify for this role through their exposure to Western-style education and literacy. These men are called "masters" (the Methodist designation for teacher–catechists), and their major roles are those of preacher and Bible reader at the service. In the main, "Chapel" closely resembles, at least in its outward form, a Methodist Sunday prayer meeting. In contrast to the healing ritual, it takes place indoors. The master standing behind a table directs the service. He begins with opening prayers. Some European-style hymns translated into the vernacular are then sung in a dirge-like fashion. This introduction is followed by the reading of a biblical passage and a sermon by the master which is interspersed with hymns. At length, someone inevitably begins the more traditional kind of Fante lyrics and chants. The structured action of the first half of the service breaks down and people begin dancing. The service concludes with several dancing collection processions and testimonials about the healing work that are given either by members or leaders who feel inclined to "bear witness to the Work."

At times, while attending these Sunday services, I felt that I was studying two separate groups or churches. The ritual separation between Chapel and the *sunsum edwuma* supports this impression. Differences in the very basis of adept-hood in the two rituals are quite obvious. Literacy is essential to the preaching master, while, in fact, I did not encounter a single healing prophetess who was literate (though many of them could recite long biblical passages). It is only through the collection testimonials and, sometimes, references in the sermon that the healing work comes into the "Chapel." And chapel seems to exert little direct influence on the healing ritual. Historically, the beginning of the chapel is understandable in the light of Nackabah's influence and his characterization of himself as "preacher."[11] From the beginning, it was Nackabah, rather than Madame Tani, who was fascinated with the modes of organization, symbols of material progress, and activities of teaching and preaching evident in the de-veloping Mission churches that grew up around the Twelve Apostles people as the years went on.

In the early years, Nackabah incorporated bits and pieces of mission ter-minology and artifacts from the Methodist and Roman Catholic missions in the Western region into the movement in a syncretistic fashion. In the early 1940s, he began entering into more serious and direct negotiations with a Welsh Pen-tecostal missionary of the Apostolic Church named James McKeown. It seems that at that time Nackabah was impressed with the "progress" of the mission churches. And, as M. C. George put it, "he had made up his mind that unless we too had a white man who could read from the book then we wouldn't prosper." For a time, McKeown met with Nackabah who he assumed to be the sole leader of the movement. Impressed with what he took to be correspondence between his own Pentecostalism and the healing work of the Twelve Apostles, McKeown set out to further "Christianize" (and ultimately control) the movement by stressing the necessity for literate leadership. In order to do this, the healing prophetesses and prophets had to be directed by trained "catechists." It was on this point that McKeown ran into the influence of Madame Tani.

The clash between Tani and McKeown came about at a meeting where McKeown stated that he would "work with them," if his catechists could be in control of the garden communities or at least preside over them as teachers. At this, Madame Tani cautioned Nackabah that it looked like the white man was going to try to make himself the "owner" of the church, a direct usurpation of her position. This revealing incident was described to me by Madame Tani's grandson and a current leader in the movement, John Aboso Mensah, in the following terms (in English):

Now there was a man called McKeown who is now the head of the Apos-tolic Church. He said he was going to Heman for a meeting there with

---

[11]Nackabah III also told a story of Nackabah on his second trip to Harris, falling out of the canoe and then appearing some hours later on a rock in the Ankobra River "preaching the gospel." Other stories also indicate that Nackabah liked to picture himself as a preacher as well as a healer.

Nackabah and my late grandmother. There, at this meeting he put it to my late grandmother and Papa Nackabah that he wanted to be the head of the church. . . . Now, Grace Tani told him that when William Wade Harris came he did not prophesy that a white man would come and be the head of the church. Then this McKeown said that my late grandmother had a "devil" [This word "devil" was no doubt translated to Madame Tani as *ab nsam*, which implied that she was a witch.] Then my grandmother said: "Yes, well, if I am a devil it is through my devilish ways that all of these prophets and prophetesses are here today." So my grandmother and all of her people immediately withdrew to Nzemaland. Still, Nackabah was fooled by this McKeown. He even said something like, "Well, a woman cannot play an Asafo drum [drum played in an all male brotherhood] and be captain of the guard." He meant that a woman could not properly establish a church by herself. So Nackabah's idea was to hand the church over to McKeown. But you see my grandmother refused. When she saw me she said, "I did not sell my church to a white man." Then I too was very pleased when my grandmother told me this very matter.

Mensah's narration shatters to some extent the older members' myth-image of the "complete work" by indicating that a rift had developed between the mother and the father of the work. However, the account also strongly highlights Madame Tani's power, authority, and influence in her position as mother. In fact, shortly after these events, Nackabah soon became involved in litigations with McKeown over other innovations. For example, McKeown tried to have the prophets and prophetesses cease using the staff-crosses, their symbols of authority, and also tried to have the calabash rattles, which had in the adepts' view unique powers bestowed by Harris, replaced with tambourines. Nackabah himself called the tambourines "useless toys." After these litigations, McKeown withdrew to Accra to head up his own Apostolic group there, and Nackabah went to Ankobra and made his peace with Madame Tani. The joint leadership and complete Work then continued as before.

It must be pointed out that due to the period of McKeown's influence and Nackabah's acceptance of the notion of having literate preachers in the movement, the church was provided with a role for males in terms of a distinctive kind of work. Today, male adepthood is tending toward a focus on the preaching and teaching role. Since this time, more and more young "masters" have come into the movement. While this trend is evident, there are still no formal training procedures sponsored by the church.[12]

I do not wish to give the impression that there are no male healing adepts. There are still a few, all nonliterate and mostly older men, many of whom were

[12]Since the 1950s, some of the masters have been talking about setting up a "Bible school" for training purposes. This has never come about although these masters would like to see it. I think that this failure to act on the idea of schools is accounted for by the primacy of healing in the movement.

trained by Nackabah and Tani or their early disciples, who act both as "pastors" and healers. But these adepts rely heavily on the younger men who have come into the movement for their literate skills in preaching. These younger men translate biblical passages into Fante idiom and draw moral lessons for behavior, much in the same way the European preachers did. They are all impressed with the power of the healers. This, by their own testimony, is the real reason why they have chosen to become teachers in the Twelve Apostles rather than some other group.

> Today this is the way it is. One person rises up and says "I am leader." Then there is litigation. Then another person too rises up and says "I am leader." Then there is litigation. But where *Nyame* is there is no litigation. Yes, in the time of those two elders there were no litigations as we see today.
> Prophetess Nyamek   Ndelah of Kikam

FRAGMENTATION OF UNITY AND
THE FAMILY MODEL TODAY

Since the early 1930s, the Twelve Apostles have gradually expanded their presence and influence from the Western Nzema and Ahanta regions around Sekondi and Takoradi up the coast and to the East. At the time of my fieldwork, the area containing the most gardens and the largest membership was localized in the heart of Fante region around the former colonial capital of Cape Coast. When the movement was confined to Nzema and Ahanta, it was possible to maintain close bonds with the mother and father of the Work through regular visits to the western region. As "disciples" were sent up the coastline to "convert the Fantes," greater distances were involved. Still, while the two elders were still alive, this did not seem to put any strains on the unity of the movement. The expansion of the church did not lead to any significant diversity in either ritual practices or ideological orientation. In fact, this is still true today. An *edwuma* performed in Cape Coast differs little from one performed in Krisin or Ankobra, and the belief system is essentially the same.

If I speak of disunity in the church today, it is because of problems in the realm of leadership that can be linked to the dilemma of "valid" succession. These problems may indeed be mediated by changes that have occurred outside the church itself (such as new modes of transportation and communication, the development of new roads and trading centers, the growing influx of literate members, and the need for the registration of churches with the Ghanaian government), but they can also be more completely understood through a consideration of the inherent tension within the church between transfer of authority "through a spirit" and the transfer of ownership through "family right." These problems have been addressed through schism and localization of authority (which tends to follow "tribal boundaries"), as well as through an attempt to maintain the mother–father model of the early movement.

When Nackabah died in 1947, no succession crisis occurred. I feel that this is a significant demonstration that succession matters were indeed still closely tied up with females' rights of ownership. Nackabah was not the one to whom the church "was given." He did not own it. At his death, his nephew simply took his place and was designated as "Junior John Nackabah (or Nackabah II)."[13] Nackabah II, as his uncle had done, used Madame Tani as his "mother" and the Work continued. In 1958 with the death of the old woman, however, a crisis of succession arose that is still having repercussions in the church today.

It is a curious fact that none of the eight children of Madame Tani ever took up their mother's work during his lifetime. This was compensated by the fame of one of her granddaughters, Elizabeth KyƐkyƐ Mensah. KyƐkyƐ became one of her grandmother's closest disciples and was noted for her adepthood in "having a spirit to heal with." KyƐkyƐ's supporters today indicate that her grandmother had made a prophesy that her granddaughter would not only carry on the Work but someday would be the head of it. There was a feeling that a valid successor had been chosen by Madame Tani herself.

KyƐkyƐ may well have been acknowledged by all as the legitimate mother, if it had not been for certain circumstances and events that occurred at the time of the old woman's funeral rites. At that time, KyƐkyƐ herself had fallen prey to a serious and "mysterious" illness. She was in a town some distance from Krisan under the care of another prophetess and was unable to attend the funeral. The funeral was presided over by M. C. George, also a famous disciple. George was a Nzema man, but, with Madame Tani's encouragement, he had led the massive "conversion" of the Fantes around the Cape Coast area.

In the midst of the funeral ritual, one of the real daughters of Madame Tani, called Bombo, was "attacked by a spirit." Though her supporters indicate that Bombo did "not know what her mother's staff looked like, under the power of the spirit that was upon her, she picked out the old woman's staff out of a pile of some 400 crosses that were present at the funeral ritual." Prophet George immediately associated KyƐkyƐ's sickness and absence with this strange occurrence and interpreted the event as "a sign." He indicated to all present that it meant that Bombo, a true daughter of Madame Tani, "should be taken as the new Mother." These events have to be set in the context of a dispute that occurred between George and some of Junior John Nackabah's people. Junior John Nackabah had not been the forceful leader and personality that Nackabah had been. It seems evident then that by proclaiming Bombo as Mother, George was making himself a Father, the defender of her rights, which rested on a direct matrilineal connection as well as a demonstration of spiritual power. There was a litigation

[13]This is based in the Fante rule of inheritance.

over this proclamation and George withdrew, claiming all of his Fante supporters as well as some of the Nzemas. This rift was the beginning of a localization of authority.

These events demonstrate the link between church rites of leadership and the importance that even male power seekers placed on a valid female personage through whom they were reckoned. Neither Mensah nor George attempted to lead *on their own*, but rather in conjunction with some female who represented true ownership as well as spiritual power. This process of localization has continued till the present, but the former mother–father model has been adapted to the process of fragmentation. After several attempts to settle the dispute, both Mensah and KyƐkyƐ and George and Bombo have now registered their churches under separate names. The Nzema group is known as The William Wade Harris Twelve Apostles and the Fantes as The Twelve Apostles Church of Ghana.

CONCLUSIONS

As I reflect on the narratives of the older people who knew them and even the younger ones who had only heard of them, the woman on the beach and the man in the bush appear to me as maternal and paternal procreators rather than as founders. They were the ones who had done both a good and fruitful work. They did this work on their own. And, as one old woman put it, "They were responsible for so many spiritual children." Madame Tani, above all, represented the whole group. In a sense, she gave the followers a feeling of direction, rightness, and legitimacy. Her work has resulted in the confidence with which members expressed that they are part of an emerging tradition. This feeling of groundedness is derived from "a new Work" that, at the same time, reflects a highly traditional aura of familial cohesion.

The model of adepthood reflected in Madame Tani's own activities and ritual innovations is still vital. It is central to any considerations of the sphere of influence and independence that females have in the focal activity of the movement, which is still definitely the healing work. Of course, this kind of female independence is not new to West Africa where women are the primary agents in commercial activity. The "garden," like the market place, is another area in which West African women not only endure but also prevail.

Plate 1 The Poro devil comes out in Sucromu, Liberia. (Bellman)

Plate 2 The devil dances with his assistants in Sucromu, Liberia. (Bellman)

116

Plate 3 Woman diviner with wand. (Mendonsa)

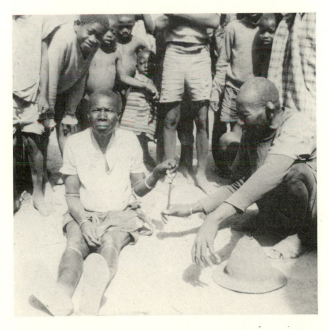

Plate 4 Woman diviner (initiate) being consulted by male client. (Mendonsa)

Plate 5 Woman diviner next to divining shrine, holding divining wand. Tumu, Ghana, 1975. (Mendonsa)

Plate 6 Woman diviner, holding divining rattle, being consulted by male client. Note ethnographer's tape recorder. (Mendonsa)

Plate 7 Yoomo Dantserebi, the *kpele* medium, waits for a client. (Kilson)

Plate 8 The Twelve Apostles in Ghana. (Breidenbach)

Plate 9 A Twelve Apostles naming ceremony in Ghana. (Breidenbach)

Plate 10 Maranke and Masowe Apostolic women elders worship together in Lusaka, Zambia. (Jules–Rosette)

Plate 11 A Maranke Apostolic woman gives instruction at a church conference at Matero, Zambia. (Jules–Rosette)

Plate 12 Maranke Apostolic women singing at the Matero conference. (Jules–Rosette)

Plate 13 A Maranke Apostolic prophet in kerek. (Jules–Rosette)

7

Women as Ceremonial Leaders in an African Church: The Apostles of John Maranke

Bennetta Jules-Rosette

Religion reflects significant changes in broader cultural conceptions. The indigenous churches of Africa provide an ideal situation for examining this process with respect to the position of women and their rise as cult leaders. Among the Apostles of John Maranke (the Bapostolo or Vapostori), one of the largest of these churches in Central Africa, women constitute the majority of the membership.[1] However, with a few exceptions, they are largely rank and file adepts. As prophetesses, a select group of women are respected as spiritual leaders and are able to challenge and check decisions made by the male council of elders. As midwives and judges at the time of marriage choice, another group of women wield a specialized form of ceremonial authority. Nevertheless, all women in the group are excluded from the hierarchy of direct political decision-making. Freed from political responsibilities, they are thought to have special expressive powers that operate chiefly in ceremonies and settings managed by male elders.

Therefore, in lieu of exercising legitimate authority, women base their leadership upon two forms of power: (1) mystical power based upon spiritual gifts, which operates like *mana*, and (2) direct control of situated interactions. I shall term the recognition of the limited exercise of power by women ceremonial leadership. Weber (1947, pp. 363–370) intended the term ''charisma'' to refer to both the spiritual appeal of a religious leader and the process of sustaining

[1]The fieldwork for this study was conducted in southwestern Zaire and in Zambia over a 14–month period of 1971–1972. Several Maranke congregations were studied in both countries with an increasing concentration of the activities of women. This research was funded by the Ford Foundation Foreign Area Fellowship Program, the Social Science Research Council, and the Academic Senate of the University of California, San Diego.

leadership in a group. I refer to the term in its dual sense as both direct spiritual power and interactional power in a religious association.[2] On the basis of this definition, I shall distinguish between ceremonial leadership based on spiritual charisma (i.e., prophecy) and ceremonial leadership based on interactional control (i.e., midwifery, marriage selection, and song). Both forms of charismatic leadership affect the male exercise of political authority; both are distinct from it. To understand the impact of these activities in the group as a whole, it is necessary to look at the formal hierarchy of spiritual gifts and ranks within the church. Within this context, the parameters of women's power become more apparent.

HISTORY AND ORGANIZATION OF THE CHURCH

Founded in 1932 by a Zimbabwean (muShona) prophet, John Maranke, the Apostolic church contains several ethnic and regional groups across central Africa. The church, which has messianic tendencies, originated in southeastern Zimbabwe (then Rhodesia) and acquired an initial following in the tribal trust lands and small towns of that area. Within the next two decades, the church moved as far north as the Zaire Republic (then the Belgian Congo) spreading a message of miraculous healing and the unity of all people. Some missiologists account for the phenomenal growth in terms of the church's acceptance of voluntary polygyny and its encouragement of polygynous marriage among its leaders.[3] This argument does not take into account the full array of cultural factors motivating the church's appeal. It is only when the relationship between male leadership and female adepthood is understood that the importance of marriage as a way of proselytizing and of maintaining stable membership emerges in perspective.[4]

The founder's own life established a pattern for the use of charismatic authority within the group. As early as 1918, Muchabaya Momberume, son of a Mozambican migrant, began to have a series of visionary experiences. During his years in Methodist primary school, Muchabaya was often sick, a tendency that he believed increased his susceptibility to visions. These illnesses culminated in a ceremonial period of death, during which Muchabaya lived alone in the wilderness. When he reemerged, he was baptized by a relative and assumed the name of "John the Baptist" Maranke. At this time, he received a calling to

[2]Weber (1947, pp. 363–373) stresses the institutionalization of group commitment and values. My emphasis on interactional charisma stresses that when such "institutionalization" occurs among the Bapostolo, many members have access to a type of charismatic authority but not all exercise equal or similar leadership.

[3]Several students of indigenous churches (Barrett, 1968, pp. 101–108; Murphree, 1971, p. 178) stress the importance of polygyny and the role of male leaders.

[4]Apostles are required to be endogamous. A member marrying a nonmenber is expected to convert his spouse to the group.

establish the Church of the Apostles. The members of John's family became the first converts and were believed to be endowed with the special abilities to preach, heal, and prophesy (Daneel, 1971, pp. 324 ff.). In 1934, the annual Passover or communion feast was held for the first time and was established as the occasion for formally vesting members with leadership ranks. The proliferation of converts during the decade following John's initial preaching necessitated the establishment of formal leadership structures as part of the Passover. Spiritual specializations or gifts *(bipedi)* were distinguished from organizational ranks *(mianza)*, comprising gradations of authority within each spiritual gift. Three high-ranking holders of each gift formed a committee of twelve ruling male elders within each local congregation. Each committee in a new area was responsible to the central committee on the Maranke reserve, and to John himself. Yearly confirmations of leaders relied on the presence of John and, after his death, on that of his two eldest sons. In this way, regional ritual and political innovations were kept under the direct supervision of Zimbabwean leaders.

Ceremonial leadership operates on a charismatic model of visionary experiences of prophets and persons who are often not in positions of political control, in contrast to the political hierarchy of persons with combined gifts and ranks confirmed at the annual Passover. Although the latter are also based on demonstrated charismatic abilities, they refer more specifically to organizational authority legitimated by the central hierarchy emanating from Zimbabwe.[5]

THE DOMAIN OF WOMEN'S POWER
IN BAPOSTOLO LEADERSHIP

Most ritual activities among the Bapostolo are distinguished by gender-marked expectations and differences in participation. The concept of Christian equality, with the expectation that men and women enter heaven side by side, is basic to Bapostolo doctrine. However, the expression of equality in political leadership is denied women. Whenever men are present at ritual events, Bapostolo women show them particular respect and express their control through interaction rather than formal leadership.[6] Women are reprimanded when their participation transgresses the boundaries of song, healing, and mediumship. During ritual, the

[5]Weber (1947, pp. 363–370) defines "charisma" as the "quality of an individual personality by virtue of which he is set apart from ordinary men and treated as endowed with supernatural, superhuman, or at least specifically exceptional powers or qualities." For Apostles, there is a charismatic element in all leadership. All church members consider themselves divinely ordained to fulfill a special mission. However, they distinguish *bipedi* or ceremonial leadership based exclusively on a spiritual gift or power from *mianza* or formal political leadership validated by authority of office as well as by a charismatic element.

[6]Through interaction, women can control and direct the sense of ceremonies and other ritualized behavior without formally acknowledged leadership roles. This is evident in their participation in song (Jules-Rosette, 1975c, pp. 150–165).

routine exercise of power occurs through song intervention. Interruption with song allows women to redirect sermon topics to present moral lessons that criticize the types of wrongdoing that they associate with men.

For men, preaching is a routine aspect of ritual leadership. Their sermons are performed in concert with a reader who presents a passage, which is elaborated upon by the speaker in antiphonal fashion. The preacher uses the entire aisle formed between the worshiping men and women to present his sermon. Women remain seated and initiate songs from this position. Young girls are taught to sit with their legs straight forward as a form of discipline. The women's interruption is a controlled contribution from this restrained position. These symbolic aspects of ritual participation must be seen in the light of a larger traditional concept governing women's behavior: *bundu*, ritualized "shame" or subservience.[7] It is the idiom through which much ritual participation and male–female interaction takes place.

In the Sabbath ceremony or *kerek*, women's song participation is complementary to that of men. In the curing ceremony, however, women perform an active and instrumental part. *Burapi* or healing power, while not confined to one sex, is associated with women's normal ritual activities. At the end of each Sabbath ceremony, women arrange themselves in rows and receive patients requesting healing. Many of these patients are women or children, although men are also among them. Healing is considered a gift of the Holy Spirit, like prophecy, baptism, and preaching. Women conceive of the healing function as a familial as well as a specific ceremonial task. Many Bapostolo women interviewed in 1972 believed healing to be the "natural" female function within the church. Others stated that they had been converted in order to heal and care for their families. When asked why she had become a healer, one woman responded, "Because it is appropriate only for women." Her answer was repeatedly echoed.

Although men designated as healers are generally viewed as extraordinary, for most women, healing is an extension of routine domestic activity, and their individuality is less important than uniform performance. One notable exception to this is midwifery, a special skill confined to the elder women healers. Midwifery entails more than the delivery of a child. It is a ceremonial process that begins with prayer and the mother's confession of sins and involves prophecy, ritual healing, song, and dance.[8]

---

[7]*Bundu*, or ritualized shame, is a feature of many male/female interactions among Apostles and within the custom of the areas in which they are located. The term *bundu* used here is a Luba term and refers to conventions of eye contact, personal placement, and modes of address. An analogous phenomenon of shame and cross-sexual modesty is found in Latin countries (Pitt-Rivers, 1971, pp. 112–122).

[8]There are few occasions on which Apostles "dance." This consists of a restrained swaying movement with few steps and does not resemble the more "spontaneous" dancing of Western Pentecostal churches, or the more traditionalistic dance steps of some West and South African indigenous churches. Dancing takes place during song sessions, exorcisms, all-night singing, at the successful conclusion of virginity examinations and birth ceremonies.

THE POLITICAL CONTROL OF
CEREMONIAL AUTHORITY:
WOMEN IN A MEN'S CHURCH

The regulation of exogamy is an essential mechanism for maintaining group identity among Apostles. This maintains the religious community as an insulated entity that can only be entered through full conversion. Even infants must be baptized, preferably by six months of age, to be accepted as full members. There is a constant effort to bring in new members from the outside through marriage and baptism. In the case of marriage regulations, women have new rights distinct from the expectations of custom. The Zairean Apostles have outlined these redefinitions of custom in a tract entitled *"Mikenji ya Tshipostolo"* (Apostolic instructions).[9] Principally, women are instructed not to marry pagans (Tshiluba: *Bena diabolo*). Provided that women of marriageable age (as young as 13) have passed the *mushecho* or virginity examinations, they are given the freedom to choose their mates.[10] These examinations take place at annual Passover and retreat ceremonies. They are revitalizations of the traditional *ciziwiso* or bride notification ceremony.[11] Elder women healers perform internal examinations on the candidates. Then all of the elder midwives judge whether the young women's marriage claims are to be honored. In principle, the young women who prove to be virgins have free choice of mates. As soon as the examination is complete, they are expected to make their requests public. In theory, the young woman's father cedes his customary authority to the council of women elders and to the young woman herself. Virginity is valued only for young women approaching marriageable age. Infertility and failure to marry are considered indications of misfortune caused by witchcraft.

Customs accepted in mission churches such as wearing a wedding gown or using the marriage liturgy are considered "pagan" by the Apostles. The bride price is also deemphasized among church members. It is still exchanged, how-

---

[9]These instructions (Tshiaba & Zivuku, 1970) composed by a Zairean elder and a Zimbabwean teaching emissary, were taught to outlying branches of the church.

[10]Murphree (1969, pp. 103–104) refers briefly to this ceremony, conducted at the annual Passover to determine marital choices and to select young women to prepare the sacramental "wine" (fruit juice) and unleavened bread.

[11]On the subject of *ciziwiso*, Holleman (1952) records:

> I have stated that no special importance is attached to the virginity of the bride any longer. Periodical examinations of unmarried girls by the female relatives have become as rare as they are said to have been common in the past; the old custom of sending the bride's family a pierced hoe as *ciziwiso* (notification) that the bride proved to be no virgin on her wedding night has, as far as I can ascertain, completely fallen into disuse because the majority of women are said to have lost their virginity long before marriage. There is, consequently, often little supervision over, or interference with, the relations between young people as long as the parents are confident that, somehow, such relations lead toward marriage. (p. 83)

ever, and this transfer constitutes the marriage ceremony and symbolizes its responsibilities. The *mikenji* formally warn against increasing bride price for personal profit for the family or as a symbol of prestigious marriage. The modernization of the bride price, represented by its translation into cash or modern goods rather than cattle and its reduction to a symbolic payment among some members, points to changing expectations in marriage alliances.[12] The Bapostolo rejection of the high bride price is an ambivalent concession toward women's autonomy. If the marriage dissolves, Bapostolo are still expected to return the original payment. This requirement provides some protection for the woman but also is a source of (negative) incentive toward marital stability. A search for the most financially secure in-law without regard for church affiliation is strictly forbidden. The young woman who has passed the mushecho is, therefore, ideally free to turn down eligible suitors and family preferences to obtain the suitor of her choice.

This freedom of choice is in apparent contradiction to voluntary polygyny. Despite spiritual caveats, familial intervention takes place to give virginal daughters to outstanding church leaders known for their integrity and their ability to provide for a family. Thus, the ideal of freedom is balanced by the reality of alliance and the use of the *mushecho* to retain church, parental, and vestiges of male control over women.

The Apostolic retreat ceremonies become the arena for courtship. Their potential as an expression of individual preference, however, is ultimately restricted by the council of women elders and by the preferences of men for their daughters' families. Nonvirgin women are stigmatized by arbitrary marriage into the polygynous households of male elders. On the other hand, the male elder who is able to support a large family still accrues prestige from both the labor and fertility promised by several wives. Thus, while a forced marriage limits the autonomy of the woman, it is a source of increased status and prestige for her spouse.

Polygynous marriages allow wives to conceive less frequently and still make a productive contribution to the family unit, while monogamous wives are pressured to rival the fertility of polygynous households. One monogamous mother stated that it was a blessing of God to bear a child in her old age. This attitude was not expressed in the polygynous households observed, where births were concentrated among the younger wives.[13]

A sense of marital and familial autonomy also influences the overall participation of women in the church. Previous research (Jules-Rosette, 1974a, p. 25) demonstrates a noticeable difference between women who revealed that they were pressured to join the church by fathers or husbands and those who were

---

[12]Bapostolo say that a low bride price is traditionally a Bemba practice (cf. Richards, 1956, pp. 43–44) and that a high payment is a modern trend, emphasized among Shona members.

[13]Comparative fertility attitudes and rates among churchwomen and their influence on attitudes toward marriage and women's power, are in need of further research.

motivated through a personal conversion experience. The women in the former category defined their membership merely as an extension of that of their husbands or families. Those in the latter used religion as a source of personal fulfillment, and were able to exercise ceremonial leadership through prophecy and song. It is possible that the young women given away in marriage tended to fit the former category, while those who at least technically passed the examination were already active members who used marriage to increase participation rather than as a source of nominal membership.[14]

Some Apostolic women were able to achieve a measure of leadership and autonomy through marriage. In this case, the women elders shared their husband's authority on interactive grounds and were addressed in an honorary fashion by the same title. This type of leadership should be distinguished from the practice of West African "clientship" or male concubinage in which women establish leadership in a group through a series of secret alliances with younger men (Bellman, 1975, pp. 186–87; Gibbs, 1965, pp. 210–11).[15] These alliances allow the woman to act as a "ritual male" and political leader. The customary access that women might have had to such power is reinterpreted by Apostles as undesirable. Similarly, the maintenance of purity by sexual abstinence as a means of transcending sexual identity is not a method through which Apostolic women acquire power. Even when powerful female prophets appear, they operate within the context of accepted familial roles and are supported by a husband who is also a major ritual leader.

WOMEN'S ACCOUNTS OF CONVERSION

As a result of the possibilities for leadership display and of the process of instruction, the types of conversion experiences described by Bapostolo women differ substantially from those of the men. Both men and women mention healing and miraculous events as part of their inspiration for conversion. For many women, problems of pregnancy, childbirth, and female disorders originally attracted them to the church. These accounts follow a universal pattern insofar as they stress spiritual inspiration and miracles. However, an emphasis on fertility and the cure of birth disorders is characteristic of women's conversion accounts.

These accounts of conversion provide a necessary background for understanding how women use ceremonial authority in interaction and the spiritual and

[14]The difference between nominal and active membership corresponds roughly to that between leadership and adepthood made by Breidenbach (see Chapter 6). It may be an even more profound distinction, however, as stressed in Barrett's (1968) distinction between persons who vaguely identify with a group and its most committed participants.

[15]This relationship is also referred to as epainogamy. Hoffer (1974) describes the case of Madam Yoko, a nineteenth–century Mende paramount chief among the Mende. She took over her husband's role as paramount chief of the Kpa Mende kingdoms and expanded her effective control through clientship alliances.

personal goals that they pursue. While many women stated that they joined the group to receive "hidden life in Christ" and "God's grace," as already indicated, many of the accounts of conversion stressed the influence of husbands and parents in pushing the women toward membership. In almost all cases, the initial motivations for joining differed substantially from descriptions of the benefits of membership. While most respondents had a mystical justification for membership, many also sought practical ends of longevity and health. No women saw their participation, as did some of the men, in terms of their spiritual calling to serve as church leaders. A sample of 31 women in Zaire was interviewed in depth. Their mean education was three years of mission primary school. Two accounts in particular epitomize the conversion experiences of Apostolic women.

The first respondent was a healer in Lubumbashi. Like many of the respondents, she indicated a direct connection between her initial attraction to the church and physical healing. However, she stated the reason for her membership more broadly, relating it to a concern for eternal life and to proselytism:

Q: Who gave you the news about this church?
A: I was given the news and the rules of this church by Kabombo Jean.
Q: What did he say?
A: I was sick for several years. He told me, first believe in God in the name of the Savior, and you will be healed.
Q: Was this person an Apostle?
A: Yes, this person was an Apostle.
Q: Why did you ask him about the church?
A: I asked him because I was suffering; I was searching for the place where I might be healed.
Q: How did you feel at that time?
A: I was filled with joy and spiritual feeling.
Q: When did this happen?
A: That happened when I believed his words.
Q: Why did you become a member of this church?
A: I became a member of this church to have external life in Jesus Christ and preach his news to others.

The second respondent, a healer in Kananga, expressed her earlier opposition to a childhood baptism. Despite this forced baptism, she had become an active member and participated in informal song sessions.

Q: Who gave you the news about this church?
A: We were baptized because our parents were baptized; no one told us.
Q: What did they say?
A: They didn't tell me anything, because I was still little.
Q: Were these people Apostles?
A: Yes.

Q: Why did you ask them about the church?

A: No, I had no ideas on that subject.

Q: How did you feel at that time?

A: I didn't want it, it didn't please me, and they ran after me to do it by force.

Q: Why did you become a member of this church?

A: So that I may also become a person of God.[16]

Many women who initially joined the church in search of cures found their faith reinforced through witnessing miraculous events. However, of more importance than such events is the active participation of women in specialized activities. Most women healers work primarily within their families. Members outside of the family seek prophetesses for diagnosis of illness and cure. In this case, their specialized skills often bring them patients and prestige outside of the immediate congregational grouping.

In addition to the active healers, four categories of women participate in specialized leadership: (1) prophetesses, (2) midwives, (3) singers, and (4) wives of leaders. In the latter two cases, leadership is mainly symbolic. Although the singers practice in groups outside of the ceremony, their influence is observed primarily in *kerek*. Leaders' wives exercise informal authority and some even conceive of themselves as co-owners of their husbands' positions. Therefore, the healer who is the wife of a baptist or elder, may assume similar responsibilities among men as well as women.

The midwives, however, form a special category. They are elder healers who may often share in their husbands' positions of leadership. Most notably, they possess a valuable body of knowledge which may be taught to others and which is indispensable to the community's survival. Midwives and prophetesses preside over the entire rite of childbirth. The power of healing as a women's activity emerges most explicitly in the context of this cooperative work.

MIDWIFERY AS CEREMONIAL LEADERSHIP

The birth of a child is a political act. The child becomes a new Apostle and his successful delivery is considered the spiritually ordained work of the parents and of the midwife. In order to give birth successfully, the mother must be "free of sin." A large part of Bapostolo midwifery, therefore, involves the ritual purification of the mother through confession and exorcism. A prophetess may accompany the midwives on special occasions. Two or three women elders experienced in childbirth work together, often in cooperation with the female members of the woman's family. With the onset of labor, healing songs are sung

[16]Similar materials are discussed at more length in Jules-Rosette (1976a and 1976c).

in the manner of all Bapostolo healing rites (see Lanzas & Bernard, 1966, pp. 200–202; Murphee, 1969, p. 102).[17] If the labor appears difficult, songs of exorcism may be introduced. Primarily, the mother is encouraged to confess all sins that may have influenced her, her husband, or her family. The prophetess questions her about her daily life as she prays for the woman. Each of the mother's movements during labor is taken as an indication of her spiritual state. If she appears to be struggling excessively with birth pains, she is considered to be in an analogous battle with Satan.

Symbolically, childbirth may be compared to the baptism ceremony because it ushers a new "potential" convert into the world. The newly born child is not formally an Apostle until baptized. This is the duty of the male elders.[18] The midwife's ceremonial role combines healing competence and prophecy with initiation. In this respect, the midwife's ceremonial task resembles that of the baptist. Thus, midwifery as ceremonial leadership and as a form of women's power conbines several spiritual skills recognized among the Bapostolo, and brings them to bear on a restricted ceremonial occasion. The midwives are also the same leaders who judge the *mushecho*. Their influence extends from marriage to the birth of each child, and they have an important impact on the entire life cycle of the maturing woman.

ILLNESS AND CURING

Healing for the Bapostolo is defined as a spiritually inspired activity for which one must be especially gifted. As an act of inspiration, it is the most basic of spiritual concerns. Apostles often refer to themselves as a church of healing and prophecy. All other spiritual gifts are considered to contain an element of healing. Hence, in the absence of an official healer, other members routinely perform some healing duties. When women healers in a Zambian congregation protested against this practice of overlap in spiritual leadership, they were informed that the most competent and spiritually powerful members of a congregation could perform these functions. Thus, while healing is chiefly reserved for women, it is considered to be within the domain of expertise of all members who have proven their spiritual worth.

In order to understand the meaning of *burapi* for women, it is first necessary to examine the definition of illness among the Bapostolo. For church members, there are no "naturally" caused illnesses. All sickness is caused by the evil

[17]Healing rituals contain a standard repertoire of songs. The most common of these, found in Shona with slight variations throughout the church, repeats the words: "I heal in the name of God in Heaven" *(Ndi rapire we Mambo mudi mudenga)*.

[18]Infant baptism is practiced among the Bapostolo and usually takes place two to three weeks after the child's birth. This practice contrasts with that of confirmation in mission churches and specific mandates against infant baptism in other indigenous churches such as the Kimbanguist church.

action of demons. Spiritual laxity, for example, anger or the transgression of food taboos, allows demon possession to occur. The Bapostolo believe that the possibility of possession is always present. The baptism of the Apostles, which cleanses the new member and makes a spiritual redefinition of social life possible, is accompanied by a comparable vulnerability. The new spiritual being may be forcefully attacked or possessed by demons. Therefore, exorcism follows soon after baptism. This exorcism is referred to among Bapostolo as *kudzungudza* or tuning.[19] It is only after tuning that one truly witnesses the Holy Spirit. The major blocks toward spiritual development are said to disappear at this point. In some cases, the "demons" that emerge during tuning appear in the form of traditional spirits.[20] They also take the form of animals and related spirit familiars. One possessed patient was observed to leap to his feet during a tuning and run off into the bush howling like a mad dog. The surrounding women who formed a cloister of curative singers were warned to move aside as he was considered beyond their control. Had the "mad dog" returned quickly for further tuning, he would have reportedly attained a form of enlightenment. With his demon exorcised, he would have found new power. For women, tuning is the major source of confirmation for their special powers; it marks their attainment of a charismatic appeal recognized by the community at large.

Tuning and visionary experiences give both men and women the right to exercise differing types of leadership responsibilities. A man may be asked to prove that he has had visionary experiences and has been truly "blessed" by the Holy Spirit so that he can preach in the Sabbath *kerek*. The tuning experience is one source of such proof. Although women can heal without the spiritual witnessing required in tuning, they cannot gain full experience in singing, cure, and prophecy. Many women expressed the wish to be tuned successfully so that they could participate more actively in the church. One stated: "We just sit there in *kerek* and 'see' nothing, while those who have been tuned have many visions."

The following excerpt from field notes describes an occasion of tuning in which the author participated. Women surrounded the candidates and sang the exorcism song. In rapid succession, young men and women (and, at times, elders) filed in to be healed and cleansed of "demon spirits."

July 1974: Matero Compound, Lusaka, Zambia
Sara sat down and was prayed over. The baptist (exorcist) rubbed her head with both hands. She stood. She said that she had no Spirit. She wanted to find the Spirit during exorcism but did not . . . Soon I was called forward. I sat down and my head was rubbed. He twisted and rolled my head in

---

[19]The importance of tuning among the Apostles is not immediately apparent. Although I became a full member of the group in 1971 (Jules-Rosette, 1976a), during my first two field visits I remained relatively unaware of the centrality of tuning for women. While both men and women are required to demonstrate spiritual achievements, tuning is one of the major means for women to do so.

[20]John Maranke (1953, Chap. 19, p. 26) describes this exorcism as part of his early healing ministry. One of the first women that he healed had been possessed by a *chikwambo* or alien spirit.

every direction. I became dizzy and said "Ameni, Ameni." Then I sat very still. My hair flew out in every direction and I felt sick to my stomach. Sara looked at me and said, "Your hair is really something else." She noticed how sick I looked and told me to go lie down.[21]

Neither Sara nor I had received the special inspiration that would qualify us for ceremonial leadership on our own. If we had been tuned successfully, we would be candidate prophetesses and could convincingly claim that all of our activities were spiritually inspired. Such visionary skills can be displayed without tuning if the healer or candidate prophetess describes the experiences and dreams in some detail. However, these descriptions must be validated by a public event in which the product of dreams becomes manifested in prophecy or cure.

Tuning establishes a crucial distinction between persons who have publicly received spiritual blessings and those who have not. Successful tuning marks a victory over evil forces; there is no need to repeat it. Conversely, recurrent exorcism is considered to be a sign of stubbornness and spiritual immaturity.

Much of the work of women's healing is routine. It involves collective prayer and singing and circumscribes their chances for advancement. Healing activities contribute a background to other ceremonies and promise a legitimate place for women's activities in exorcism and prayer.[22]

Even when they sing within exorcism ceremonies, women are often spectators rather than involved participants. To achieve recognized expertise, one must maintain relative immunity to the attacks of evil forces while simultaneously exercising an identifiable skill. It is for this reason that midwifery stands in marked contrast to routine women's healing. The following distinctions may, therefore, be made among the tasks and routine activities reserved for Apostolic women:

Ceremonial Leadership	Expressive Leadership
Prophecy (includes formal grade)	Healing (includes formal grade)
Midwifery	Routine healing
Morality songs (women's sermons)	Songs of exorcism and healing
Virginity examination	Free choice of mate
Women's decision–making	Singing and prayer
Successful tuning	Songs of exorcism

In each case, expressive leadership is the prerequisite for a modified form of ceremonial leadership among women elders. The exercise of leadership in prophecy, women's discussion groups, virginity examinations, and women's

[21]This discussion is excerpted from field notes taken at a Bapostolo retreat in Matero Compound, Lusaka, Zambia. The experience described marked my first extended personal contact with tuning.

[22]This background participation explains Aquina's (1967b) contention that women are never full members of the church.

preaching (the singing of didactic songs in *kerek*) relies on having achieved and demonstrated spiritual "purity" through tuning, visionary experiences, and worship. Ceremonial leadership presupposes spiritual achievement as witnessed by the entire group and confirmed by the male hierarchy. However, it does not rely on the presence of male members for its exercise. Women's retreats, marriage selection, and childbirth represent occasions when women alone assume both spiritual and interactive control.

SOURCES OF WOMEN'S CEREMONIAL LEADERSHIP

Women use contact with male leaders to establish their own authority. Through tales of their association with leaders like John Maranke, women establish a form of "ceremonial leadership through association" (Jules–Rosette, 1974a, pp. 1–2).[23] In establishing their presence as witnesses to important historical events, these women demonstrate their ceremonial authority. On one occasion, Marie Tshibola, a healer and wife of a major Zairean leader, reminisced about a meeting with John Maranke. As Marie built the story, she repeated the names of the leaders who were present and gave the details of their conversations with the founder.

John Maranke had preached a short sermon during which Mbolela, a Zairean leader, stood and began to sing.[24] As he sang, the Holy Spirit inspired the congregation and everyone became blessed. This blessing, like the tuning experience, gave those partaking of it a special spiritual status. It was through the *account* of this experience that Marie was able to affirm her expressive leadership. Marie's account was "a tale of power" rather than a mere description of events.[25]

The following excerpt is taken from Marie's account of her meeting with John Maranke:

Lusaka, July 9, 1974
In front of a gourd tree, we arrived at John's yard, where our party all went to meet him. They brought us water on the women's side there; the women in charge of the food came and went with the water. We went into the house—into John's enclosure. They had me wait with Baptist William, who said, "No one shall wash all over."[26] No one came to greet me . . .

---

[23]This work stresses the importance of accounts of miraculous events as a source of charismatic leadership among the Bapostolo.

[24]The practice of rising to sing is frequently the breaking point between ordinary and ritual settings, and is used to denote the importance of a ritual occasion for the Bapostolo. Spiritual powers are believed to overcome church members when ecstatic singing is achieved.

[25]Castaneda (1974) describes such a use of accounts of spiritual skill by the shaman Don Juan.

[26]That is, he was declaring it a ritual occasion, *tshijila*, involving abstinence from washing the whole body and from sexual activity. *Tshijila* is regularly invoked on the Sabbath eve and before retreat ceremonies.

I stayed with that mother there. Her husband stayed, no one was in the Spirit, he finished speaking. Then Mbolela sang:

(Kevulanda) yo yo yo
My little Lord, the apple of my eye,
(Kevulanda) yo yo you avele-
(Avelesa, avelesa, avelesa) of love (avelesa)-

John stood up. When he was in the middle, the Spirit of God flew over, flew over the enclosure. Aha, mother. Father, stop. Father, stop. (An aside.) Spirit of God (azomutayi) like t–t–t–t–t–t–t–t–t–t–t. John said, ''Let's pra——y.'' We prayed . . . the Holy Spirit [was everywhere]. We were in the Spirit, until John said the words ''Let's pray.'' We prayed, we prayed until the end. We shook hands, he shook my hand, we kissed each other. Moblela kissed all of them. The ones who didn't all get to kiss each other were sad. The one who's dead, who was he, Muteba Pierre, that one who died, Mobolela, the singer, Mbila David, John Masaniji [and their wives], were there. They said hello. John spoke to give a little speech, like nothing, to explain—ah, ah . . .

Marie's account of power gave her two forms of special privilege: direct contact with John Maranke and immediate inspiration from the Holy Spirit. On the basis of these expressive sources of inspiration, Marie could make organizational claims to power as a master singer and a blessed member of the church. Her position was reinforced as the wife of a leader, and her ceremonial leadership allowed her to sit in on important church decisions.

BURAPI AND PARTICIPATION AS A HEALER

Confirmation in a spiritual gift is generally accompanied by a series of visions. These ratify the gift and present the healer or the prophetess with concrete knowledge about spiritual performance. Once an inspired gift is confirmed, the candidate must learn a series of new practices. My own confirmation as a healer and apprentice midwife provided me with a point of departure for understanding the experiences of other members.[27] In this case, the initial baptism was treated as a visionary experience. Through such visions, I was shown the differences among several types of medicines and was instructed that only one, a small vial of water, would be permitted to me as an Apostle. My account of these visions, along with a prophet's verification, was treated as sufficient grounds for confirmation.

I was, nevertheless, surprised to be selected among those to be confirmed. The head evangelist of the Zambian group who had accompanied me to the

---

[27]These experiences have been described in Jules–Rosette (1975a, 1976a).

Passover celebration called me forward for prayer. The prophets touched my head lightly and pulled back the veil worn by Apostolic women. This was the sign of confirmation, yet I possessed no knowledge of the healing process. Had I been judged capable of and ready for the duties of faith healing, or had I simply been confirmed as a woman in good standing within the church? I soon found that, in a sense, both of these assessments were correct. The confirmation did not *make* me a healer in terms of practical performance, yet the prophets had judged that the time had come for my training. Ceremonial leadership could be acquired only through appropriate instruction.

A Zambian leader indoctrinated me in the realities of salvation. He explained that I was now obliged to follow the commandments of the Bible, or I would burn by eternal fire that would consume the soul as well as the flesh (see Jules–Rosette, 1975a, p. 89, for a detailed description of these experiences). This generalized statement was intended as a specific instruction about "right living" and set the tone for my instruction as a healer. A few days later, a retreat ceremony was arranged. Women's living quarters were separated from those of the men, and the confirmed healers were instructed in their duties. Just before sunrise, the elder healers would pass through the encampment awakening the newly confirmed members. The elders were maShona, and they told the secrets of healing in their language. These accounts offered a public rationale for the appropriate position of women in relationship to men and guidelines for the types of social expression formally expected of women.

Over the course of my training as a healer, an inventory of practices was presented to me indirectly. I was taught to kneel behind the patient while praying for him or her and to observe a specific sequence of physical manipulations. While the cure itself is believed to occur through faith, women's healing relies upon a series of ritualistic practices as opposed to miraculous intervention. The healer is taught to touch important nodes of the body in which physical problems may reside: the head, shoulders, torso, arms, legs, and feet are touched in that order. Women may touch all the parts of the body except the top of the head. Demons are said to reside in the hair on top (as opposed to the sides) of the head. Although women generally use the *karapi* or prayer stick during this process, it is not required. Men may use their staffs rather than simply their hands, especially in the case of serious illness. The occurrence of several persons praying over a single individual is not rare. During any given healing ceremony, an entire group, generally composed of women bystanders and healers, prays and sings.

The techniques of bodily manipulation are presented in a cursory manner. When I was instructed at the initial retreat ceremony, I was told to observe the other women, then to kneel behind a patient. My first patient was a six-month-old child. I was instructed to prop the child up and to touch first the sides of his head and then the rest of the body. The child survived, but I had no sense of "helping" him. Gradually, I became aware of symptoms of acceptance or resistance. If the patient refused to lift his arms toward Heaven when the healer raised them, a sin or transgression might be indicated. If the patient rolled his head when one touched the sides, some form of possession was indicated. These nonverbal cues learned through the process of healing were signals for the novice faith healer to call upon more specialized practitioners such as prophets to diagnose illness or evangelistis to hear the patient's confessions.

Other aspects of the nonverbal behavior appropriate to the healer were also taught indirectly.[28] On one occasion, when I had completed the ceremonial aspects of the physical healing, I rose abruptly. The patient continued to sit quietly on the ground. An elder healer who had witnessed the incident whispered, "Never rise before the patient. Tell the patient that you have finished and wait for the patient to get up." This instruction had not been given to me before. It became relevant only when an error had been witnessed. Similarly, if the healer performs the ceremony alone, the patient is asked to sing the healing songs. Refusal to sing is regarded as a sign of resistance to cure. These nonverbal cues become apparent only when one learns about and participates in the process of curing. Apostles seldom speak of these signs or cures independently of the occasions upon which they occur.

Confirmation as a healer is not a terminal process. It merely begins with the approval of the prophets and elders. The early abstract instruction sessions combined with routine healing and prayer for women and children with minor ailments began my learning as a healer. However, further inspiration was required to progress beyond routine healing. In my case, this inspiration consisted of a reconfirmation and "power prayer" made by the Bapostolo leaders from the church's center at Bocha. They did not deny my original confirmation at this time but instead suggested that further spiritual inspiration was necessary, since I had not originally known what to expect as an initiate. This inspiration would enable me to pass from routine healing to the more miraculous curing of chronic illnesses, if I were able to preserve and pursue the healing forces.

This anecdotal information stresses the combination of inspiration and hierarchy involved in the healer's position. For healing to go beyond routine practice, a publicly witnessed instance of spiritual inspiration is necessary in the form of successful tuning, power prayers, and visionary accounts. This inspiration is similar to that required to achieve interactional status as an important singer and ceremonial leadership as a prophetess. Healing as women's power is thus subject to the same requirements for spiritual leadership as any other confirmed rank within the church. It is both spiritually validated and classified as part of the church's internal leadership structure. However, it never endows women with general political leadership. Whereas men often achieve special

---

[28]In his description of the *mitote* or peyote meeting among he Yaqui Indians, Castaneda (1971, pp. 37–41) describes such nonverbal behavior as mutual "cuing" among participants in the interaction.

prominence as spiritual healers, women seldom achieve this individual recognition except through midwifery and prophecy.[29]

The council of women elders, insofar as it exists, operates during the mushecho to regulate the collective marital welfare of the group. In other cases, the women within a given congregation meet in subgroups of healers, in singing groups, and in educational or sewing circles on an autonomous basis (cf. Jules-Rosette, 1974a). Outside of the instructional meetings for women healers and prophets, these subgroups are not formally or ceremonially required within the church. Where these groups do exist in several of the Zairean congregations, women who exercise ceremonial leadership among themselves are able to transfer this participation to the congregation as a whole. Their exercise of interactive power is built upon a background of internal cooperation and ceremonial "rehearsal" for the larger event.

Ceremonial leadership, therefore, is the limited exercise of power in practical decison-making and ritual settings. During the Sabbath service, the *maharikros*, or special singers, regularly intervene and redirect discourse in sermons.[30] This intervention controls the topics presented and the order of speakers. Insofar as singers regularly engage in this practice, they too acquire ceremonial leadership through collective participation. Singing is the basis upon which many women's subgroups form in Bapostolo congregations. These members practice strategies for intervention in *kerek* and sing for healings and exorcisms.

Specialized women leaders, whether prophets, healers, or healer–midwives, must demonstrate an extraordinary spiritual experience, although their powers are seldom viewed by men as exceptional. On the basis of their expressive experiences, a claim may be made for the exercise of spiritual and ceremonial leadership among Bapostolo women at the expense of political participation. The fact that direct political participation is denied them enhances the spiritual mystique surrounding Bapostolo women and supports their ability to attempt to veto political decisions on the basis of ceremonial authority, since self-interest is presumably not involved.

It is my conclusion that the necessity and ability to heal a patient is essential for achieving specialized ceremonial leadership. These curative activities are extensions of traditional expectations of nurturance on the part of women, and in no way challenge the political hierarchy that excludes them.

There is, thus, far less differentiation in appropriate leadership tasks for women than there is for men. Women, as stated before, are far less likely to

[29]These are "prophet-healers by the angels" who diagnose and heal through special powers given to them by the angels.

[30]*Maharikros* is the plural of *harikros*, described by Apostles as derived from the English "high cross." See also Murphree (1969, p. 99) and Aquina (1967b, pp. 203–219).

receive the mythic renown of male healers. To achieve this, a woman would have to assume the role of a ritual male, as occurs in some forms of traditional mediumship (cf. Colson, 1969, pp. 69–103). Such a role is largely not permissible among Bapostolo women.

A complete picture of the contribution of women to Bapostolo life would take into account their economic situation as well as their ritual contributions to the group. In changing urban settings, this economic contribution varies. It also alters in terms of whether nuclear or polygynous cooperative homes are most prevalent in a given congregation and area. However, regardless of this contribution, the church as a whole regulates the leadership contribution of women and their symbolic importance.

Women are not instructed in the skills of public oratory, argumentation, and collective decision-making. The Bapostolo, like many other indigenous churches, include those headed by women (ritual males), earns the status of a man's church. In many indigenous churches, even those women who do assume positions of leadership are not able to transfer them to other women on an hereditary or a legalistic basis (Martin, 1971, pp. 113–120). The label of a man's church is not based on its admission of polygyny, which in effect offers women a variety of life-styles from which to choose and supports their relative autonomy in mate selection. Instead, it is based on the relative absence of women from the church's oral lore, contemporary myths, and ongoing political processes.

It is in this sense that healing, as a routine although still spiritually ordained activity, is women's power and forms the background for other forms of political and ceremonial leadership among the Bapostolo. The ceremonial authority that Bapostolo women exercise commands the respect of both members and outsiders in their communities. Yet, it holds no promise of advancement or of direct participation. Instead, like the new marriage selection ceremonies, the exercise of ceremonial authority among women offers them the incentive to remain representatives of a traditional social order in which the legitimate authority for political decisions ultimately rests in the hands of men.

INDIGENOUS CHURCHES
AND LOCAL ADAPTATIONS
OF WORLD RELIGIONS

Introduction to Part III

Bennetta Jules-Rosette

The chapters in this section examine groups that self-consciously define themselves as churches as well as offshoots of world religions. In many instances, these churches directly reflect the impact of external influence upon African societies, as Fabian emphasizes in his discussion of the Zairean Jamaa movement. The Masowe Apostolic church, founded by an independent prophet and stressing millenarian themes, maintains an identity separate from both traditional and mission organizations. Like other Apostolic groups, it combines Christian doctrine with traditional religious practice (see Jules-Rosette, 1975b; 1977). Kileff and Kileff describe the church's revitalistic preservation of a number of traditional customs relating to the status of women including polygyny, *nhaka* (levirate), and the separation of the sexes in many everyday activities. The group also condemns sorcery and many aspects of traditional practice, substituting a new hierarchy of spiritual practitioners. Like the Maranke case analyzed in Part II, the Masowe Vapostori illustrate a rigid separation between men's and women's ceremonial work and a great discrepancy in their sources of access to legitimate authority in the group.

The economic structure of the group both requires and facilitates life in town. To market the wares produced in its small cottage industries (cf. Jules-Rosette, 1975b, pp. 1–15), the church requires proximity to an urban center with a variety of consumers. Because its doctrine forbids wage employment, they remain in town without involvement in the major business enterprises of urban life.[1] Although marginal, the group is not without political impact and is re-

[1]Note that this phenomenon is not unknown in the United States. Small religious groups that live communally often establish business enterprises to support their way of life. This is common among the "new" or alternative religious groups based on both Christian and Eastern religions.

147

garded by secular community leaders in Zambia as an important source of mass political support.[2]

On the national level as well, the urban indigenous churches are part of the development of popular culture across Central and Southern Africa. Their music and the symbolic forms through which they identify themselves have filtered into the larger society in Zaire and Zambia. Syncretic ritual practices have become part of the larger moral culture in which the urban churches operate.

In contrast to these more independent developments, the Jamaa and Balokole movements developed within the Catholic and Angelican missions, respectively. While the Jamaa wished to retain the major beliefs and rituals characteristic of Catholicism, under the leadership of Father Tempels, they attempted to incorporate philosophical elements of traditional African religion (such as "vital force" and an understanding of animism) into Catholic doctrine on a philosophical basis. The concept of familyhood is tied to the roles of Jesus and Mary as reconceptualized in Jamaa. Monogamous marriage became the foundation of Jamaa with the assumption that the partners take on the characteristics of the trinitarian figures. Resolving the marital relationship doctrinally made the husband–wife unit the focus of theological change. Despite these modifications of orthodox Catholic theology, the initial preference of the movement was to remain with the Catholic Church. More recently, internal pressure has led to schism and the sectarian development of its doctrine and organization. As is the case with the Harrist church, there are many Jamaa offshoots such as the Katete in the Kasai province. These sectarian spinoffs carry aspects of the movement's male and female symbolism to an extreme by reinterpreting biblical texts with an active and somewhat animistic use of the family (cf. Mayoyo, 1971).

The East African Revival or Balokole is a Protestant renewal movement that has its theological roots in the American Great Awakening and other Western revivals. One of the key features of joining the revival was open confession of all past sins and testimony of conversion. Even after joining, repeated confessions were necessary to reinforce membership. The lack of success of some mission endeavors to elicit full commitments from new converts was one of the factors stimulating this requirement in the revival. During the mid–1930s, the revival went through a highly charismatic phase with members attesting to receiving strange visions and hearing voices that confirmed them. The personal acceptance of Christ as a savior is at the core of Balokole belief and practice, and it must be demonstrated to the religious community at large. Robins demonstrates this through women's accounts of the conversion experience.

The conversion accounts illustrate that women have avowedly resolved crisis situations in their lives through the salvation experience in Balokole. In particular, they portray their former lives as transgressing the taboos and requirements of both traditional society and mission Christianity. As a result, they

---

[2]This situation, of course, differs cross-nationally. The general feeling in Zambia was that the Vapostori did not deflect from political commitment but rather were a major source of it.

encountered misfortune at the hands of the spirits. The revival provided its members with a new morality and the promise of freedom from the misfortunes caused by alien and ancestral spirits. Women deprived of their positions as special *emandwa* cult leaders by the rise of subsequent cults were able to resume positions of ceremonial leadership in the revival movement.

Quimby describes a syncretic form of Islam as it is practiced by the Dyula community in Bobo-Dioulasso, Upper Volta. Like the members of some of the indigenous churches, women in this community were traditionally deprived of political control and were kept in the background during ceremonial performances. The women participated only in certain rites that provided them support in difficult social situations or gave them a source of release, while leaving the political control of the community's activities to the men. Social change in Dyula was accompanied by the secularization of some of the community's rites. Services previously presented by religion were taken over by secular institutions: schools, courts, and hospitals. New developments in the economic status of women during this process have resulted in the return to traditional customs of modesty and to early marriage to govern their conduct. In addition, Islamic law has been reinterpreted to restrict certain rituals of release performed by the women with the assumption that these rites would promote their social and economic autonomy.[3] Both the internal dynamics of the community and the processes of social change that it has undergone have altered orthodox aspects of Islam in Bobo–Dioulasso.

PRIESTS AND PRIESTESSES IN THE NEW CHURCHES

Both the indigenous and separatist or spinoff movements redefine the activities of women within their respective hierarchies. The women of the Apostolic groups preserve positions of mediumship and symbolic power inherent in the local cultures from which they arise. The official ritual separation of the sexes, a division reminiscent of that in the traditional religious associations, allows for the parallel and complementary development of male and female ritual leaders. The expressive leadership of women is recognized through their indirect participation in ceremony through song, gesture, and curative activities.

Both the Jamaa and the Balokole provide women a means of redefining unpleasant, restrictive past experiences. The Jamaa ideology of marriage elevates women to a new position and offers a certain freedom from traditional obligations. The Balokole confession and ritual activities offer a method of transcending the political restrictions of the Nyabingi cult and returning to the older,

---

[3]A similar situation can be observed in the Apostolic churches. As the women become increasingly financially independent, ritual constrictions are placed on them to assure their conformity and subservience to the male political hierarchy.

mystical power associated with the *emandwa* secret societies. Through relative ritual separation, the power of men and women leaders is retained. The Jamaa emphasis on the balanced family model of ritual fulfillment, and the transposition of this model to a promise of individual salvation indicates a new way of symbolizing the doctrine of spiritual equality. The ritual separation of the sexes implicit in mission teachings and Paulme doctrine is not attained until it has been transplanted into familiar cultural idioms.

OVERVIEW

The articles in this section demonstrate the crosscutting themes of religious acculturation and new balance achieved between gender-linked ritual and social activities. In contrast to groups discussed in Part I, these churches model themselves with reference to Western organizations despite their rejection of, or ambivalence toward, them. They all wish to be recognized by dominant world religions: Christian or Islamic. They classify themselves with regard to these religions. While the Apostolic groups do not consider themselves separatist, they are biblical fundamentalists and are intent upon proving the extent of their orthodoxy to other Christian organizations. Nevertheless, they stress their autonomy from existing Western denominations and from all other indigenous associations, no matter how similar in name, doctrine, and rhetoric (cf. Jules-Rosette, 1977).[4]

The Jamaa and Balokole movements remained internal to their missions of origin, until accusations of heterodoxy and the schismatic process forced them away. Even, then, the Western religions remained a ritual and theological point of reference to them. They considered themselves to have revitalized these religions and to have made them applicable to the "African" way of life. They welcomed the label of revitalistic rather than heterodox or schismatic groups. The Islamic followers of Bobo-Dioulasso project a similar relationship with orthodox Islam. A comparison may, nonetheless, be drawn between the "transplanted" and "traditional" groups discussed in this volume. All groups are preserving significant traditional symbols and beliefs from animistic belief in spirits and ancestors to attitudes about ritual comportment. The difference among the groups is based not so much on their willingness to draw upon external doctrine but instead in their interest in accepting new external forms of expressions and publicly proclaiming their adherence to them. The distinction is by no means "evolutionary," even in a symbolic sense. Rather, the continuum from cult to church in contemporary Africa represents the wealth of innovative cultural forms used by both rural and urban groups as a means of adjustment to rapidly changing social environments.

---

[4]This strict separation allows the groups to maintain their own autonomy in a highly competitive religious and social environment.

8

The Masowe Vapostori of Seki: Utopianism and Tradition in an African Church

Clive Kileff

Margaret Kileff

Throughout contemporary subSaharan Africa, syncretic religious movements are prevalent. This chapter describes an indigenous church in Zimbabwe that has combined both Christian and traditional Shona religious elements. However, the resulting syncretism led to a church unlike its predecessors. The members of the Apostolic Sabbath Church of God hold beliefs and lead life-styles that differ from both traditional Shona and European culture. These differences are reflected in the persistence of a gerontocracy and a patrilineal system of political control counterbalanced by the idealization of ceremonial authority for women. Women function as spirit mediums and special singers and are regarded as the guardians of the group's spiritual power. They may advise the men but they do not wield direct and autonomous political power.

The Vapostori code of ethics contrasts in several ways from Western Christian teachings. The Vapostori do not allow their members to work for Europeans. In addition, they teach:

> . . . that the poverty of Africans was the result of the greed of Europeans who had received all their wealth from the technical knowledge made available to them by God who they had rejected. The [Vapostori] church promised that God would reward Africans in Heaven and that Europeans would be condemned to Hell. It also taught that at some time in the future technical knowledge would be made available to Africans through the prophets. (Garbett, 1967, p. 317)

The prophet and leader, Johane Masowe, also stressed, in a manner typical of many indigenous churches, that European missionaries had hidden from Africans the knowledge and power contained in the Bible and that this was now available to his followers through revelation by the Holy Spirit. Thus, the Vapostori church members were able to set up a system of social relationships autonomous from the mission hierarchy. This had the effect of creating meaningful relationships in a time of rapid culture change. In the larger context, Jules–Rosette (1973) writes:

> The growth of independent churches on the whole illustrates the importance of religion in resolving cultural conflicts and in sustaining meaningful forms of personal association in societies where communal and kinship relationships are rapidly changing. (p. 174)

The Masowe Vapostori maintain an independence from the larger European and African community. They do not work for Europeans, nor do they raise crops or keep cattle like their African neighbors. The Vapostori are self-sufficient artisans, and their identity is sustained in part by their robed dress, shaven heads, and beards. By participating minimally in the Europeans' educational system they have further insured the intergenerational continuity of their way of life and religious beliefs. This relative rejection of formal education has led to a revitalistic response toward the role of women that maintains them in a politically subservient, domestic position, in spite of their access to prestige through mediumship. Like the Maranke women, Masowe women possess ceremonial and not political authority.

THE LIFE OF JOHANE MASOWE

There is little documented information about Shoniwa or Johane Masowe[1] other than that found in correspondence of colonial government officials who witnessed, with some anxiety, the success of the young prophet in attracting a "fanatic" following. Another source of information about the early history of the sect and its founder is the piecemeal accounts of Masowe's followers. The details related by older people who knew Masowe and traveled with him are inexact and tend to be embroidered by each raconteur. It is, however, interesting to note that many of the myths and legends about the prophet correspond to incidents reported in the records of government officials suspicious of his activities.

Shoniwa was born in 1915 in Musaringa Village in the Gandanzara area of the Makoni Tribal Trust Land about 30 miles northeast of the town of Rusape. It is reported that from childhood, Shoniwa displayed extraordinary behavior. He addressed every adult male as "Baba" (father). He was familiar with Christianity through the teachings of Methodist missionaries in his area (Murphree, 1969, p. 61).

As a young man, he left his rural home and went to work in Salisbury and later in Norton, a small town south of Salisbury. Some say Shoniwa fell ill and died in Salisbury; others say he died in Norton or Gandanzara. His grave was

---

[1]In Shona, Masowe means "an open place." Masowe instructed his followers to worship in open places and not to erect church buildings.

being dug and the family called together, when he revived and told the poeple he had been with God. He spent three days in the Marimba Mountains, where he received the Holy Spirit. God commanded him to teach others so that they too might be saved. He was given a wooden staff, long white garments, a Bible, and a new identity. Thenceforth, he wished to be known as Johane Masowe (Sundkler, 1961, p. 324). His message to the people was that they must not work for Europeans. They must destroy their government-issued registration certificates. They most forsake traditional witchcraft practices and destroy paraphernalia associated with these practices. His followers would not die and would receive the Holy Spirit themselves in preparation for the judgment. They must not build churches but worship out-of-doors. It is also reported that Masowe cautioned believers not to plow or plant crops. It was promised that Moses and Elijah and the prophets would come down from Heaven and make war with the Europeans and drive them out of the country.

He claimed a divinely changed identity: Shoniwa was dead; Johane Masowe now lived as the Messenger of God. Official documents from the period refer to him as one claiming to be John the Baptist (Rhodesia National Archives, Salisbury, File S1542 M8B). Today, his followers call him the Messiah. There has been a transition over the years from his role as Messenger of God to that of intermediary *with* God. This contrasts with the Maranke Vapostori interpretation that John Maranke was the "mutumu," or Witness of God and not a Messiah. On the other hand, Johane Masowe has become for his disciples a black Messiah, usurping the role of Christ.

FOUNDING THE MOVEMENT

Masowe's earliest work took place in the areas around his home in the Makoni Tribal Trust Land. He moved from place to place, preaching and baptizing those who accepted his message. It is likely that as is typical of this kind of movement, his relatives were among his first converts. It is not known how Masowe delegated leadership during this early period, but it is probable that he retained direct control of his followers. Unique to his movement has been a secretive character that is not found in the similar and contemporary movement of John Maranke.[2] Outsiders have been prevented from finding out about much of the secret lore, and even members who have not had direct contact with Masowe are shielded from the hidden doctrines of his group.

Masowe rejected the use of Christian sacraments other than baptism, and he retained exclusive right to baptize converts. His radical ministry was met with skepticism from traditional leaders who feared usurpation of their authority, colonial administrators who were anxious about the anti-European character

---

[2]Sundkler (1961, p. 323) refers to Masowe as the "secret Messiah."

of his teachings, and missionaries who were angry over the loss of present and potential converts. Both traditional leaders and missionaries complained to government authorities that young people and women were attracted by Masowe's teaching, forsaking traditional respect for parents and husbands. This appeal of the Masowe and similar groups to women is often attributed to the social pressures of polygynous marriages as well as to possibilities for women's ceremonial leadership through healing and spirit mediumship.

Official correspondence refers to Masowe as a "charlatan" and a "religious fanatic."[3] His activities were viewed with suspicion and contempt. It was alleged that he was using religion as a veil for subversive political activities.

The National Archives files contain an eyewitness report of the behavior of some of Masowe's followers. They are referred to as Apostolics. The observer was an Anglican missionary whose account was incorporated into a letter of complaint:

> The Apostolics have established themselves upon a hillock not a quarter of a mile away. They have no church building. They prevent their children from coming to school . . . they come and sing and shout round the church every night.

Especially irksome to authorities was the fact that Masowe was not practicing under the supervision of European Christian missionaries. He was detained for questioning, kept under close surveillance, and jailed at least once on a charge of not carrying a registration certificate.

Between 1932 and 1947, Masowe moved about with his followers who were called "vaHosanna," first in Zimbabwe and later into South Africa and Botswana.[4] Masowe did not settle in his home area and establish his sect there. Members of the movement who traveled with him at this time say the group moved because of disputes with tribal authorities in the areas where they lived.

In 1943, the group crossed into south Africa and lived in Pretoria and Johannesburg. Later, they moved into Botswana in order to secure the necessary documents that would allow them to live in South Africa (Sundkler, 1961, p. 324). In 1947, Masowe led his followers to live in the Korsten squatter area near Port Elizabeth on the southeast Coast of South Africa. During the 15 years the VaHosanna lived in Port Elizabeth, they supported themselves by selling handmade items such as baskets, furniture, and metal buckets. They came to be known as the "Korsten Basketmakers" and remained a discrete community unassimilated into urban squatter life. The main Masowe migration center in Lusaka, Zambia, is now also called Korsten.

During this time, members of the sect carried identity cards or certificates

---

[3]These accounts are contained in correspondence between the Zimbabwean colonial Native Commissioners for the Rusape chiefdom and the central office in Salisbury in 1933, File S1542 M8B 1933.

[4]This appellation apparently derived from the preference of Masowe's followers to shout "Hosanna" as a greeting and as an expression of religious fervor during services.

that were designed to resemble the hated government-issued passes required to be carried by all Africans in the Republic. The Vapostori claim that they carried these church certificates instead of passes. The adoption of such traits is evidence of the relationship between the church and other political structures.

During these years, Masowe traveled back and forth to Zimbabwe, converting and baptizing those who desired to join his group, the Apostolic Sabbath Church of God. Individuals and families moved between Zimbabwe and the community in Port Elizabeth. Many who were converted remained in Zimbabwe. Masowe spent a great deal of time away from the Korsten community.

In the late 1950s, Masowe left the Korsten community for the final time. His mission was to evangelize and to baptize. Those who lived with him at this time believe he traveled to Zambia, Tanzania, Kenya, and into the Zaire.[5] In Masowe's absence, a man named Jack Sithole assumed leadership of the community. Sithole died in 1962, leaving the group with leadership dispersed among several elders. Since Masowe was the only person who could select a successor, the group has been left with a dilemma that remains unsolved.[6]

Sundkler visited the Korsten community in the late 1950s after Masowe's departure and before Sithole's death. At this time, Sundkler was interested in Bantu messianic groups and in the distinctions between those and ordinary Zionist churches. Sundkler believed that Masowe and Sithole were the same person, that Jack Sithole was a disguise that Masowe presented to the outside world (Sundkler, 1961, p. 325). This confusion increased the mystery surrounding the founder.

[5]Today, there is a group of Masowe's Apostles living as a self-contained community in a large house in a fashionable Nairobi neighborhood. Jules-Rosette's (1975a) recent book about the Apostles of John Maranke contains the following description of Masowe's followers who live in the Marrapodi area of Lusaka, Zambia:

> Unlike other independent churches, such as the Apostles of John Masowe, which also originated in Rhodesia, the Maranke groupings did not establish community-wide cottage industries. The Apostles of Masowe, known as the "Hosannas," because of their singing style, and as the "Basketweavers," on the basis of their trades of basketweaving and tinsmithing, live in self-sufficient communities that are adjacent to those of the Maranke Apostles in Zambia and Rhodesia. The Masowes share the profits of this work to buy large communal homes where they live and worship together. As these communities expand, emissaries are sent to establish communal quarters in new areas. While a few of the Maranke Apostles live together on farms in Zambia and Zaire, outside of Rhodesia their pattern is less communal and blends more easily with the variety of family styles already found in urban areas. (Jules-Rosette, 1975a, pp. 332–333).

[6]Johane Masowe died on September 18, 1973, after the field work was complete. The impact of his death on the sect offers a topic for future research. It is not known where he died, but I was informed by a letter from one of the Seki group that "the body of Father Johane was flown from Ndola [Zambia] to Rhodesia, and we took his body from Salisbury airport to Rusape and we buried him at Gandanzara on September 28, 1973. More than 1,500 people attended the funeral."

In 1955, the South African government began to protest that the presence of the Shona Korsten Basketmakers ''was in contravention of the Union's immigration laws'' (*African Daily News*, June 7, 1962). The government of then Rhodesia negotiated with the South African authorities over the next seven years to persuade them to allow the group to remain in the Republic. On March 23, 1962, the local government was notified that members of the sect born within the territory were to be repatriated (*African Daily News*, June 7, 1962). In anticipation of this, representatives of the sect had been brought to Salisbury in 1960 to view possible sites where the community could be resettled as a whole: ''as . . . a religious sect this appeared to be necessary'' (*African Daily News*, Aug. 20, 1962). Two sites were offered to the group—one in Zimunya township near Umtali in the eastern part of the country and one in the Seki Tribal Trust Land near Salisbury. No decision was reached at this time. The delegation representing the Korsten Basketmakers traveled on to Botswana to explore the possibility of settling there after their expulsion from South Africa. This probe apparently yielded unsatisfactory results.

On June 7, 1962, the first refugees from the Korsten community in Port Elizabeth began arriving at Plumtree, the rail stop just inside the Zimbabwean border. Between two and three thousand people were eventually housed in tents and huts that had been erected as temporary shelter in the transit camp. Members of the group report that their people were disgruntled with the forced removal. Some quietly left Korsten and moved to other cities in South Africa before the police arrived to oversee the removal. Once in Zimbabwe, about half of the people rejected the offer to resettle them there and continued on to Zambia. Those who remained in the transit camp at Plumtree continued to negotiate with the Minister of Native Affairs in Salisbury for a site where they could settle and continue to live as a distinct, self-sufficient community. Because of their involvement in small-scale production of straw and tin goods, the Korsten Vapostori insisted that they must live where they could have easy access to urban markets. This issue was the heart of a dispute that lasted several months before members finally agreed to accept a 100-acre site fifteen miles south of Salisbury in the Seki Tribal Trust Land. They were granted the right to occupy the land free of charge for three years, after which time rent would be collected for each occupied residential stand.

THE SEKI COMMUNITY

Masowe's repatriated followers settled on the 100-acre site of bush land in the Seki Tribal Trust Land, 15 miles south of Salisbury. There are more than 50 semiautonomous congregations of the Apostolic Sabbath Church of God living in other parts of Zimbabwe, but the community at Seki has played a unique role in the history of the movement.

Physical Setting

The Vapostori village is located in Zimbabwe's high veld plateau with its temperate climate and light sandy soils. The village is situated beside the main road leading into the city. This road was paved several years ago and offers easy access to Salisbury in all weather.[7] Buses now serve the area, drawing people into the sphere of urban influence.

The community is reached by traveling half a mile along a dirt track from the main road, until one encounters the rows of square, brick houses. A small, round metal sign informs the visitor that this is the home of "The Korsten Basketmakers." Overhead, a single black wire dips down from the tall poles that have followed the dirt road, and disappears under the corrugated iron roof of the nearest house. This small, two–room brick structure is used as an office and storage room. Inside the office on a small rickety table, the wire joins a telephone, installed in February, 1973. Members say it enables them to conduct business transactions with greater facility and to keep in touch with groups of their church living elsewhere in Zimbabwe. The Vapostori share a party line with Nyatsime College, St. Mary's Mission, and businesses in the nearby center.

The village has been laid out in small, equal stands or lots. At present, 80 stands are occupied by houses. On each stand is one or more small structure, usually a square house and several round thatched huts. Most of the houses are made of brown, sun-baked bricks with corrugated iron roofs, windows, and sometimes a concrete floor. The huts serve as kitchens and storage rooms. The homes are small, containing two or three rooms. Less prosperous families live in traditional thatched huts, but all aspire to build modern brick houses when they have enough money. The village is laid out in two long parallel rows of houses facing each other across a wide grassy area. Running in between and perpendicular to these long rows are four shorter rows of houses, two at the south end of the village and two in the middle. This creates two open squares in between the houses. Women carry water from a nearby well in large metal containers. The government plans to pipe water into the village during the coming year.

As one walks through the village, bicycles are in view everywhere. A few cars and trucks can be seen. The Vapostori appear to enjoy a higher standard of living than their rural neighbors. Many of their homes are furnished with couches, beds, chairs, and tables. Radios and even tape recorders are not an uncommon sight.

---

[7]The government plans to develop the area both as a dormitory suburb to house urban African workers and a factory site in an effort to decentralize industry, relieving the congestion in Salisbury. This is similar to the South African policy of developing "border industries" on the edges of Bantustans, but differs from the latter in its proximity to a major urban center.

Economic Life

Although land is available to them, the Vapostori only have small gardens and do not rely on agriculture for their food. They have abandoned the traditional Shona reverence for and ritual uses of cattle. This has been a practical necessity of their migratory and basically urban life during the past 40 years. Rural Vapostori living in other communities may have cattle, but their economic and ritual importance has diminished. The emphasis is on being self-supporting craftsmen. In this way, they can participate in the cash economy without accepting the servitude of employment in the urban labor force. They remain economically independent of wage labor and free to observe the Saturday Sabbath and to meet for prayers at other times during the week.

Visiting the community on any day but Saturday, the air is filled with a chorus of metallic taps as men and their sons are busy shaping sheets of galvanized metal into containers of various sizes and shapes. These are generally referred to as "tins" or *mabava*, since they are commonly used for bathing and washing. Sheets of metal are purchased as raw materials and are beaten with hammers around metal rails, until they are the appropriate shape. Making tins is the most common vocation among men in the village. Sewing scraps of cloth into quilts and bed covers is a common activity for women. The people buy scraps from clothing factories in Salisbury. The work requires a sewing machine which is regarded as a major purchase by the Vapostori. Once in possession of a sewing machine, a family is in a position to make clothes for themselves and for sale to others.

Basketmaking is a common craft practiced by the Vapostori. Both men and women make baskets, and the labor is generally divided, with some members of a family splitting the poles and others weaving the strips into baskets, sleeping mats, and chairs. Still other members of a family cycle into the city with baskets to be offered for sale to passing motorists from a street corner. The Masowe women do the bulk of the marketing of small goods in town, and they have become entrepreneurs in their own right. Through these means, they provide partial support for the subunits of their polygynous families. A few Vapostori work with wood or leather. Men who are wealthy enough to afford a car or truck make money by hauling people and goods. They hire out their vehicles to other Vapostori and to people in neighboring villages. Most Vapostori men aspire to own a car. One man in the village owns a small van from which he sells fruit, candy, and other food items in the urban townships.

Vapostori men and women market their goods in Salisbury and throughout the country, especially in the Tribal Trust Lands, at mine compounds, and on large agricultural estates. Most of their customers are Africans, although they do make some products specifically for the European market such as dog baskets, bird houses, patio chairs, watering cans, and mailboxes. Men and women travel separately to sell their goods. Vapostori craftsmen have areas that they visit regularly, staying out for several days or weeks at a time. During a trip they may sell goods, take orders, and collect money for goods already delivered. Women are away from home for shorter periods. Their trips are arranged easily in polygynous households, where domestic duties and child care are shared. The men say that their wives are allowed to keep most of the money they earn to spend on themselves and their children and to buy raw materials, cloth, or yarn for future products. The Vapostori state they are forbidden to deposit their money in banks, until the government is "in just hands." In the meantime, they rely on keeping it hidden in their houses or carrying it with them.

Social Organization

In traditional Shona life, religious and political institutions are interwoven, with one validating and reinforcing the other. As discussed in the introduction to this volume, in the Vapostori community, religious leaders are also secular leaders. The life of the community revolves around the religious commitments of the sect. Just as the traditional *masvikiro* (spirit mediums) are consulted before a chief is selected, the *masvikiro* and *vaprofita* in the Vapostori sect are relied upon to communicate the choices of the Holy Spirit for leadership roles. Each category of leader is dependent upon the others for support and validation, and no one person or group can exert undue control (see Table 8.1). Church doctrine prescribes behaviors that regulate all aspects of daily life, and church elders resolve conflicts between members.

Table 8.1 Office Holders

	Males	Females
Muvengeri	1	—
Vaparidzi	21	—
Vaprofita	3	3
Masvikiro	1	—
Vakota	3	—
Vaimbi	39	81
Total	68	84

Among the Vapostori, polygyny is the ideal and has been attained by 70% of the men in the Seki community (see Table 8.2). As is traditional among the Shona, the first or senior wife has a higher status than other co-wives. The Vapostori say that a man's wealth is measured by the number of wives and

Table 8.2 Types of Marriages

	Males	Females
Monogamous	25	25
Polygynous	68	179
Divorced	1	0
Total	94	204

children he supports, but men are warned not to enlarge their families beyond their financial capacity. They are fond of pointing out how much better able they are to take care of polygynous families than many nonmembers are of monogamous families. There is considerable advantage in polygyny in cases where wives and their children are producers as well as consumers. Only very young children do not participate in the making of products for sale. In many tribal areas of Rhodesia, however, land is scarce and additional wives and children may outstrip the productive capacity of the land.

Family units are usually composed of a man, his wife or wives, and their children. Thirty-seven percent of the heads of households reported the presence of other people in the household related to them or to their wives. Seventy percent of the men surveyed have more than one wife. There are several large extended families in the community, consisting of two or three generations of males and their wives and children. In one case, the head of the family has six wives. In adjoining houses live his adult sons and their wives and children. This homestead consists of a number of stands surrounded by a barbed-wire fence that serves to demarcate the boundary of this extended family. Most families are, however, divided because of the many dislocations experienced by this group. Many of the Vapostori have relatives living in Zambia from whom they separated in 1962, when the community divided. Both the Lusaka and the Nairobi Vapostori communities are based on polygynous communal households with a cottage industry method of economic support. Women contribute equally to this economic sustenance and support their own family units autonomously.

Vapostori women are easily distinguished by their unusual appearance. Women and girls wear white dresses, aprons, and turbanlike head coverings. The dresses are modestly styled with high necks, sleeves, and long skirts. Men wear ordinary Western clothing but shave their heads and wear beards. The Vapostori say that their shaven heads are a symbol of their servitude to God and of sorrow for their sins. Their beards represent the glory of God. These features of clothing and grooming provide a visible sign of their separation from other groups. They say that they are often ridiculed, especially the women, because of their appearance. This, too, serves to reinforce their identity with the group.

In everyday life, there is strict separation of the sexes. This is also found in traditional Shona culture. Women prepare meals and serve them to their husbands who eat in separate groups with other men. When addressing males, women must kneel with eyes downcast. When riding in cars, the women sit together in the back seat and the men in the front. Men and women also sit separately at religious services. Women are expected to be subservient to their husbands in all matters. Contrasted to this is the fact that women are able to occupy the powerful positions of *masvikiro* (spirit mediums) and *vaprofita* (prophetesses) in the church leadership hierarchy and to express their spiritual control through ceremonial authority.

Church members must abstain from drinking alcoholic beverages and from smoking. They do, however, drink a weak, homemade brew called *mahewu* that is made from millet. They observe food taboos as listed in the Old Testament, including abstinence from pork. They do not eat carcasses of animals that have died, and are forbidden to keep ducks, dogs, and cats. The Vapostori say that *mashavi* (evil spirits) reside in dogs and cats. Gambling and adultery are considered sinful, as are all activities, such as violent sports, that involve physical contact. The Sabbath is observed from sunset on Friday until sunset on Saturday. No work or business may be conducted during this time, and members are instructed to spend their time praying, reading the Bible and participating in worship and healing services. These are ideal behaviors, and the church code provides ways of dealing with infractions. Teenage boys are a source of considerable concern to their elders. Some are known to drink beer and smoke at the nearby Chikwana Beer Garden.[8]

ATTITUDES TOWARD EDUCATION
FOR WOMEN AND MEN

Education of children is a controversial topic in the community. The villagers refuse to send their children to government or mission schools, saying that there they will learn immorality, be exposed to other religions, be allowed to participate in sports, and be encouraged to compete and to fight. It is said that girls will learn disobedience to men. As is also emphasized in the subsequent discussions by Fabian and Quimby, indigenous churches do not necessarily enhance economic and educational opportunities for women. Instead, women become the symbolic retainers of custom, and their enforced conservatism remains an essential defining theme of the church. The practice of avoiding government schools minimizes stress arising from contact with contradictory values, and guarantees that the young will be socialized within the village. Literacy is valued for the purpose of reading the Bible, but education is seen as unnecessary and threatening.

Within the community there is a small school. Classes are held in the mornings inside a small brick building, but pupils overflow into the surrounding yard. One teacher is responsible for instructing several hundred students. The school has only minimal materials and equipment, and the curriculum emphasizes religious instruction and memorization of Bible passages. It was founded by several younger men in the community who felt very strongly that

---

[8]During a meeting with church members in the office, I felt something under my foot. Investigation revealed an unsmoked cigarette lying on the floor. Church elders immediately began rebuking several young men who were present and one who was absent.

Vapostori children should be educated. The church elders strongly opposed the school but eventually relented. Table 8.3 shows the number of years of education of men and women in the Seki community. Seventy percent of the women and 40% of the men surveyed have no formal education. At the other extreme are several young men in the village who are pursuing a Junior Certificate by means of a nine–year correspondence course.

Table 8.3 Years of Education of Adults in Seki Community

No. of years of education	Males	Females
0	55	158
1	2	3
2	15	9
3	14	14
4	19	19
5	10	10
6	9	4
7	5	2
8	5	3
9	1	2
Total	135	224

Although rejecting the servitude of the industrial society, the Vapostori seek to enjoy the benefits of it in the form of consumer goods. They purchase most of their food, including maize meal, the staple in the Shona diet.[9] The Vapostori homes are well furnished, and most adults are well dressed. Money is the preferred form of exchange, although, when selling in rural areas, goods may be exchanged for food. Aspirations for material possessions center on bicycles, sewing machines, radios, cars, and furniture. This orientation is in contrast to rural orientations toward cattle as a desired goal and is a direct break from the economic and ceremonial conventions of customary Shona rural life.

ORGANIZATION, RITUAL, AND BELIEF

Organization

The Seki community is one of more than 50 semiautonomous congregations of the Apostolic Sabbath Church of God living in Zimbabwe. Within each congregation, there are varying numbers of men and women occupying positions in the leadership hierarchy. The hierarchy is extremely flexible, with people being promoted to positions of leadership based on their individual characteristics and merit rather than on the needs of the system.

Leadership for the congregations is centered in the Gandanzara area of the

[9]Sadza, a stiff porridge of boiled maize meal, is the basic ingredient of the Shona diet.

Makoni Tribal Trust Land and the Dwedzo area of the nearby Chiduku Tribal Trust Land. Church elders living in these areas where the sect originated supervise the Zimbabwean congregations, sometimes traveling to visit them in a Land Rover owned by the church.

Leadership Hierarchy

The *muvengeri* or evangelist is the ceremonial and political head of the congregation. He is responsible for administering the church code and must be present at all religious rituals. He interprets church doctrine and directs the people in how to live. There is one *muvengeri* in the Seki community. This office may only be held by men who have first served as *vaparidzi*.

Twenty-one men identify themselves as *vaparidzi* (sing., *muparidzi*) or preachers. Their duties include organizing church services, calling the community to prayer, receiving visitors to the community, settling small disputes in families, and conveying more serious matters to the *vakota* or judge and the *muvengeri*.

The *masvikiro* (sing., *svikiro*) and *vaprofita* (sing., *muprofita*) are the women and men who become possessed during religious ceremonies. The *vaprofita* are more powerful and have higher status than the *masvikiro*. Women often occupy both of these roles. During possession, both *masvikiro* and *vaprofita* speak in tongues.

The *svikiro* is the spirit medium in traditional Shona religion who communicates with various spirits. Among the Vapostori, this role has been modified so that the communication conveyed by the *masvikiro* is from the Holy Spirit. They deal with matters of concern to the whole group and may advise members about their behavior in relation to the church code. The *masvikiro* may also predict marriages between eligible young people. Although women may become *masvikiro*, there are no females in the Seki community who hold this office.

The *vaprofita* or prophets are also possessed by the Holy Spirit and have the power to reveal individual sin. The Vapostori say that the *vaprofita* can look into the past and find the causes of illness and misfortune. They also have the power to predict illness, to heal, and to predict the future. They are believed to be able to foretell rain. These abilities lead a great deal of ceremonial force to the position of the Vapostori women as spiritual leaders despite their exclusion from the major occasions of decision–making. The *vaprofita* must be able to discern the Holy Spirit in a member before he can assume a leadership position. They must experience this a number of times and may subject the candidate to scrutiny by *vaprofita* from other congregations before pronouncing him worthy.

Both *vaprofita* and *masvikiro* speak in tongues during possession. Their messages are interpreted by other *vaprofita* or *masvikiro* or by the *muvengeri* or the *vaparidzi*. The glossolalia become an undifferentiated medium that may be given content by the interpreter. In this way, all church officers have an opportunity to manipulate behavior and belief—the *masvikiro* and *vaprofita* through their possession and dream interpretation, and the *muvengeri* and *vaparidzi* through interpretation of glossolalia. Dreams are also an important source of interpretative material and are frequently reported and interpreted by various church officers.

The *vakota* (sing., *mukota*) are men whose political role is similar to that of a judge. There are three *vakota* in the Seki community, and they are respected for their fairness and honor. They preside over meetings of church elders, where disputes among church members are settled. The emphasis is on consensus and compromise, and the similarity to the traditional Shona chief's court, or *dare*, is striking. After hearing both sides in a dispute and assessing the feelings of other church elders, the *vakota* give their judgment. There is no upward mobility from the position as there is between the ranks of *vaparidzi* and *muvengeri*. One of the *vakota* in the Seki community is responsible for collecting monthly rental fees of $1.25 paid by each stand holder to the District Commissioner.

The role of *vaimbi* (sing., *muimbi*) constitutes the lowest category in the leadership hierarchy and is occupied primarily by women. During religious services they function as a choir. Their singing is a background for other parts of the services and provides demarcation between parts of the service. Songs are sung in Shona and usually consist of a single sentence or a phrase that is sung over and over again with variations in pitch and tempo.

During religious services, singing is used to call the Holy Spirit and to create a mood conducive to possession. Singing is a significant part of Vapostori life. They are known to other groups because of their unique style. In the Seki community, 39 men and 81 women identified themselves as *vaimbi*. From the rank of *vaimbi*, women can rise to become *vaprofita* or *masvikiro*, and men may rise either to *vakota* or to *vaparidzi* and eventually to *muvengeri*.

The Vapostori say that the Holy Spirit chooses people to occupy these roles within the church hierarchy. Choices are revealed through the *vaprofita*, and only those who are exceptional in their devotion to church life are chosen. While leadership and mobility within the church are flexible, they are also a source of conflict. There are no definite rules stating how many positions are available at each level of the hierarchy. Theoretically, Masowe is the head of the church. He chose the first leaders from among his faithful apostles but left no mechanism for succession to those positions of leadership. Many of his original converts are still living in the Seki community and occupy positions to which they were appointed by Masowe himself. When they die, the community will have to evolve ways to fill their positions and neutralize conflicting claims for these positions.

RELIGIOUS RITUALS

Religious services are always held outside in an open place. This is how Masowe directed his followers to worship. In the Seki community, members usually congregate in the grassy area between the rows of houses. This space is not marked in any special way but becomes sacred ground as people gather there for prayer. When the Seki Vapostori are joined for services by other groups, they move their meeting place to the open fields near the village. Such meetings may last for 24 hours or more, and shelters are built for the visitors.

The place where the service is held is designated the *masowe*, and all must remove their shoes before entering. The male office holders—*muvengeri, vaparidzi, vakota, masvikiro,* and *vaprofita*—sit in a row facing the congregation. This row is designated as *vebati vemabasa* (the place of the people of works). At the front of the congregation sit the male members followed by the male *vaimbi*. Behind them are the female *vaimbi*, female *masvikiro*, and female *vaprofita*, followed by ordinary female members.

The service is usually conducted by several *vaparidzi* and the *muvengeri*. They take turns reading the Bible and interpreting what has been read. During the services, church officers and members may wrap in white toga–like garments. However, male members do not have a distinctive uniform as is common among many independent Christian sects. During the services, singing is begun by the *vaimbi*, but all members are expected to join in. Any member may become possessed by the Holy Spirit and begin to speak in tongues. Possession is the aspiration of all worshipers and is manifested by body tremors and glossolalia. During services *vaprofita* may attempt to heal people by holding their heads and praying for them. They also diagnose the cause of the illness.

Treatment of Illness

As in customary Shona religion, the causes of illness and misfortune are sought in the social order rather than in Western scientific thought. Vapostori are strictly forbidden to use Western medicine or to seek medical treatment outside the village, either from doctors or from traditional Shona *nganga* (herbalist-diviners). In the case of traumatic accidents such as broken limbs, a mupostori would go to the hospital to have the bone set and return to the community to have the *vaprofita* search for the cause of the accident in the antecedent behavior and social relationships of the injured person. This is an important example of the syncretism of belief and practice.

Although the Seki community is located 15 miles from the most modern hosptial in Zimbabwe, nearly every adult woman surveyed had lost one or more babies at birth or in the first year of life. The most dramatic case is a woman who lost all ten of her young children to diseases in a three-year period. The *vaprofita* attributed this misfortune to an irregularity in the way her marriage had been contracted. This woman's male relatives were said to be angry because the traditional *mombe yeumai* (cow for the bride's mother) had never been paid. This was done by the woman's husband, and she has since borne another healthy child.

People who break the code of conduct prescribed by the church are identified and examined by the *vaprofita*. Depending on the severity of the infraction and the repentance of the sinner, a member may be put on probation. During this time, he will be prayed for and watched and may ultimately be reinstated. The severest form of punishment is exclusion from the group.

Marriage Customs

The Vapostori do not exchange *lobola* (bridewealth) at marriage unless the bride's male relatives are not church members and demand it. A marriage is marked by feasting and is believed to be finalized at the birth of the first child. Infertility is not grounds for divorce, since polygyny offers the possibility of producing offspring with another wife. Young people are able to express choice in the selection of marriage partners, but some marriages are arranged by fathers or are foretold by the *masvikiro*.

Since polygyny is widely practiced, conversion is relied on as a source of marriageable women. Because of the wide association of Vapostori in the Seki community with groups of church members living in other parts of Zimbabwe, marriages are contracted across a wider social space than in the past. Divorce is permitted if a spouse breaks the church code, but the offending party may not remain in the church. At the death of a man, his wives may be inherited by his brother. This is a traditional Shona custom called *nhaka*. If the wife or wives refuse, they have the right to return to their parents, but the property and children of the deceased man remain in his patrilineage and fall under the control of his eldest surviving brother or, if there are no brothers, to his eldest son. Thus, women remain part of the patrilineage and continue to be subject to their husbands' families.

Protection from Spirits

The Vapostori have abandoned traditional Shona customs relating to supplication and sacrifice to the ancestors. Instead, they say their prayers are given only to the Holy Spirit. Vapostori who are devout in their prayers are filled with the Holy Spirit and cannot be possessed by the *vadzimu* (ancestral spirits) or be influenced or harmed by the *ngozi* (avenging spirits) or *mashavi* (evil spirits). Vapostori cannot become victims of pagan witchcraft. Pagans who are possessed by *vadzimu* or *ngozi* or *mashavi* at the time of conversion must be exorcised by the prayers of the *vaprofita* The Vapostori say that the Holy Spirit fills the place of the other spirits and protects the person from their return.

Baptism

Baptism is the only Christian sacrament retained by Masowe when he founded his movement. Through baptism, people are believed to be cleansed of their sins and to become part of the church. Masowe is the only person who was able to baptize. Due to his long absence from the group before his death, no one has been baptized since before the group left South Africa in 1962. The Vapostori express anxiety over the fact that their children and recent converts have never been baptized. They offer special prayers for these people. Throughout the church, the result of this failure to baptize has also resulted in intense schisms between the fully baptized members and the newer converts.

CONCLUSIONS

The Masowe Vapostori in the Seki community have formed a viable economic, social, and spiritual community. Despite, and perhaps because of, stresses and strains of culture change, dislocation, and discrimination, the community has survived and prospered. The syncretic aspects of the church, in which elements of both Christianity and Shona tradition have been creatively melded, have served to preserve and strengthen the community in times when outside forces place particularly heavy pressures upon the church of Johane Masowe. Women within the church occupy a position of ceremonial authority that is tied to the Shona customs of spirit mediumship. Their powers of prediction and healing are considered awesome. They also maintain considerable economic independence as polygynous spouses. Yet, their activities are limited by customary Shona patrilineal control and by the central location of political power in the hands of the fully baptized male elders.

9

Man and Woman
in the Teachings
of the Jamaa Movement

Johannes Fabian

INTRODUCTION

Investigations of the role of women in ''changing'' Africa typically envisage the following scenario: In traditional society, especially with polygyny being a common institution, most women had a low status.[1] That situation worsened upon first contact with Western economic and educational systems, because women were in some cases denied even limited access to the new avenues of progress. Only when modernization began to affect traditional institutions, notably the family, and to transform subsistence economies into cash economies, did women find opportunities for emancipation as small entrepreneurs and as leaders in religious and parapolitical movements. Depending on the kind of study conducted, claims have been made for all of these avenues as major factors in changing the lot of African women.

I will place these reflections in a different frame, one that accommodates the scenarino outlined above, but takes account of the fact that ''modernization'' and ''emancipation'' are never sufficiently understood if viewed only in terms of behavioral input–output models. Like all social processes, they involve the creation and transformation of cultural content—images, symbols, metaphors that pervade and inform action. Investigations that omit that dimension are little more than manipulations of extraneous ''indicators'' (power, income, education, and

---

[1]It must be noted, though, that many anthropologists and other social scientists have been aware of the *high* status of women in traditional societies. That was also the point of departure for Barrett's (1968, pp. 146–150) attempt to introduce the assertiveness of women as a major step in his analysis of African indigenous churches.

so forth). These indicators which, by definition, must remain unchanged in the course of a study, then turn into projections of the measuring system on to that which is to be measured.

What should a different scenario look like? First of all, one would have to keep in mind that all our investigations into women's roles in Africa, traditional or changing, are likely to be filtered by or expressed in terms of the fundamental fact of colonial domination. Consciously or not, that relationship of domination–submission is conceived in terms of cultural images among which the male–female relationship has been a key symbol. It is not surprising then that *within* the dominated society, male domination and female submission would be found to constitute the key to understanding social relations and process.

Applied to the phenomenon under investigation—the new religions in Africa—this perspective had to produce or reinforce stereotypes and preconceptions regarding the role of women. "Religion," especially in its Christian and syncretic forms, somehow had to be a "natural" vehicle for the emancipation of women.

Let us assume that, at least psychologically, relationships between the West and Africa have become sufficiently decolonized so that the present historical situation no longer condemns us to metaphors of male domination and female submission. We would then be free to reopen investigations with a number of different assumptions such as: (1) that African traditions in precolonial times defined male–female relationships first dialectically and then (sometimes) hierarchically; (2) that religious movements of the colonial period were symptoms of the vigor of tradition first and then, at times, reflected dissolution and admixture, and that the role of women in these movements should be viewed accordingly; (3) that in the postcolonial period, movements and their ideologies and languages turned out to be deeply embedded in an emerging popular culture and that, consequently, the role of women in new religions should be understood in that context and no longer only in terms of the survival of traditional forms or the impact of missionary churches.

With these assumptions as a guideline, I will examine the role of women as defined in the teachings of the Jamaa movement in the Shaba region of Zaire.[2] *Jamaa* (literally, and not quite accurately, translated as "family") is the popular and, at times, massive response among African Catholics living in the urban industrial towns of the Zairean copperbelt to the teachings of Placide Tempels, a Belgian missionary widely known as the author of *Bantu Philosophy* (originally published in 1945). The movement assumed that name and the basics of its present organization in 1953 in workers' settlements of the mining company near Kolwezi. Since then, membership has generally been restricted to adult, married

[2]Concerning the ethnography of the Jamaa, see especially Fabian (1971) and De Craemer (1965, 1973). Work on Jamaa texts on which this paper is based was supported by a grant from the Wenner–Gren Foundation for Anthropological Research, New York, whose aid is gratefully acknowledged.

couples, either practicing or former Catholics, who have to undergo several degrees of initiation. For many years, the movement stayed within the mission church although, from the start, tensions existed between its lay–centered enthusiasm and the conservative bureaucratic inclinations of most members of the clergy. Fairly early, it was affected by schism and heterodox dissent. More recently, as the combined result of internal developments and the influence of ecclesiastical and political authorities, the movement seems to have taken a sectarian course.

BANTU PHILOSOPHY

When Tempels founded the Jamaa, he acted in full awareness not only of traditional models (especially from the Luba–Shaba culture that he knew best) but also of the kind of colonial projections on to traditional culture that I mentioned earlier. He had rejected European stereotypes of polygyny as "typically African," pointing out that the traditional institution of marriage could only be understood in the light of basic principles of Bantu thought (see Tempels, 1944–1945, and my comments on that paper, 1970, pp. 6–7, 1971, pp, 27–28). But in view of these early signs of what was later to become a central theme of his teachings, one is surprised that in *Bantu Philosophy* he hardly mentions the role of women. It is as if the basic project of that book—to describe Bantu thought as conceived in a hierarchy of forces—had made it all but impossible to raise problems that could not appropriately be described in hierarchical terms. Undoubtedly, that conspicuous absence of women in *Bantu Philosophy* gives credence to Tempels' latter-day African critics who maintain that the work was not so much a study of Bantu thought as it was an attempt to define and justify the *relationships between* "Western thought" as Tempels saw it and "Bantu thought" (again, as Tempels saw it). That relationship he described as one between rigid, static, manipulative, aggressive thought (Western) and fluent, dynamic, intuitive, compassionate thought (Bantu)—an eloquent, if oblique expression of the male–female key metaphor that Tempels shared with the colonizers. *Bantu Philosophy* did not treat the male–female relationship; it was the metaphorical enactment of such a relationship.[3]

Bantu Philosophy, despite its considerable literary impact at the time, did not make a religious leader out of the missionary–ethnographer. That role was assumed by Tempels after he had experienced the repressive powers of the "civilizatory mission." His book brought him several years of forced exile in Belgium and a personal crisis that once and forever ended his solidarity with the colonial enterprise. When he returned to the Congo he arrived with a new message that eventually became the doctrine of the Jamaa movement.

[3]For an analysis of the historical context of *Bantu Philosophy* and a critique of recent critiques, see Fabian (1970).

The change was dramatic. In the teachings he gave to his movement, Tempels now made male–female relationships the central topic. His earlier conceptions of vital force and of a hierarchy of forces became subordinated to the principles of love and complementarity. There is hardly a page in his later published (see Tempels, 1962) and unpublished writings, as well as the many instructions I heard and recorded in the field, in which this theme did not appear, albeit often in veiled allusions and images recognizable only to the initiated. Not surprisingly, when Jamaa doctrine extended these notions to its conception of the Trinity and of the roles of Jesus and Mary, this had to create conflicts with orthodox Catholic theology.

This reorientation toward male–female relationships was accompanied by a thorough reevaluation of traditional models that Tempels began to employ more and more in showing the practical consequences of his teachings.

JAMAA CONCEPTIONS OF MALE– FEMALE RELATIONSHIPS

What do we know about the traditional role of women in the culture(s) from which the Jamaa recruits its members? Several difficulties stand in the way to a clear answer. For one thing, members of the movement come from at least 15 different groups in Shaba and Kasai alone. Precisely because southern Zaire is made up of closely related language groups inhabiting roughly similar ecological zones and formerly controlled by vast precolonial "states," these groups tend to stress ethnic differences in most modern contexts. The Jamaa did not *find* a common tradition; it had to create one. Tempels, prophet of a new culture, is also one of our major informants about the old one, inasmuch as he was one of the many missionary–ethnographers who, until recently, were our only source of knowledge. It is, therefore, not only difficult but epistemologically doubtful to attempt to reconstruct the "true" tradition in isolation from the historical and intellectual context that produced the Jamaa as a new religion.

In view of this situation, one is not surprised that the images of the traditional status of women held by observers, supporters, and members of the movement often appear to be contradictory. On the one hand, these ideas did not conform to my expectations. Most of the people I interviewed on the subject gave me statements that echoed the findings of the Reverend Father Colle (1913), a "classical" Luba ethnographer to this day:

> . . . Among the Baluba–Hemba, the woman occupies a
> position which is not given to her in many African
> populations and tribes. She is relatively respected,
> in the village as well as in her family. Occasionally,
> she has her say, and her word often will be accepted
> over that of her husband. In her house, she does as
> she pleases; she accepts marriage freely, she can be

a chief or *masangune* (elected elder). In litigations,
she is admitted as a witness. Often, she is more
persuasive than a man; the young woman is more intelligent than the young man. Her advice has about
the same weight as that of a man. In gatherings, she
sits where she wants (except if privileges have to
be respected). On nights of drinking, she even drinks
with the men. In the Buhabo sect, the *sango–nkazi*
are served by men. There are many women who are
village chiefs. In sum, she is more or less equal to
man, in public as well as privately. (p. 349, my translation)

Accordingly, one finds in Jamaa discourse and imagery many instances in which
traditional models and customs are used to expound the new doctrine. This may
be in the form of references to pacts of monogamous marriage *(lusalo, mak-
widya)*,[4] to the role of the couple in traditional hunters' associations *(buyanga)*,[5]
and to the respective symbolic and ritual roles of Mwant Yaav, the Lunda
emperor, and his first wife. It also carries over into the literary form of marriage
counseling *(shaurio)* that looks remarkably like the speeches by parents
documented from the tradition (Peeraer, 1939, 1943).

On the other hand, Jamaa teaching often seemed to contradict these positive evaluations. In instructions about marriage and in other contexts, speakers
frequently insisted that women were traditionally treated like slaves *(batumwa)*
and that it was only the Jamaa that gave them dignity and equal rights. In the
following excerpt from a conversation with a Jamaa member, both views occur
side by side:

kwa namna ya maungano kati ya	As regards the way wife and
bibi na bwana: mababu wetu wa	husband are together, our
kwanza walijua kabisa/ lakini:	first ancestors knew all
kulikuwa kitu moja akosa/ kwao/	about that. But there was
babibi yao balikuwa kama watumwa:	one thing that was lacking
esclave/ kwa namna moja/ ndio	among them. Their wives
*hiki Jamaa ina*changer*/ anageuza*	were exactly like slaves.
ile/	That is something the Jamaa
	has changed.
lakini kwa mapendo enye ya	But as far as mutual love be-
kupendana kati ya bwana na bibi:	tween husband and wife is
mababu wa zamani: les ancêtres*:*	concerned, our ancesors did
balifanya bitu: yenye hatuwezi	things that even we, their
hata sisi watoto wao sasa/	children, are not capable of.
balikuwa banasaidia babibi yao:	They helped their wives, even
ku hata kushota maji: hata	to fetch water and carry fire-
kubeba mizigo: hata kufanya	wood, or what not.
kitu gani/ hata iko anatembea	And when someone was travel-
na bibi yake hivi: yee hataweza	ing with his wife he could not

[4]The term *makuidya*, describing a custom similar to the *lusalo*, was given to me at Kikondja
(Shaba); see also the entry *–dyà* in Van Avermaet and Mbuya (1954).

[5]On the use of *buyanga* in the Jamaa, see Fabian (1971, pp. 14–15).

kuikala kama bibi hajaikala
hapana/ ndio ilikuwu bububu
wetu wa kwanza/ bakuwa na ile
respect *ile/ baliendelea paka*
vile/

stop if his wife had not
stopped, too. This is the way
our first ancestors were, they
had this respect, and this is
the way they used to live.

lakini pa kitu kamoja kenye
balikuwa nabo: kenye Jamaa ana-
geuza ni: utumwa/ walikuwa wana-
tumia wale wabibi yabo sawa
watumwa/ comme esclaves/ *kwa*
mambo moja/ balikuwa wanawafan-
sia mambo inye ya utumwa/

But they had one small thing
that the Jamaa changed, and
that was slavery. They used
their wives like slaves, now
and then, and did things to
them that belong to slavery.

ile Jamaa anageuza/ bibi si
mutumwa/ anamuona kama mutu/ mi
bwana niko mutu/ bibi ni mutu
kama miye/ hapana mutumwa/ ni
mutu kama miye/ ndio kakipande
kamoja unaona: Jamaa inageuza
kwa namna ya kuwa ya mababu
yetu wa kwanza/

The Jamaa changed that. The
wife is not a slave. [The
Jamaa] regards her as a person.
I, the husband, am a person.
The wife is a person like me.
She is not a slave, she is a
person like me. You see,
that is a small matter
where the Jamaa changed the
ways of our first ancestors.[6]

Plain and slightly redundant as it may seem, this statement contains many of the complex ideological twists that make it impossible simply to ascribe progressive (or regressive) tendencies to the teachings of religious movements such as the Jamaa. By using a seldom heard Kiswahili term for ancestors (*mababu*: in Shaba the usual word would be the Tshiluba loan-word, *bankambo*) the speaker makes it clear that he talks about a *remote* past, a time of "beginnings" (*mababu wa kwanza*). To depict ancestral accomplishments in mutual love and respect between husband and wife he uses counterimages derived from current ways in which female subordination is expressed. Carrying water or firewood are women's chores a man would consider shameful. As we shall see later, marriage in the modern context is often characterized by separate lives of husband and wife. All this is related to the attitude of "respect," a key value likely to be cited in any comparison between times of old and the present. In view of the counterimages invoked, one does not understand very well why the ancestors are being accused of treating their wives like slaves. The point is that the speaker is not interested in accusations. He qualifies the change brought about by the Jamaa as recognition of personhood (*umuntu*, one of the most important doctrinal terms), which the Jamaa characteristically conceives as an *intensification* of tradition—of "what we always wanted." *Umuntu* is the object of the search for a new consciousness appropriate to a society that is to the core urban and "modern" and for which the village past serves as a positive mythical foil.

---

[6]From a conversation recorded by the author on June 26, 1966, at Luaba. The speaker was in his thirties and a member of the Jamaa in Malemba, northern Shaba. Concerning standards of transcription and translation, see Fabian (1971, p. 228).

IDEAL INTERRELATIONSHIPS EXPRESSED
IN JAMAA DISCOURSE

This positive attitude to the past involves neither naive glorification nor does it cause the movement to close its eyes to concrete problems of the present that are in the way of its ultimate goals. With respect to marriage and male–female relationships, the prophetic message of the Jamaa is not one of achieved solutions but of projects based on diagnoses of social evils that are surprisingly astute.

Several devices are employed in Jamaa discourse to deal with the question of male–female relationships. One is the mythical fixation of primordial events and situations. Another one is what could be called an ontological definition of the problem. A third one consists of a selection of concrete pragmatic contexts in which mythical models and ontological principles are supposed to be realized. All this could be followed through to the levels of ritual, dreamlife, and everyday action, but for the sake of clarity and brevity, I will consider only the first three.

I distinguish between ''levels'' of mythology, ontology, and pragmatic context for reasons of descriptive and analytical convenience only.[7] A more thorough interpretation of Jamaa discourse would have to take account of many textual features (such as genre, style, individual and regional variations). Here, I will present only some results obtained from the study of numerous taped, noted, and, occasionally, written texts. Greatly simplified, the main elements of Jamaa thought concerning marriage and male–female relationships are defined and interconnected as shown in Fig. 9.1.

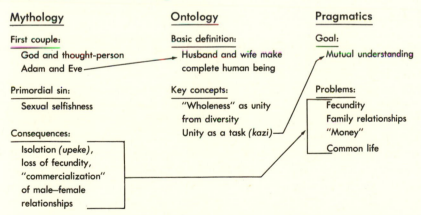

Figure 9.1 Jamaa conceptions of marriage and male–female relationships.

Starting with the left column (mythology), the first and fundamental tenet of all stories of creation is that God ''thought'' himself a companion *muntu mawazo* (thought-person) before he created mankind. I was unable to determine

---

[7]For the results of a componential analysis of Jamaa terminology see Fabian (1971, Chap. 3, esp. pp. 160ff.).

how many members of the movement subscribe to the belief, held by some, that this thought-being was "Myriam" (later on "realized" as the Virgin Mary). There is little doubt that, either in direct statements or as an implication of its doctrinal tenets, the Jamaa places male–female relationship at the beginning, and that it differs in this respect from orthodox Catholic theology.[8]

Adam and Eve, the first human couple, were to live the same "unity in thought" that God had with his companion.

ni kuungana ku mawazo/ kuwa ndoa	To be united in thoughts: true
ya kweli ya kuungana ku mawazo/	marriage means to be united in
ile ilikuwa hata na ule baba wa	thoughts. This is how it was
kwanza na ule mama wa kwanza/	with the first *baba* and the
si tunajua ule mana wa kwanza na	first *mama*.
baba wa kwanza? ni nani? ni	Do we know this first *mama* and
Adam na Eva/ kumbe ni bale	this first *baba*? Who are they?
balituonyesha ndoa ya kweli/	It is Adam and Eve. Therefore
	it is they who show us true
	marriage.[9]

Jamaa teaching is less explicit about what went wrong with the first couple. Like certain earlier Christian interpretations of Genesis, it obviously does not think that the primordial sin was merely an act of disobedience, a transgression of an arbitrary taboo. In all versions I have seen, it "humanizes" that event, alluding to a lack of love and mutual understanding. One account, for example, contains a veiled reference to sexual selfishness (masturbation?) and gives a graphic description of the consequences: loss of fertility and sexual disharmony. When Eve realizes what she did . . .

akaona na macho yake/ sasa ana-	She saw with her eyes and she
anza kueikia haya: na mateso:	felt shame, suffering, and
na upeke paka pale . . . Eva akarudi	loneliness . . . Eve returned to
kwa bwana wake: kinya pasipo	her husband, silent, without
kusema kitu ao kuoma mwili ya	saying anything and without
Adam/ ao Adam anamuita yeye	asking Adam for his body.
kuitikia tena: hapana/	And when Adam called her, she
	did not consent any more.

When God chases them from his field *(shamba)*, his curse is expressed in almost Marxian terms, a diagnosis of a root evil in modern society is perceived by the Jamaa:

munaanza kuuzishana mwili nili-	You begin to sell to each other
mupa wa mapendo . . .	the body of love I gave you . . .
kumbe mwendeni mukauzane na ile	So go and buy each other with
mali yeni mutapata ku jasu	the riches [bridewealth?] you

[8]To be accurate, I should say "from dominant Catholic theology." On the role of Franciscan (Scotist) theology in Tempel's thought, see De Craemer (1973).

[9]From a *mafundisho* (instruction) on marriage recorded by the author of May 6, 1967, at Kolwezi. The speaker is one of the female leaders of the Jamaa.

yenu . . .
wababa na wamama: kuku kwetu
hatuone ile mawazo?

wabibi wengine wanakatala kuo-
lewa: wanataka paka kwenda na
kuuzisha ule mwili wa mapendo ku
franga/   .
. . . na wengine nwanaume wanaacha
ao wanakatala kuowa: wanasema
twiko wambalaka/ wanataka paka
kwenda kuuza ule mwili ku franga/

make from your sweat . . .
Fathers and mothers [address-
ing audience], don't we see
this among us?

Some women don't want to get
married, they just want to go
and sell this body of love
for money.
. . . and some men leave [their
wives] and refuse to marry.
They say, we are bachelors.
They just want to go and buy
that body for money.[10]

Jamaa discourse is replete with statements, standardized formulas, and examples *(mifano)* stressing the ontological unity of man and woman (Fig. 9.1, middle column). It is a unity that grows out of diversity and is maintained through complementarity. Superficially, this may resemble the well-known pleas for harmony that American society seems to know as the only antidote to women's liberation. Jamaa thought differs in two respects. First, it is concerned with unity, not equality. Or, to put it differently, it promotes goals and tasks *(kazi)*, not rights. Second, it always envisages male–female unity in a concrete context that, for this society, is marriage as a child-producing institution. But, as Tempels pointed out long ago, marriage in this society cannot be reduced to legal, contractual relationships between one male and one female; it always entails obligations between groups of relatives. Also, because fecundity is such an all-encompassing value, there is always the potential of extending the child-producing unit beyond the two initial partners. That, according to Tempels, was the rationale for traditional polygyny (its economic foundations notwithstanding), and that is the background to modern-day derivatives of polygyny even in their most alienated and "commercialized" forms.

In a *mafundisho* on the origin and meaning of Jamaa, the following passage clearly expresses the dialectical, processual conception of male–female relationships:

muangarie vile huyu paka muntu
huyu moja/ muntu tu mawazo/ hata
pale Mungu anakuwa kumuweka mu
dunia: tunaona huyu muntu: Mungu
anamupa nyumba mbali mbali/
nyumba muke na nyumba mume/ ni
pahali pa kusema na sisi tufanye
kazi/

tutafute ile kintu kilikuwa na

See how this human being when
it was with God was only one
human being, thought-person.
But when God put it on earth
we see that God gives to this
human being different houses:
a female house and a male
house. What this says is
that we should work.
Let us search for the thing

---

[10]From a written document prepared by the groups in the Kolwezi area; see Fabian (1971, Appendix IV).

Mungu tangu zamani/ kama Mungu
alitufanya wantu wa kimo kimoja:
pengine tulitaka kushindwa namna
ya kufanya kazi/

that was with God in times of
old. If God had made us identical, perhaps we would have
failed to do the work.[11]

Several years later, the same (female) speaker (as in footnote 9) gave this description of marriage problems:

tulibakia mu ndoa siku mingi:
bibi na bwana: she kuwa umoja ule
bapadri balituonyesha nao siku
ya ndoa hapana/ tunakuwa: bibi
na mawazo yake/ bwana na mawazo
yake/
mu nyumba balituambia asema:
hamutakuwa bantu mbili hapana:
mwee bibi na bwana mutakuwa muntu
huyu moya/ pale tunaingia ndani
ya nyumba tunakuwa mukubwa na
mudogo/ tunakuwa chefu na mu-
tumwa/

kumbe sasa bumoja bwetu ni wapi?

We have been married for a long
time, wife and husband, but
the unity into which the priests
joined us on the day of our
wedding we do not have. The
wife has her thoughts, the
husband his. They told us,
in your house you are not
going to be two persons.
You, wife and husband, shall
be this one person.
When we entered the house we
were senior and junior, chief
and slave.
So where is our unity now?

To achieve unity is not just a salutary task, it is an existential necessity rooted in the complementary nature of man and woman. This is vividly depicted in the following passage from an instruction on marriage:

Mungu anatangulia kutuonyesha
mufano mukubwa kabisa kabisa:
katika sisi wenye bantu/ kama
minajisema niko peke yangu:
minajionyesha hii mukono asema
ni mukono mwanaume ni mukono
mwanamuke/ huyu asema/ hii
jicho asema ni jicho ya ngambo
mwanamuke/ hii jicho ya ngambo
mwanaume/ sababu gani Mungu
alituumba vile?
alituumba kwa kujua asema:
atakuwa na wake huyu/ lakini
huyu atapata: ni ule atakuya
kumuonyesha ku bumuntu bote
buzima akuwe yee wote muzima/

For a long time God has been
showing us a very great example indeed. Here I am.
Should I tell myself I am
alone by myself, I only have
to show to myself this arm.
It is the right (male) arm.
And this one is the left (female) arm. This eye is on
the left (female) side, this
eye is on the right (male)
side. Why did God create us
this way? He created us so
we should know: (This man)
is going to be with his (wife)
here so that she will show
him with the help of everything human how to be complete.[12]

[11]From a recording made in 1963 by Msgr. Malunga, now Bishop of the Kamina diocese. The speaker is the one referred to in footnote 9.

[12]From an instruction on marriage recorded by the author on May 10, 1967, at Musonoi. The speaker and his wife were among the first followers of Tempels.

The basic value of complementarity is clearly reflected in structures of organization and leadership. Depending on the history of a Jamaa group, women may assume leading roles, but to my knowledge this has nowhere resulted in a significant predominance of women. Here and there, I found signs of role differentiation between organizers (mostly men) and spiritual leaders (mostly women). But given the low value the Jamaa places on formal organization, these developments, otherwise typical of charismatic movements, have remained rudimentary. Although I cannot presently explore this, I should point out that the strongest factor in maintaining complementarity over hierarchy has been initiation which, in form and content, is pervaded by images and rites of complementarity (see Fabian, 1971, p. 166 ff.).

THE RESOLUTION OF MARITAL PROBLEMS IN JAMAA

Unity and complementarity are not only preached as abstract principles. In the right column of Fig. 9.1, I listed some of the concrete issues that are often the subject of discussions and exhortations. Studying a great number of Jamaa texts, one is struck by the degree to which these issues seem to have become terminologically standardized and "stylized." The pragmatic dimension of discourse, identifying projects and programs of action, thus becomes predictable. In fact on balance, the movement seems to be more concerned with identifying problems than with giving solutions.

One example of standardization is found in the much repeated triad of *masikilizano* (mutual understanding), *masaidiano* (mutual help), and *mapendo* (love). I noticed other signs of standardization when I looked again through my field and case notes, trying to determine typical incidents, topics of conversation, sources of conflict, and concerns regarding male–female relationships. I found that these can easily be grouped under the following four headings:

Fecundity. Offspring are the main goal of marital union. But this should not be misunderstood as concern with biological reproduction only. In traditional society, fertility was the focus of highly elaborated beliefs, rituals, and "magic" practices. As a concept, it allowed numerous and subtle metaphorical extensions beyond its literal meaning. In the Jamaa, many of these were replaced or redefined through the notion of spiritual fecundity *(nzazi ya roho)* that even a childless couple may achieve by initiating and thus "engendering" *(kuzala)* new members to the movement. Stability of childless marriages and deep emotional identification among the spouses are frequently cited as the most impressive achievements of the movement. Conversely, many couples claim to have become fertile after and as a result of joining the Jamaa. In this respect, the movement fitted so much into the mold of traditional "secret" societies and fertility cults that numerous cases were reported where unmarried women (some of them prostitutes in the sense of *femmes libres*) made the journey upcountry from Lubumbashi to Sandoa or Kamina in order to seek fertility in Jamaa groups.

Nuclear Family Versus Extended Kin Groups. Like other urbanites who have become orientated toward a nuclear family, Jamaa members must come to terms with the traditional claims of the husband's and wife's extended kin groups. I found that in their outward behavior, members of the movement tended to meet their obligations and respect customary and legal procedures (such as payment of bridewealth). Within the Jamaa, however, kin relationships are redefined in ways that are well summarized in the following admonition:

kumbe mu kati yetu: kama tuli-
isha kuona: tuache mapendo ya
kutuma mpembeni/ mapendo yetu
ibakie katika nyumba yetu/ na
mama na mi: tukuwe kitu kimoja/
ni kule kunatokea hata mufano
minaita bibi yangu asema ni mama/
kwa sababu yee anakombola mama
yangu/ ni yee anakombola baba
yangu/ yee abakombola chizazi
yangu chote chizima: ni kule
minamuita jina ya mama/

Therefore, as we have seen,
let us give up squandering
love on the side.
Our love should stay in our
house Mama and I, let us be
One.
This is the reason why I call
my wife "mother." It is because she replaces my mother,
she replaces my father.
She replaces my whole family,
this is why I call her by the
name "mother." (see footnote 12)

Money problems. Most discussions about practical problems of marriage and male–female relationships involve "money." This concerns above all the modalities of bridewealth *(mali)* which, under the conditions of an inflationary cash economy, has become subject to market fluctuations and manipulations. Jamaa people do not oppose the idea of bridewealth as such, but fight excesses that made the custom lose its traditional symbolic significance. Cash continues to play an important mediative role once the marriage is concluded. Jamaa husbands are known to share their wages with their wives *(kubalula)* beyond the necessary allocations for food. Jamaa women do the same if they have a source of income. Given the scarcity of cash (the equivalent of U.S. $60.00 would be considered a good monthly wage) and the precarious economic situation in which most of the population live, "money" is a constant and concrete problem on which members of the movement must test and prove their convictions.

A Common Way of Life. One of the major obstacles to developing stable and satisfying relationships in a nuclear family situation is the persistence (and degeneration) of traditional patterns, in which husband and wife used to identify with separate peer groups based on division of labor and leisure activities. In the towns, the absentee husband, spending much of his time with one or the other *liaison* or in bars, often serves as the counterimage to the Jamaa husband. The movement stresses commonality in daily life: common meals, participation in household chores, and long and intensive conversations among the spouses. Contacts outside the nuclear family are provided by the common activities of the Jamaa and especially through the establishment of longlasting networks of friendship and spiritual kinship through initiation. To be sure, this can in turn create problems, especially if husband and wife do not embrace the message with equal fervor. On many occasions, I questioned members and leaders about this point. Typically, they would admit minor difficulties and imperfections only to retreat to the ontological principle of unity. In any case, the mechanics of initiation that always require participation of the couple would make separate involvement inconceivable.

A NEW RELIGION IN ITS LARGER SOCIAL CONTEXT

Having briefly exposed the pragmatics of Jamaa discourse, I should like to raise once more the question that initiated this discussion: In what sense does this religious movement define or transform societal conceptions of male–female relationships? Since I wish to formulate an answer that could be valid beyond the confines of the Jamaa, I find it necessary to insert here a brief recapitulation of the theoretical and methodological principles that up to now have been guiding my interpretations. The argument could be summarized as follows:

1. An important indicator of the specific makeup of a system of beliefs is a distinctive doctrinal terminology. As can be shown on formal grounds and through comparison with other special languages, such as the teachings of the Mission Church, the system of Jamaa beliefs has its own internal structures and external boundaries. It constitutes what could be called the semantic context of the movement.

2. Within the system of doctrinal language, classes or levels of concepts and terms can be distinguished roughly along the lines indicated in Fig. 9.1: mythology, ontology, and pragmatics. If one wishes to examine the significance of doctrinal language for action, one should concentrate on terms and concepts located on the pragmatic level. This should be the point of articulation between words and deeds, ideology and action.

3. Two models—both of which I would now regard as potentially misleading—often serve to conceptualize that articulation. One is the impact model or one of its many variants: A charismatic movement as beliefs-in-action initiates or redirects change in a social system not merely as response to internal imbalance but also an "external source of change." The metaphor underlying this model seems to be derived from celestial mechanics, hence the emphasis on impact. Another model explains *why* a charismatic message may become a source of change that is external, i.e., not reducible to the inner exigencies of the social system it affects. It is usually derived from Max Weber's notion of an *Eigengesetzlichkeit* (autonomy) of belief systems. Despite the fact that Weber

(and Parsons) insisted that this autonomy was a matter of "logic," i.e., of the specific intellectual makeup of a belief system, it seems to me that the underlying metaphor was a historical one. I propose that *Eigengesetzlichkeit* expresses the basic Christian conversion metaphor: Specific and new courses of action are rooted in acts of faith, in embracing beliefs that have a logic of their own, which is beyond human negotiation.

Undeniably, this key metaphor has had a profound influence on viewing articulations between intellectual and social cohesion from Durkheim's (1965) collective representations to T. S. Kuhn's (1962) paradigms. It always involves a *petitio principii*, surreptitious affirmation of that which it sets out to explain. And it had the insidious effect that any social process anywhere in the world could be absorbed by and its interpretation adapted to a peculiar Western conception of relationships between belief and action.

Let me now return to the phenomenon under consideration, male–female relationships as defined in a charismatic movement, and report on a "discovery" that has helped me to articulate my doubts about these models. I spent two periods of fieldwork in the Shaba region of Zaire, both in about the same social context, i.e., among urban wage earners, craftsmen, small entrepreneurs, and hangers-on, both also with intensive efforts to master the Shaba variety of Swahili. From 1966 to 1967, my time was exclusively devoted to the Jamaa, and my social basis was the mission. From 1972 to 1974, I did research on conceptions of work in a metallurgical plant, in a small furniture factory, and among various groups of artists (popular painters and actors). I was then based at the National University. Between the two stays, I had devoted five years to the study and analysis of Jamaa texts. When I returned to Zaire in 1972, I thought of myself as a fairly fluent speaker of Swahili.

The discovery I alluded to came about when I came to realize that my competence in Jamaa discourse proved painfully inadequate in contexts outside the movement. I became aware of the degree to which I had been captured by a closed universe. Paradoxically, I began to recognize Jamaa terminology everywhere and in contexts I did not expect to find it. As the time went on, I recognized not only terms but phrases, formulas, and entire rhetorical structures (such as didactic questions typically used in Jamaa teaching), comparisons between "now" *(sasa)* and "then" *(zamani)*, definitions such as *mapendo ni kusikilizana* (love is mutual understanding).[13] I must admit that, at first, I was tempted to trace these elements back to direct Jamaa influence on popular speech and rhetoric or, perhaps, to a kind of religious–moral discourse that the Jamaa shares with other movements in the area. In some instances, I was able to trace

---

[13]To check on these hunches, I analyzed, among other documents, a recording of the sound track of a TV panel discussion on the topic of marriage (Telézaire, Lubumbashi, *Sisi kwa Sisi*, February 9, 1973). None of the four male and two female participants was, to my knowledge, a member of the movement. Yet, the transcript contains numerous Jamaa-like formulas and discussions of all four problem areas described earlier.

such connections and establish that speakers who sounded Jamaa to me were, in fact, active or former members.

What I observed could have two implications. Either my claims that the movement had developed and was, in fact, somehow constituted by a distinctive language were unfounded, or I had come upon tangible proof of the transformatory impact of the Jamaa on Shaba society.

I cannot accept the first possibility, because I still think that the evidence on which I based my analysis of Jamaa discourse is too overwhelming to allow more than revisions of detail. The second interpretation, diffusion from the movement to the wider society, is tempting but, as I see it now, inadequate. Instead of assuming that even a movement of such importance as the Jamaa should have an "impact" on the wider society, we should explore a more obvious possibility: If everyday discourse in Shaba sounds so much like Jamaa (especially in its pragmatic aspects), it is because the movement is part of, perhaps an intensification of, popular consciousness. This would allow us to abandon impact-and-conversion models, and conceive of charismatic activity as an aspect of social processes comparable to emerging expressions of a new urban folk culture in the visual arts, dance and recorded music, improvisational theater, sports, and other recreational activities.

Theoretically, we always postulated that charismatic leaders and their followers succeed to the extent that they speak the language of the people. In practice, the discovery that this is, in fact, the case can come as a shock, revealing to us that we went too far in letting ourselves get caught in our interpretive schemes and our enthusiasm for the unique qualities of religious enthusiasm. I think as we explore the outer limits of the *significance* of new religions, we must also consider the possibility of their *insignificance* in initiating and shaping social realities.

That research on movements and new religions became so important may have something to do with the fact that, consciously or not, it allowed us to approach changing societies in terms of specific groups, visible leadership, unified ideologies, and distinctive activities. At a time when anthropology began to lose its "tribes" and "kinship groups" in the upheavals of decolonization, movements became the perfect analytical substitute. I think that we will now realize how much these movements have been part of processes in the new mass cultures of Africa. We should apply whatever theoretical and methodological sophistication we have gained from the study of religious enthusiasm to the often exuberant expressions of those new cultures.

10

Conversion, Life Crises, and Stability among Women in the East African Revival

Catherine Robins

The importance of conversion to Christianity in freeing women from many of the constraints of their traditional social roles in African societies has long been noted by administrators, historians, and anthropologists, as well as by apologists for missionary activity (Weber, 1964, p. 105).[1] In Christian movements of indigenous African origin, women have been prominent, particularly in ritual roles. Through their elaboration of ritual roles and their tolerance of expressive religious behavior, indigenous religious movements have created an outlet for women largely absent from the more orthodox mission setting. This paper will examine conversion to one such movement, the East African or *Balokole* Revival, in the geographical area of its origin, southwestern Uganda.[2]

The East African Revival is a large-scale movement of renewal institutionalized within the Protestant churches of Uganda, Kenya, Tanzania, Rwanda, and Burundi.[3] Originating in the activities of the Ruanda [sic] Mission, an ultraconservative offshoot of the larger evangelical Anglican Church Missionary Society,[4] the movement has its theological roots in the great English and

[1]This paper is based on research carried out in Uganda between September, 1970 and April, 1972. The assistance of the Kigezi District Administration, of the Church of Uganda, Rwanda, and Burundi and of the brethren of Kigezi is gratefully acknowledged.

[2]*Balokole*, literally "saved ones."

[3]No sociological study of the East African Revival has yet been published. For an analysis of the development of the Anglican Church in Buganda that contains much information on the Revival there, see Taylor (1958). For a theological evaluation, see Warren (1954).

[4]The Church Missionary Society (CMS) enjoyed a virtual monopoly over Protestant mission work in Uganda. For an account of the controversy that prompted the split of the Ruanda Mission from the larger CMS, see Hewitt (1971, pp. 461–74).

American revivals of the eighteenth and nineteenth centuries. By 1935, when it was firmly established within the churches of Rwanda and southwestern Uganda, it had assumed a thoroughly indigenous character despite its European origins. The evangelical theological emphasis on the necessity of a radical personal experience of conversion and commitment—being "saved" by Jesus—gave rise in that setting to distinctive group structures and normative emphases, including a puritanical code of personal behavior. Nuclei of "saved" Christians emerged within Protestant congregations; open confession to past sins and testimony to conversion became prerequisites to entering the fellowship of the saved. Ongoing participation required the commitment to "testify" through repeated confessions of sin within the group, and to engage in aggressive evangelization among those outside the movement.

The first of the Rwanda Mission stations, at Kabale, the District headquarters of Kigezi, was established in 1921, following about ten years of sporadic mission activity by African evangelists from the adjacent district of Ankole. While the missionaries prayed for a "revival" from the first year of their work the religious life of the district during the next several years was characterized not by massive conversion to Christianity but by repeated confrontations between followers of a traditional spirit mediumship cult of the female deity, Nyabingi, and the missions and administrations.[5] The last of these, in 1928, followed by a few weeks the dramatic conversion to Christianity of a medium of the cult. Her conversion, which brought large numbers of her followers temporarily into the church, generated false hopes of a mass movement toward Christianity among the missionaries.

These hopes were short-lived as her followers drifted away. The military defeat of the last anticolonial rebellion in the same year apparently brought to an end hopes of successful religiously-based resistance to European colonization. More importantly, from the point of view of the missions, it seems to have destroyed the credibility of much of the remaining apparatus of traditional worship in the district, leaving the way open to competing belief systems. Some further description of the social context of the Kiga and Hima societies of colonial Kigezi is essential to a full understanding of the rapid spread of the Revival and of its impact on traditional norms of behavior in those societies.

THE KIGA AND HIMA OF KIGEZI

Kigezi District lies in the extreme southwestern corner of Uganda. Like most colonial administrative units, it is composed of diverse ethnic and political groups. In 1931, it contained about 226,000 people, making this area of roughly 2,000 square miles one of the most densely populated parts of the country

[5]There is a considerable literature on the Nyabingi–inspired risings in Kigezi. It includes Philipps (1928, pp. 310–21), Bessell (1938, pp. 73–86), Hopkins (1970, pp. 258–336).

(Thomas & Scott, 1935, p. 503). These are divided into four major sociopolitical zones, administratively united but culturally distinct. Two of these, Bufumbira and Kinkizi, will not be considered here. Rather, attention will be concentrated on the Kiga counties of central and southern Kigezi and Ruzhumbura, the area to the northeast, bordering on Ankole. These were both areas of massive involvement in the Revival and early mission influence.

The Kiga, inhabiting the colonial counties of Ndorwa and Rukiga, are an acephalous agricultural population who had escaped domination by any of the surrounding centralized kingdoms in the precolonial period.[6] Sharing language and religious traditions with these neighboring areas, they have nevertheless developed a sense of independent cultural identity. The clans who make up the Kiga people are of varied geographical origins; older informants remember traditions of migration north from Rwanda as late as the nineteenth century. But there is sufficient cultural homogeneity to legitimate generalizations about Kiga society as a whole. The best account of Kiga culture and society is given by Edel (1957), who lived in the District in 1932 and 1933.

The people who occupy Ruzhumbura are divided between a small pastoral minority of Hima and a much larger majority of people who cultivate for subsistence. All identify themselves as Hororo, a designation deriving from and symbolizing their political autonomy in the precolonial past under the kingdom of Mpororo.[7] This region, despite its cultural likeness to the larger kingdom of Ankole, refused to be incorporated into it, becoming instead a part of Kigezi District under colonial rule. Agricultural Hororo resemble in all respects the Kiga to the south, and there have been considerable migrations of Kiga into the area in search of land or refuge from political disturbances. The Hima Hororo of the District live much as do their counterparts in Ankole, although by the early 1970s, exclusive pastoralism was becoming almost impossible in Kigezi, where population density was too great to allow free movement of cattle. Among Hima of Kigezi, social separation was maintained through the elaboration of prohibitions, both against social contact with Kiga and agricultural Hororo, and against the practice of agriculture or the use of vegetable food excepting beer. This caste etiquette, perhaps the most distinctive feature of Hima society, served as well to insure the political predominance of Hima ruling families. In Kigezi, rudiments of the precolonial political organization of Ruzhumbura were maintained through the British appointment of county chiefs from within the ruling family.

No ethnographic account of the Hima of northern Kigezi has been written. But their closeness to the pastoralists of Ankole makes it possible to rely on the detailed descriptions of Nkore Hima that exist. Indeed, the most fully studied Hima area, Nyabushozi County in northeastern Ankole, has long had affinities

---

[6]The District is presently divided into six counties: Ndorwa, Rukiga, Ruzhumbura, Bufumbira, Kinkizi, and Rubanda. The last of these was created late in the colonial period.

[7]This kingdom is believed to have disappeared during the eighteenth century. On the origins of Mpororo, see Morris (1962, pp. 17–23) and Karugire (1971, pp. 190–93, 224–30).

with Ruzhumbura in Kigezi; both social relationships and more permanent patterns of migration have linked the Hima of these two areas throughout the colonial period.[8] Two aspects of the societies of the Kiga and Hima would appear to be particicularly relevant to the problem of conversion among women: the roles of women in the persistent features of traditional belief and practice, and the socioeconomic matrix of marriage and family life.

Edel's information on precolonial religious life is fragmentary, and many practices had all but disappeared by the time of her residence in the District, but she gives a picture of the religious life of the Kiga that differs little from that of other peoples of southern Uganda (Edel, 1957, pp. 129–72). Divination and healing were practiced, various observances relating to spirits of ancestors *(abazimu)* were carried out, and a more centralized but still rudimentary version of a widespread cult of tutelary deities *(emandwa)* still functioned. Within ancestor observances, divination, and healing, women had no differentiated roles beyond the provision of beer, always their responsibility. It was in the cults of the *emandwa* that they apparently enjoyed particular prerogatives. Rudiments remained of a specialized cult, the *emandwa z'abakazi* or *"emandwa* of the women," restricted to women devotees and focused on the problem of barrenness (Edel, 1957, p. 146). It was a cult of spirit mediumship, whose followers passed through a ritual of initiation before enjoying the benefits of access to the spirits.

By the 1920s, the ritual centrality of these and other nonlineage-based observances had given way to the cult of Nyabingi. By the end of the nineteenth century, this cult, which may in its inception have resembled those of the *emandwa* in providing means of coping with the recurrent difficulties of daily life, had become highly political in intent. With the emergence of a "priesthood," a fraternity of mediums who assumed the life-style of minor chiefs, demanding tribute and distributing patronage, mediumship becomes a means of aggregating power. The role of medium, traditionally occupied by women, was increasingly taken over by men. With the significant exception of Muhumusa, a Hima woman who used her ritual position in military action against both Rwanda and the British and German administrations, most Nyabingi priests detained or executed for anticolonial resistence in the early twentieth century were men.[9] With the usurpation of power by men within the cult and its subsequent total suppression, the ritual functions it offered to women were eliminated altogether.

---

[8]A full-length monograph on the Hima of Nyabushozi has recently been published, Elam (1973). Stenning (1962) also carried on research in northeastern Ankole during the 1950s. A number of brethren from Ruzhumbura had migrated to Nyabushozi, the most sparsely populated part of Ankole, in search of cattle and land during the late 1950s and early 1960s. They retained close ties with *Balokole* in that area, and during the course of my research, a couple of preaching teams visited Kigezi from that area.

[9]She is commonly described as a widow of the Rwanda Nwami (king) Rwabugiri but was, in fact, Hima (personal communication, Alison Des Forges), 1972. Muhumusa is celebrated as a folk heroine of resistance in Kigezi, and innumerable rural bars and restaurants are named for her. See Hopkins (1970) and Pauwels (1951, pp. 337–57), for a list of *bagirwaor* priests of Nyabingi arrested by British and Belgian authorities.

In the subsistence economy of Kigezi, women had few specialized roles. They were responsible for the bulk of the work associated with the production and preparation of food, including beer, as well as for general domestic labor. By the early 1930s, the cash sector of the economy was still poorly developed. A few women were employed by others in agricultural labor, and labor migration and employment with Europeans, largely taken up by men, were slowly growing in importance (Edel, 1957, p. 89). Women in Kiga society had no independent economic base and little time. While they exercised considerable discretion in the use of economic resources, ultimate control over the products of their labor always rested with their husbands (Edel, 1957, p. 95).

Marriage among the Kiga symbolized the transfer of a woman's productive and reproductive capacities from the household and economic unit of her father to that of the husband (Edel, 1957, pp. 50–71). It was exogamous, patrilocal, and, by preference, polygynous. Cattle were exchanged in bridewealth. Women were given little choice about whom they married, and were powerless to prevent the introduction of a second wife into the household. Elopement did occur, and it was not unknown for girls to run away in protest against a proposed husband. Marriages by elopement, however, had ultimately to be regularized through the exchange of cattle (Edel, 1957, p. 56).

Sexual relations before marriage were severely punished; in common with the people of Ankole and Rwanda, the Kiga regarded premarital pregnancy as a serious offense. Where the identity of the father was known and marriage had taken place prior to the birth of the child, it nevertheless had to be delivered in the bush and killed, an act followed by ritual cleansing of the woman. Where pregnancy was thought to result from incest, the woman herself might be put to death (Edel, 1957, pp. 65–66). This extraordinarily severe attitude toward premarital sex was accompanied by a high degree of tolerance of sexual relations outside of marriage, provided these conformed to an accepted range of relationships and circumstances. Women were permitted, and expected, to sleep with their husbands' brothers and blood brothers. A young woman married to an older man was similarly allowed access to the sons of his earlier wives (Edel, 1957, pp. 66–67). After marriage, relations were characterized by the usual pattern of male dominance, with men free to beat and abuse their wives within socially recognized limits (Edel, 1957, pp. 59–60). Divorce, while unusual, was possible. An unhappily married woman could either return to her family, an action discouraged by relatives reluctant to return the bridewealth, or run away with another man. Fertility was highly valued, and only after her first pregnancy did a woman assume the status of a fully married woman.

This pattern of female subordination was, Edel notes, slowly being eroded by the British administrative requirement of consent. Kiga girls were nominally free to refuse an undesired marriage. In practice few did so, although some, Edel suggests (1957, p. 64), attempted some kind of protest. Where preference was exercised, it was directed toward monogamous marriage to younger men.

While the social structure of Ruzhumbura differed significantly from the

Kiga areas to the south, religious practices were similar. The Hororo, like the Kiga, practiced divination, carried out observances to the *abazimu* or ancestors, and believed in the power of the *emandwa*. In these, the practice of Hima and agricultural Hororo differed little. The Hima of Kigezi would appear by the early 1970s to have had no remaining practices relating to kingship; unlike the pastoralists of Ankole, they observed no royal cult.[10] The cult of Nyabingi, however, had many adherents by the end of the nineteenth century, an affinity that may be explained in part by its special ritual and historical connections with the kingdom of Morporo.[11]

For Hima women in both Ankole and Ruzhumbura, the transition marked by marriage was a radical one. Roscoe (1923, pp. 75–76, 116–17) noted the dramatic contrast between the behavior and physical appearance of Hima girls and women.[12] Fifty years later, Elam (1973) made similar observations. Up to puberty, little sex role differentiation was evident between boys and girls. All children herded small livestock, played together, went virtually naked, and mixed freely with adults of both sexes. Female children appeared to have enjoyed a remarkable degree of freedom up to at least the age of eight or nine (see Roscoe, 1923, pp. 116–17, although Elam, 1973, pp. 85–86, places the transition somewhat later). Girls deemed ready for marriage preparation were removed to the exclusive company of women, were given covering garments (usually hides), and were systematically fattened to conform to the Hima ideal of female beauty through the consumption of large quantities of milk, the only food normally taken by women in Hima society. They were taught the few skills essential to the woman's economic role: basketry, the care of milk pots, and the preparation of butter. Above all, girls were protected from the stigma of possible premarital pregnancy. Both Elam (1973, pp. 53–57) and Roscoe (1923, pp. 120–22) agree on the traditional attitudes toward this offense. Pregnant girls and the putative fathers, if they could be discovered, were drowned or expelled from the encampment. At best, such girls sought refuge among neighboring agricultural Iru with whom they sometimes intermarried (Roscoe 1923, pp. 120–21).

Marriage itself symbolized the dramatic transition in the life of a woman from the preadolescent condition of chastity, relative social freedom, and economic usefulness, to one of extensive sexual license within socially defined limits, and economic parasitism. Prohibited from any contact with cattle and fed on large quantities of milk, the adult woman's economic role was restricted essentially to consumption. It was only in bearing children that she contributed to the life of the group and, as among the Kiga, barrenness was heavily stigmatized. After marriage, women entered a condition of semiseclusion. Completely covered in skins or cloths, with even their faces veiled, they could only be seen by close relatives. In addition, they wore large numbers of heavy copper or iron

[10]The royal drum, Murorwa, symbolizing the power of Mpororo, had long since disappeared.
[11]Pauwels (1951, pp. 337–38).
[12]Roscoe's study is the classic ethnographic account of the people of Ankole.

bracelets or anklets, indicative both of the wealth of their husbands and the lack of physical activity that characterized their lives.

Hima marriage was patrilocal and polygyny was practiced, although it was not extensive.[13] Hima women were married young, occasionally before puberty, and no consent on their part was required. Marriage itself symbolized both a woman's passage from her father's to her husband's household and her assumption of new sexual roles (Elam, 1973, pp. 90–205). While closely guarded from outsiders, Hima women were permitted, and indeed expected, to engage in extensive sexual relationships with various categories of men, including husbands' brothers and blood brothers. Living arrangements after marriage were characterized by an unusually low level of residential and social differentiation. Among fully pastoral Hima, living quarters, always temporary, were very small, and customary prohibitions on proximity found in most societies, were often absent. Elam (1973, pp. 38–41) found adolescent brothers and sisters, daughters and mothers-in-law, and even co-wives sharing sleeping quarters in the same huts. This lack of residential differentiation was perhaps symbolic of the married woman's largely residual economic status in the kraal. With the warning of her reproductive capacities and sexual attractiveness in old age, the position of a woman in the household became even more ambiguous. This, then, was the traditional social context within which the Ruanda Mission operated between 1921 and 1935 in large parts of Kigezi, and from which the Revival emerged.

THE AFRICAN CHURCH AS A VEHICLE FOR THE REVIVAL

The volatility of the religious life of Kigezi District in the early colonial period has already been suggested. The last confrontation between agents of Nyabingi and the Missions and Administration was followed, however, by a brief period of relative quiescence before the outbreak of the Revival in 1935. During this period, the newly established church developed certain distinctive features that can be seen to have later facilitated the patterns of conversion that came to characterize the Revival. Two aspects of social structure are of special interest: the extreme decentralization of church organization and the lack of external supervision of evangelistic activities.

The Ruanda Mission's founders, both medical doctors, quickly established an institutional centre at Kabale, the district headquarters, with hospital, church, and evangelists' training school. But much evangelization during the 1920s and early 1930s was carried on by local itinerant preachers, often semiliterate themselves. Their efforts gave rise to an extensive network of out-schools and churches, usually one-room huts supervised by a single teacher. Here, rudiments of reading and writing sufficient for assimilation of the Gospels and basic doctrine were taught. Through these classes, candidates for baptism were instructed.

[13]See Elam (1973, pp. 90–205) for a complete discussion of Hima marriage.

The Bible in the Nyoro translation could be easily read by literate Kiga and was readily available to all newly baptized converts. Spreading through these informal patterns of evangelism, the church grew quickly; by 1933, there were almost 4,000 baptized members and about 265 out-stations and rural churches in the district.[14]

In Ruzhumbura to the north, the church made somewhat less rapid progress in this period. Among the Hororo agriculturalists, strong identifications of Protestantism with Hima dominance somewhat diminished its appeal, and the Roman Catholic White Fathers actively competed for their allegiance.[15] Baptism records do not fully describe the early Christian community in Kigezi, but we know that young men were predominant. Quick to see the advantages of literacy in gaining mission or government employment, many came to "read," as baptism studies were always described.

The spread of the Revival after 1935 cannot be directly linked either to these early efforts of the missionaries. Rather, it represented the culmination of a series of largely spontaneous individual experiences of conversion from 1935 onward. Originating among catechists and teachers, "salvation" or *okujunwa*, as the movement came to be known, spread widely, and conversions of "pagans" and those familiar with little more than the rudiments of Christian doctrine were noted during the first year. By 1936, the Revival had taken on some aspects of a mass movement. Large numbers of people were gathering in village churches, praying and singing well into the night. While the movement remained nominally orthodox in doctrine, conversion was marked increasingly by charismatic phenomena—visions, voices, trance states, and uncontrolled shaking.[16]

Within two years, the movement had spread into Ruzhumbura, where these manifestations took on even more dramatic form. Throughout this period, missionaries made few efforts to control these situations while expressing concern about their inability to do so. Fearing a dampening of the enthusiasm that seemed to be encouraging conversions, they restricted their activities to the discouragement of mass phenomena that seemed likely to cause difficulties with the local authorities and to efforts to reassure them of the movement's innocuous character. Much of the local activity was left in the hands of African catechists and the Ganda pastor, working out of Kabale, who was the only ordained African in the district. In this way, the lay leadership of the movement remained intact. In 1938, the evangelistic work of the district was put in the hands of the English missionary most closely associated with the Revival. A medical doctor, he was

[14]These figures are derived from the baptism register, St. Peter's Church, Kabale.

[15]The Catholics established a large mission and school at Nyakibale, near the Protestant central church in Ruzhumbura. Conflict between the two groups was frequent and sometimes violent throughout the colonial period.

[16]These conditions entered the local vocabulary. The period of religious enthusiasm is described by older informants as *okucugusibwa*, a word of unknown meaning that was unfamiliar to missionaries who had worked in the District at this time.

released from hospital duties to devote full time to church work and served, in effect, as Rural Dean of the district up to 1946.[17] His personal sympathy with the movement's evangelistic methods and the continued shortage of other European personnel in the district during the war years ensured the development of an ecclesiastical structure in Kigezi compatible with the methods and objectives of the emerging Revival.

NORMS AND VALUES IN THE REVIVAL

How can the Revival movement be described? Operating within the transplanted church it lacks clearly defined organizational forms. It must be defined, instead, in terms of practice and belief.[18] The central religious fact in the life of a Revival "brother" is the experience of conversion or acceptance of Jesus Christ as "personal savior." To be saved is not an act of will but, rather, an experience. It is accessible, however, only to those who are open to it and genuinely repentant of their sins. It is always immediate and unmistakable, and it marks a radical discontinuity in the life of the believer, whether professing Christian or not. In both a theological and social sense, he achieves a new identity.

In the early period, conversion was often marked by a dramatic and frightening encounter with the Christian supernatural in the form of visions, voices, or dreams. While these manifestations never became necessary conditions of salvation, they were widely accepted as authentic, particularly in the conversion experiences of those formerly outside the church. For the newly converted Christian, whatever his background, incorporation into an existing fellowship of the "saved" was dependent on willingness to give evidence to the group of repentance of past sins through open confession. This custom, described by one observer as "ordeal by confession" (Taylor, 1958, pp. 103) generated intense controversy within the Mission and the church.

For all, behavioral conformity to the rigid norms of the Revival community was expected following profession of conversion. In the absence of any clear biblical injunctions on many areas of daily life, standards emerged that represented a synthesis of indigenous cultural values and nineteenth–century evangelical prejudices. To the obvious transgression of theft, murder, and adultery were added polygyny, drinking, smoking, and dancing. Personal adornment of any kind was rejected as a manifestation of "worldliness," and all traditional religious practice and many customs having little religious content were branded as "pagan." In Kigezi, where many were converted from outside the church,

---

[17]This was Joe Church. As a doctor and unordained man, he could not, of course, act as Rural Dean.

[18]There are several descriptions of the "liturgy" of the Revival fellowship meeting, based on observations in different parts of East Africa, that agree in all significant details. See, for example, Warren (1954, pp. 118–21) and Stenning (1965, pp. 272–73).

traditional practices reinterpreted in Christian terms were sometimes incorporated into the life of the fellowship. The criteria that ultimately determined the acceptability of a practice, however, never compromised the standards of Christian morality represented by the ultraevangelical Ruanda Mission. Rather, traditional values tended to govern those areas on which the Mission and Bible were silent. This can be seen both in the early tolerance of conversion phenomena, such as visions and shaking, and in the subsequent highly selective acceptance of traditional norms of clan exogamy and payment of bridewealth within the new community.

As the spiritual fervor of the early period cooled somewhat, patterns of meeting and worship were shortened and routinized. By 1936, in many parts of the district, small nuclei of saved Christians within larger church congregations were meeting two or three times weekly for prayer, mutual confession, hymn singing, and the reception of new followers. Within these groups, distinctive norms of interpersonal conduct developed, facilitating the maintenance of the puritanical standards of personal moral conduct expected of the brethren.

The most important of these were complete openness among the brethren, and a temporal equality that reflected their commitment to the spiritual equality of all believers. The immediate social structural consequences of these emphases were a highly decentralized social structure of independent leaderless fellowship groups varying in size from five or ten to, perhaps, fifty and the acceptance of a pattern of consensual decision-making within these groups.[19] Differentiation between leaders and followers was denied legitimacy in the community of the saved. In practice, certain individuals within each group did assume greater authority, subject always to control by others through charges of sinfulness or pride. Group sanctions were exercised against those seen to be seeking leadership or attempting to reach important decisions, however personal, without reference to the group.[20]

Incorporation into such a community inevitably underminded existing associations of kinship and friendship for the new believer. The fellowship, constituted as a quasi-kinship group, assumed many of these functions for the brethren. Saved Christians were rigidly endogamous, and suitable husbands and wives often were selected and always approved of by the group. For poorer brethren, bridewealth was supplied by the fellowship and marriage was presided over by the group. More significantly, perhaps, senior members of the Revival opened their households to converted adolescents fleeing pagan homes.[21]

From the outset, evangelistic activities occupied a central place in the life

---

[19]An interesting illustration of this pattern in practice is given by Smoker (1971, pp. 96–108).

[20]One of the leading brethren was bitterly criticized by more conservative older brothers for his decision to accept a graduate fellowship to study theology in the United States, a step taken without consultation with the community.

[21]The most important of these was a Kiga leader living in Ruzhumbura, who took in a number of adolescents. This tradition is still maintained in Buganda among older more conservative leaders.

of the fellowship. The relations of the brethren with those outside, both pagans and nominal Christians, were governed by efforts to bring them to the point of conversion. Central to the protocols of successful evangelization was the statement of testimony, a highly personalized account of conversion. Revival brethren testified at every opportunity. In the early period, much preaching was carried on in markets and on roadsides, and special efforts were directed at close kin and friends. Here, preexisting social networks were activated for the purpose of bringing friends and relations to a realization of the need for their own conversion. In densely populated Kigezi, contacts among agriculturalists were frequent, and public preaching easily attracted large crowds.[22] In Ruzhumbura, among Hima pastoralists, extensive itineration, carried on in the exchange of cattle and in negotiation of bridewealth, provided a means of communicating the message of the Revival.

By mid-1936, the organization of evangelization was routinized through the establishment of preaching "teams." These small bands of converts, often of very diverse social composition, traveled about the country on foot, sometimes camping in village churches and holding weekend meetings for preaching and the reception of new believers into the fellowship. In Kigezi and Ruzhumbura, the existing network of out-stations facilitated their traveling, while the egalitarian norms of the movement insured the participation of women and girls. They preached in groups or in mixed teams, and their absences from home sometimes generated intense conflicts.[23] They also served as graphic evidence of the new status enjoyed by women in the Revival fellowship. Early preaching always featured testimonies while stressing the perils of damnation and the need for swift and unconditional repentance and acceptance of Jesus as "personal savior."

Testimonies rapidly became stereotyped through repeated telling, conforming to the evangelical conversion cycle of sinfulness, repentance, and realization of the power of Jesus to save. As such, they described in highly personal terms an individual's passage into the Christian community. At the same time, as Stenning (1965, p. 271) and others have noted, they reflected the central concerns of the societies in which the Revival developed. Through the catalog of sins they invariably presented, the norms of both communities—the traditional and the Christian—were made explicit.

By looking at several accounts of conversion in the Revival, we may be able to see beyond the individual concerns to the social dimensions of this phenomenon. We will look first at the testimonies of two Kiga women, both of them familiar with the church prior to conversion:[24]

[22]One informant, a young man from northern Rwanda, clearly remembered the crowd that collected for the visit of a preaching team to a neighboring hill during his childhood.

[23]See the entries of the District Commissioner in the *District Tour Book*, Kagunga, Ruzhumbura, Aug. 8, 1945, and Kebisoni, Ruzhumbura, Sept. 19, 1946, Kigezi District Archives. Both refer to fines levied on church teachers for taking girls out on preaching missions.

[24]These and the testimonies of Hima women that follow were tape recorded in Kigezi in 1971. The texts are literal translations of the testimonies.

Everina B., Kiga woman in her fifties

[Her father was a priest of an *emandwa*. She defied him by going to "read" at the church and was baptized before her marriage. When her husband, a nominal Christian, left work as a teacher and went to work for the government, he started drinking heavily. He urged her to stop going to or working for the church. Their children were refused baptism because of the drinking.]

It pained me much to see that I was a Christian and my children could never be baptized. We became very rich and my husband decided to marry a second wife, and from then onwards, he rejected everything about religion. He rejected me, too, although we remained together at home. Then, when I was at home feeling very miserable, a voice, perhaps a voice of God who created me, told me to return to the ways of the church . . . I obeyed the voice and returned to the ways of Christianity. I began to cooperate with the brethren. I now started attending church services, going to work [communal labor for the church] on Tuesdays, and even paid church funds.

As I was sitting in my house, I heard the voice of the Lord, telling me to accept Jesus in my life. There was no preacher present nor was I in a fellowship meeting. Only I heard the voice saying, "Accept Jesus in your life." I accepted Jesus . . . now a child could be baptized providing one of his parents was a true Christian . . . and my children were baptized. Then Jesus forgave me all my sins—those concerning my sorrowful life, those about the separation between my husband and me, those about looking after my children on my own, and many others . . . My husband rejected me completely, and I had to bring up my children on my own . . . Poor 'though I was, Jesus helped me to raise the money with which I sent some of them to school . . . My husband is very rich . . . but there is no connection between us.

Judith K., Kiga woman of the same age

[Her father practiced traditional offerings to one of the *emandwa*, and she assisted him. She began studying for baptism and then eloped.]

In eloping I found that I was to be with that women [she points to a woman who is present in the room] . . . Our man was a Christian, but he didn't want to go to church. When he died, we started going to church, but at first I refused, saying that we used to prepare beer. How can I stop drinking it? So our old one [the senior wife] went on alone, and she was baptized and saved. Later, I left beer, and I was taught and baptized . . . Myself, I said, "I can't be saved . . . what shall I gain by being saved?" I stayed a Christian, but I still committed adultery, and I was not able to give birth . . . I had a pregnancy, but I miscarried. From then, I was barren. When she got saved, I kept laughing at her, saying that she had gone mad. And I said that I would never be saved . . . Do I become saved so that I can start giving birth? . . . Later, it was on Thursday, when the voice called me and came to me in our church, Hamurwa, and then I was saved.

These testimonies, which typify the experiences of a large number of Kiga women in the fellowship, bear certain common features. The women had some contact with church prior to their conversion and considered themselves at least nominal Christians. Both had come from pagan homes with which they had broken through their efforts to read for baptism. But conversion was precipitated for each woman by a set of personal circumstances that we may define as a "life crisis." For each it was an experience perceived as a direct confrontation with the Christian supernatural.

Some of these crisis situations can be characterized as "traditional," typical of Kiga society, particularly the tensions aroused by a polygynous household, and the stigma attaching to infertility. Others are specific to the emerging Christian culture in Kigezi such as denial of baptism or the desire to be accepted as a full member of the church through salvation. Indeed, by the mid–1940s, failure to be converted into the Revival was widely seen as an inability to meet the full institutional requirements of the church, as the refusal to baptize children of parents who drink alcohol suggests.[25] Two distinct types of crisis or stress situations can be identified, then: those that reflect a woman's failure to cope with traditional demands, and those that arise from an inability to meet the new and rigid standards of the Christian community. In both cases, conversion provided a means of coping with these pressures.

Among preponderately pagan Hima girls and women, pressures of the first kind, derived from customary social situations, were of overwhelming importance in the conditions surrounding their conversion into the Revival. As the accounts of their conversion illustrate, these crisis situations clustered around the central social role played by the Hima woman: wife and sexual object. They also reveal the particular dilemmas of members of a caste-stratified society. Let us look at two such accounts. The first woman was converted in adolescence.

Faith B., Hima woman, born about 1930

I was born in a big pagan family, and they did not allow anyone to go to church. But in 1941, I heard that there was *okujunwa* [salvation], that anybody who entered *okujunwa* would never go to Gehena . . . The power of God . . . found me in the home . . . It was a Sunday. I escaped and went to the church. I found people preaching. That day I didn't go home. I believed and became saved. Then I stood in the church and told all my sins. When I was still a girl, I used to commit fornication with boys. I used to steal . . . I was a girl of sorrows, because my father died when I was still

---

[25] In requiring total abstinence, the churches in Kigezi were exceeding the requirements of the Anglican Church of Uganda of which they were a part. This equation of Revival standards with those of the full church was a continual source of friction in relations with the Bishop of Uganda.

very young, and I used to cry. The sin of fornication caused that disease [venereal disease] when I was still young. My father left me with my brother who made that sin with me, who slept with me. When I felt I should be saved, I thought I would be ashamed when I repented, but I saw that other girls had repented and in their testimony said similar things to mine.

They used to beat me every day. It did not stop me. They even stopped me from going to church . . . They would bruise my body, and blood would come through my nose and mouth. But I would hear a person of great strength telling me to continue . . . until my brothers no longer beat me but determined to give me nothing to wear . . . one of the Christians gave me a mat. I slept on it during the night and covered my body with it during the day. Soon the mat was flying in tatters. They gave me a skin. The skin covered only the front. Some women were ashamed of my nakedness, so one gave me a piece of cloth . . . After I was saved, I ate chicken [a traditional prohibition among Hima]. For it was a deed for women to eat chicken. My parents refused to give me milk for three years. We, my sister and I, ate and drank water. I didn't know whether I would be getting married because of the disease I had mentioned . . . but getting married and producing children I could do without, as I had already been saved. But in July 1944 God gave me a home.

The testimony which follows is of a woman converted as an adult.

Faith K., Hima woman about fifty years old

I was born in a pagan home . . . When I was already married, in 1941, I heard that there was *okujunwa*. When I heard about *okujunwa*, I didn't at first accept it, because I thought it wouldn't do any good for my sins I had already committed . . . When I reached the church, I found there people with whom I had grown up repenting, and those with whom I had sinned were repenting. And I had done many deeds. I committed adultery. I used to steal. I used to go looking for beer with a group of men wherever they went. I used to do many things anywhere, anytime, even in the bush . . . In 1941, December, I believed and became saved. But then I had a husband, and we had one child. When I became saved, he sent me from his home. When he sent me home, I put away my rings from the legs and arms, and I covered myself with a piece of cloth like this from there. When I ate a chicken, put off those bracelets and the cloth, he sent me away. I agreed and went to my father's home. My brother sent me away too. I went to stay in other people's homes. Meanwhile my brother became saved. He took me home again. My husband accused me in court, but I refused completely. From there he sent me away completely, and his dowry was returned to him. I preached, told my testimony to people, and went with

Jesus. While I preached and gave my testimony, God gave me Ernesti K., and we married in the church.

These testimonies reflect similar concerns to those of Kiga women. But they also focus on certain distinctive features of Hima society in Kigezi. Unlike the Kiga women whose testimonies have been examined, these women had little or no experience of the church prior to their contact with Revival preaching. Through repeated testimony, the emphasis on the totally pagan background of the new convert has become exaggerated.[26] The nature of Hima society and the late expansion of the church into Ruzhumbura give credence to claims that they were largely unfamiliar with Christian teaching at the time of conversion. Like the Kiga women, they describe a condition of extreme "moral depravity," probably exaggerated, before conversion. Here, however, significant differences in emphasis can be identified. As Stenning noted in writing of the Hima of Ankole (1958), those saved in the Revival tend to describe their former sinfulness in terms of transgressions both of traditional and Christian norms of conduct. The full catalog of sins is comprehensive. It includes drinking, traditional worship, adultery, fornication, and stealing, as well as sexual transgressions such as incest and sexual relations "in the bush," both strongly sanctioned in traditional society.

We have suggested that certain situations of "life crisis" tend to become foci of conversion among women in Kigezi. Among the Hima women of Ruzhumbura, these surround marriage and sexual relations. In a society where adult women are largely confined to these social roles, marriage and sexuality become of overwhelming concern. The most common to these is probably the dilemma posed by an unwanted marriage. Of the women interviewed, two were converted in adolescence at a time when they were faced with the prospect of marriage to pagan men chosen for them by their families. Others, converted after marriage, record a history of serious conflict with their husbands or husbands' kin, men who in traditional society would have had sexual access to them. For the Hima woman, the conflict created by contact with Christian teaching was particularly acute. While polygyny was not generalized, the patterns of sexual behavior allowed to and expected of a woman were totally incompatible with Christian moral standards. That the Revival was not simply a refuge for Hima women rendered sexually unattractive and socially marginal by old age, as Elam contends (1973, p. 215), is clearly shown by these testimonies. His observation that membership "virtually precludes unmarried girls and young wives" is not supported by available evidence. Many of the older generation, as these testimonies demonstrate, were converted in their youth as adolescents and young wives, and large numbers of young women with infants are still visible at gather-

---

[26]Testimonies of Hima brethren typically began with a phrase that literally translated means, "My family were very, very pagan."

ings of the saved.[27] It would appear, then, that the "crisis of aging" is only one life crisis among women met through conversion.

This transition was a radical one. How did the new community of converts provide a solution to the difficulties created by this break with tradition? Through the kinship functions they assumed—their selection of husbands and wives and provision of bridewealth—the brethren facilitated the detachment of new converts from the old life while maintaining their own norms of group endogamy. To adolescents not yet ready for marriage, they provided refuge, clothing, and food. In a community where caste etiquette rigidly proscribed contact between Hima and Kiga, one Kiga evangelist advertised the radical character of the new community by taking young converts from both groups into his household. And Hima converts signaled their rejection of tradition through widespread violation of caste prohibitions, behavior that served to further isolate them from unconverted kin and friends. On conversion, Hima women, as we have seen, rejected both food prohibitions and established conventions of dress and deportment. As these accounts suggest, the sanctions exercised by families of converts followed traditional lines. Access to milk for sustenance and hides for clothing, always controlled by men in Hima society, was denied to converted women and girls.

It is not always possible to separate the crises that precipitated conversion from those that followed upon this change of status. Entry into the community of saved Christians frequently exacerbated existing sources of tension within families, as wives were encouraged to free themselves from the constraints of customary control by their husbands. Widespread disobedience by converted wives and children was noted with concern by African officials and by the district commissioner, and more than once was brought to the attention of the Mission. In 1938, in remote Kinkizi, on the Congo border, the District Commissioner observed that:

> The present revivalist enthusiasm of the CMS [Ruanda Mission] had been particularly powerful in this Saza . . . The result has been particularly disturbing to the women, who have refused in some cases to cultivate at all, and have forsworn beer, tobacco, and beads, and made a habit of night services—the resultant hysteria has caused a good deal of ill feeling.[28]

Four years later, the same complaints arose about the effects of the Revival on women:

[27]This was particularly striking at a convention of some 6,000 brethren of a schismatic faction strongly supported in Nyabushozi, held in Kampala in 1970. At local meetings in Kigezi, including one at which a team from Nyabushozi were present, both young women and large numbers of men were in evidence. Elam cites a sex ratio in the movement of four women to one man based on "census data." In view of the absence of any recorded statistical data on the composition of the movement, it is difficult to see the basis for his statement. He may be using figures on church membership to generalize about the Revival fellowship, but they represent, at best, 10 to 15% of those on church rolls.

[28]*District Tour Book*, Kinkizi entry, April 1, 1938, Kigezi District Archives.

> Considerable dissatisfaction was caused throughout the District by the teaching of the more advanced members of the "Twice Born" movement [the Revival] as it has led to the undermining of parental control over children and more especially over young women.[29]

Analysts of indigenous churches in Africa have greatly emphasized the selective adaptation of local movements to such strongly rooted customs as polygyny and ancestor veneration. Barrett (1968, p. 116), for example, argues that in failing to recognize the centrality of polygyny to the life of many African groups and its place as "a necessary element in the economy, a matter of prestige for men, a guarantee of security for women, and a foundation of family, clan, and tribe," the missions laid the way for the formation of independent movements.[30] But these and other accounts of conversion in the Revival suggest that women come into the movement seeking religious legitimation for the *rejection* of polygynous unions rather than a religious accommodation with polygyny. The Revival fellowship offered social support and religious legitimation to radical departures from customery marriage. Women, in particular, were offered new social and ritual roles within the fellowship. They participated in preaching teams and carried on personal evangelism; through their association with the church, they became literate. In the presence of Revival norms of consensual decision-making, they exercised equal control with men over the choices central to the life of the fellowship.

A broader view of the processes surrounding conversion is suggested by this attempt at understanding conversion in the East African Revival. While the experiences of Kiga and Hima women in the early Revival reveal only one aspect of a larger phenomenon, they call into question some of the dominant interpretations of this process. Studies of conversion into African religious movements have tended to stress the cognitive element, the ability of such movements to provide alternative explanations of social reality to men and women faced with unfamiliar social situations. In writing of religious change in West Africa, analysts such as Horton (1971, pp. 85–108; 1975, pp. 219–235) and Peel (1968) have interpreted the acceptance of Christianity in both its mission and independent forms in terms of its ability to explain unprecedented misfortunes in a time of rapid social change. Stenning, adopting a wider approach, has suggested (1958, p. 12) that the religious life of the Hima of Ankole in the late 1930s was characterized by a "ritual, dogmatic and . . . moral vacuum" filled for some by entry into the fellowship.

In looking at the life experiences of women, we would emphasize the moral and ritual aspects of religious change. The Revival, unlike many indigenous churches, offers neither simple explanations of misfortune nor supernatural means of coping with it. Healing is not practiced and the religious enthusiasm of

---

[29]Kigezi District *Annual Report*, 1942, Kigezi District Archives.

[30]Barrett (1968, p. 118), however, emphasizes the strict monogamy of the Revival brethren.

the early period, central to the conversion of many older brethren, has largely been eliminated.[31] The fellowship did, however, offer radical alternatives to existing modes of behavior in Kigezi, where traditional religious practice had lost all viability. And this was of particular importance to women. The decline of the *emandwa* of the women and their replacement by the cult of Nyabingi whose ritual offices had been usurped by men and turned to political purpose destroyed the credibility of the only remaining means of religious recourse left to women in dealing with recurrent life crises. The Revival filled this vacuum, not by providing alternative supernatural means of manipulating fate, but by creating a new society.[32]

---

[31]Stenning (1958, p. 115) characterizes the attitude of the brethren toward disease and healing as "compulsive hygiene." He explains this in terms of their tendency to equate illness with sin. The attitude of Kigezi Hima brethren toward illness is distinctly Western and rational, not only in their scrupulous hygienic measures but in the inordinate amounts of time they spend in visiting the sick and attending clinics. Examination of early testimonies suggests that the movement may, in the enthusiastic period, have served some of the therapeutic functions of a cult of affliction, not in providing for physical healing but in meeting psychological stress among women.

[32]See Robins, C. E. *Tukutendereza:* A study of social change and withdrawal in the *Balokole* revival of Uganda. Doctoral Dissertation, Columbia University, 1975.

11

Islam, Sex Roles, and Modernization in Bobo-Dioulasso

Lucy Quimby

In the late nineteenth century, the Dyula community in Bobo-Dioulasso, Upper-Volta, numbered between five hundred and a thousand inhabitants. Sia, as the town was then called, consisted of a cluster of five small villages. The dyula lived in one of them. Nearby villages contained colonies of Dyula related to those in Sia. An extensive network of trade routes connected Sia with communities to the south, northwest, north, and northeast. The Dyula had come to Bobo-Dioulasso from Kong, where they had overthrown the rulers and established their own dynasty near the beginning of the eighteenth century (Quimby, 1972, pp. 11–12, Binger, 1892, p. 365).

Dyula males unquestionably dominated this society. Patrilineal and patrilocal, the identity of the various Dyula lineages revolved about the activities of their male members and ancestors. A description of the social structure must, therefore, begin with an examination of these lineages and their interrelationships. As one might expect of men in a militaristic society such as this, they both denigrated and feared the domestic, nurturant sphere of life to which they relegated their women. The public religious rituals of the Dyula community illustrate the community's understanding of the proper role of each major social group, including women. When a period of rapid social change in the twentieth century eroded many of the political and economic bases of male dominance, men turned to religious ideology and ritual to defend their dominant position. Many of the women demonstrated the reality of their new independence by refusing to modernize their religious ritual according to male directives.

In the nineteenth century, Dyula patrilineages were of two occupationally specialized and historically distinct kinds, the *sonangui* and the *karamoghou*.

Sonangui males were a warrior elite who based their military power on horses imported from the north and, when they became available, guns imported from the coast. They lived in a symbiotic relationship with their *karamoghou*, male Muslim clerics who eschewed political or military activity and devoted themselves to Muslim scholarship, including the making of charms, and to long–distance trade. This type of complementary alliance between a ruling group whose interests were mainly politico–military and lineages who defined their identity in terms of Muslim scholarship and an avoidance of worldly politics was common to many parts of West Africa (Curtin, 1971, pp. 11–24).

Both *sonangui* and *karamoghou* are of Malinke origin. At least one of the *karamoghou* lineages traces its *isnād*, or transmission of scholarship, back to the fifteenth–century scholar, Al-Hajj Salim Suwari of Dja (in Massina) (Wilks, 1968, pp. 177–78). *Sonangui* society was politically unstable. In theory, each *sonangui* lineage owed obedience to the *gurutigi*, the oldest male of the earliest living generation. When he died, the next oldest man of his generation became *gurutigi*, until there were no more members of that generation. Then the succession passed to the oldest member of the next generation. In practice, the *gurutigi's* sons apparently often resented having the leadership pass to their uncles, and they sometimes left to conquer new territories for themselves. Distance guaranteed the desired degree of autonomy.

Sonangui wealth depended largely on tribute extracted from conquered populations. Military action, actual or threatened, was usually necessary to insure the payment of this tribute. Protecting trade caravans also required military force. *Sonangui* males were often belligerent and aggressive in order to maintain their political position. The ideal *sonangui* male was forceful, domineering, and always ready to take violent action, (Bamori Watara, March 25, 1970; the names and dates cited here and in subsequent pages refer to conversations between the author and individuals in the Dyula community in 1969 and 1970).

Domestic violence was also common. Wives and children were beaten. Members of other lineages traditionally had the power to stop fights between two *sonangui*; this allowed the preservation of family life without destroying the military honor of the disputants.[1] As one old man summarized the violent aspects of the male *sonangui* self–image, "In the old days, if you slapped a Watara, you died for it."

Sonangui males were preoccupied with power. The order and generation of one's birth conferred a certain political position. Also of crucial importance was a man's reputation as a warrior and the size of his military following. Important men recruited a following from among members of their own families and by buying and capturing slaves. Powerful men had very large families. Wives were

[1]The Watara were *senanku* or "joking cousins" to the Kulibali. Members of each group relied on the other for assistance, required each other's presence at certain religious rituals, and had the right to limit each other's violence and help negotiate each other's disputes (Ladji Babu Watara, March 16, 1970; cf. Dieterlen, 1951).

useful as bearers of children. Male children could become warriors, and female children could be exchanged for wives for their brothers. These exchanges of women in marriage cemented politically useful alliances. A strong leader often had more than thirty wives, both slave and free.

The *sonangui* and the *karamoghou* with whom they allied themselves understood the universe according to a cosmological model that was the same for both groups in its broad outlines. According to this model, life on earth included both visible and invisible beings and events. *Jinn*, mentioned in the Quran, were like humans but usually invisible. They could take any shape. *Wokoloni* were tiny men with their feet attached backward who had access to secret powers. *Subaghau* were people who secretly ate other people's souls. Visible, publicly observable events like a battle often had hidden aspects as well—the power of a victorious warrior depended not only on his physical strength and military training, but also on a whole array of super–human protections whose preparation was the secret knowledge of trained *karamoghou*.

Ruling over both the visible and invisible realms and determining their activities was God. He controlled the earth, heaven, and hell and areas beyond. He was eternal. Dyula society thus operated under a dual system of command. The *sonangui* ruled the areas they had conquered, while God controlled the universe from on high.

This understanding of the structure of the universe had different implications for the *sonangui* and the *karamoghou*. *Sonangui* men were interested in what they could get through their political and military activity. The spiritual leaders of the *karamoghou* community believed that the best way of strengthening the influence of God's way on earth was to avoid taking on the responsibilities of government themselves. The ideal *karamoghou* male was a man close to God who spent his time in prayer and studying Muslim theology and law. By such means, the *karamoghou* thought they were assured a place in heaven.

The *sonangui* depended upon the *karamoghou* to mediate their relationship with God. The clerics linked man to God in the rites of passage and the various annual rites. They made charms to influence God's use of His powers in relation to humans. Engaged as they were in strongly competitive behavior, *sonangui* men were interested in anything that would give them an advantage over their rivals or enemies, and the *karamoghou's* relationship with God provided them with access to the unseen world. Each *sonangui* lineage had a *karamoghou* lineage that "belonged" to it. The ties were ritual, economic, and political. In return for speaking with God on behalf of the *sonangui*, members of the *karamoghou* lineages received goods and political protection. *Sonangui* fathers sometimes gave their daughters as wives to *karamoghou* men free of any marriage payments.

Sonangui men seemed to have acknowledged the value of the Islamic tradition chiefly through their relationship with the *karamoghou*. Aside from an often minimal participation in Muslim community rites, the *sonangui* of Gouiriko were not themselves observant of Muslim mores. They drank huge quantities of *dolo*, a fermented brew. They neglected the five daily prayers. The name *sonangui* itself means "one who makes sacrifices," that is, sacrifices to Malinke spirits or ancestors. The *sonangui* preserved elements of their pre-Islamic religious heritage, such as the observance of *tana* or ritual behavior associated with lineage totems, and belief in the return of the *ni* or vital spirit of a dead ancestor in each child being born. Facial scarification was another non-Islamic practice. In spite of these lapses in behavior, from the Muslim view, they identified themselves as Muslims through their alliance with "their" *karamoghou*.

One of the major social divisions was, thus, that between warrior *sonangui* and religious *karamoghou*. Another was that between men and women. Women were *not* included in the positive role definitions of *sonangui* and *karamoghou*. A woman's inclusion in one or the other of these groups was based on her family or marital alliance.

Men defined women as lacking in the essential attributes of the *karamoghou* and *sonangui* roles. For the *sonangui*, anyone who didn't fight was "like a woman." *Sonangui* war garments were dangerous to women; a pregnant woman standing down wind of one would miscarry. For the *karamoghou*, following Quranic ideas, women were legally inferior and ritually unclean. Legally, a woman's testimony was equivalent to half that of a man, her proportion of an inheritance was less than that of her brothers, her rights in marriage were less than those of her husband. When her husband died, she belonged to one of her brothers-in-law. Ritually, women were a source of pollution. A menstruating woman was unclean and might neither pray, fast, nor have sexual intercourse with a man. Men washed after intercourse to rid themselves of impurities. The Dyula claimed that the *toto*, a species of robber rat that displayed an interest in human possessions, was originally a man who went to sleep after intercourse without doing his ablutions and died in that polluted state (Kokasori Watara, July 6, 1970; Bamori Watara, May 16, 1970).

Women presented other dangers. Men felt that male impotence and, at times, social and economic failure were the results of a wife's "hard-headedness." Women, therefore, posed an essential threat to the masculinity of both *karamoghou* and *sonangui*. To avert this, a bridegroom usually consulted a learned *karamoghou* to discover the most auspicious day for his marriage and received charms to bolster his potency. Men showed considerable interest in charms to control women. *Karamoghou* knew a variety of charms that a man could use to obtain a woman he desired (Numutye Watara, July 6, 1970; Bassori Iabete, July 29, 1970).

Men usually belittled the influence of women upon the history of family and lineage relationships. They denied that women were ever important enough to be the cause of major quarrels between families. The men of a lineage were acutely conscious of the need to maintain unity, and they ate together out of a common pot each evening. As each man put food in his mouth with his hand and returned his hand to the pot for another mouthful, he exchanged "dirt," in the form of saliva, with the men of his lineage. This level of intimacy helped bind them together (Badawa Watara, Feb. 24, 1970).

Nevertheless, these men were in competition with one another for wives. Older, more powerful men could marry as many women as they could obtain and keep; younger men, thus, had difficulty finding wives. Because the preferred marriage was between second cousins, a married woman had certain opportunities to play off one man against another, her father and brothers against her husband and her husband's family. Men either had to agree that women were unimportant or risk cleavages in the male solidarity of the lineage. The use of secret charms to settle disputes was an important resource.

The potential difficulties raised by the males' need to discipline their wives influenced the patterns of exchange of women among lineages. *Sonangui* fathers allowed *karamoghou* men to marry their daughters, but the Dyula considered the reverse arrangement too dangerous. Were a *sonangui* man to beat the daughter of a *karamoghou*, he would have to live in fear of the *karamoghou's* magical powers (Bamori Watara, May 16, 1970).

Mary Douglas (1966, pp. 141–45) suggests a correlation between beliefs that women carry pollution and societies in which women have the opportunity to pit one man against another, challenging the masculine power structure. Dyula society is a case in point.

A more positive view of women's powers appears in the epic tradition of Malinke society. Traditions about Sunjata, for example, make his success dependent upon the help of his mother and sister. His mother, whose superhuman strengths were so great that Sunjata's father was able to deflower her only after threatening to kill her, protected him in his childhood and youth, His sister saved him from evil powers on two occasions (see Niane, 1965). This view of women as the power behind the throne is typical of Malinke epics, which reenforce the supposition that claims about the minimal role of women in Dyula family relations represent masculine ideals rather than a more threatening reality.

The other side of the masculine fear/repression complex was an appreciation of women as socially useful in some ways. Primary among these was the capacity to bear children. Family size both reflected and contributed to social power. A man's grown children were his supporters, politically and economically.

The most important woman in any man's life was, without doubt, his mother. Men explained that a mother would do for her child what no one else would—take care of him when he was small and weak or sick. Women here, as in most African societies, carried their babies strapped to their backs. Lacking diapers, they simply didn't worry much about urine, and to control the disposition of feces, a mother gave her infant periodic enemas, blowing the fluid up his anus with her mouth. Some forms of illness in older children and adults required the same treatment. A mother's willingness to suffer such extremes put her sons in great debt to her. The affectional bond between mother and son was stronger than any other in that very competitive society, and a woman looked forward to dependence on her grown sons when she became old.

Female children in *karamoghou* lineages sometimes acquired enough learning so that as mothers they were able to teach their sons the alphabet and simple texts. Many biographies of famous *karamoghou* refer to early lessons from their mothers. The role of a mother in the socialization of a warrior was less clear. However, she was known to defend his interests whenever possible against his half-brothers (Al–Hajj Muhammed Sanogho, May 26, 1969).

What evidence there is about women's view of themselves indicates that they saw their sphere as the domestic one primarily centered around childbearing and nurturance. In a preindustrial society in which land was plentiful, the death rate high, and children providing one's support in old age, childbearing was an important activity. Legally the wards of their menfolk, excluded from leadership of the whole community in politics or religion, women were a disadvantaged group, yet one with its own definite sense of identity and importance. Clearly, the society could not survive without their powers of procreation and nurturance.

The charms that women sought from the *karamoghou* demonstrate their concerns. Foremost among these were charms to promote fertility. This reflects women's awareness that both their value as wives and their security in later adulthood depended upon the bearing of healthy male children. Women also sought charms to control their husbands' sexual activities. Some of these guaranteed impotence in extramarital affairs. Sexual jealousy, combined with economic dependence on their husbands, made charms of this type attractive to women (Quimby, 1972, p. 87).

As in other societies where sex roles are clearly defined, there was room for the exceptional woman of a ruling family to take on certain roles that were traditionally male. Guimbe Watara was such a woman, a unique phenomenon in Dyula society, a total aberration from the normal pattern of sex roles. The daughter of Jori Watara, king of Gouiriko, she followed typically male paths to success. She had a reputation for being able to ride horseback and fight "just like a man." Her father died when she was three, and his brother and successor Bako-Mori, eventually delegated her to be the family's representative in Bobo-Dioulasso, where she evidently maintained her position through a combination of political acumen and military power. She had a band of armed retainers, mostly slaves, whom she used to protect herself and to lend to her allies to increase her prestige and put them in her debt.

When the explorer, Louis Binger, traveled through Bobo-Dioulasso, he stayed with Guimbe, and when he left, she sent her retainers to escort him on the next stage of his journey. Local tradition tells that Binger was very ill when he arrived and that Guimbe nursed him back to health with a cure that included enemas, which she administered. The intended moral of this anecdote bears on the politics of the colonial period and an intention to bolster a claim to a privileged position vis-à-vis the French. More interesting in the context of sex roles is the idea that Guimbe's claim to Binger's (and, therefore, French) alliance combined both the masculine provision of bodyguards and the mothering provision of intimate medical care. (Bamori Watara, May 10, 1970; Hebert and Guilheim 1967, pp. 139–64).

Community religious rites provided a kind of social theater through which members expressed and reaffirmed the social order. Each group demonstrated its accepted role. Brief descriptions of three types of community ceremony follow—a funeral, a marriage, and a celebration of the Muslim fast month of Ramadan.

In the event of death, family members of the deceased washed the body, wrapped it in a shroud, and buried it. As men and women of the community heard the news, they went to visit the family of the deceased, often bringing a contribution to the funeral expenses. This was a solemn occasion, and visitors usually sat quietly, the men sitting in one part of the family's courtyard and the women in another.

On the third day, the men came together to perform the funeral ceremony. They wished God to pardon the dead person's sins and welcome his soul into heaven. The *gurutigi* of the decreased's lineage invited one or two men from each lineage to view the sacrifice that he had prepared for the occasion: a large dish of kola nuts and a text of *Dalā'il al-Khairāt* or, roughly translated, "Guide to Happiness." Each lineage representative took one kola nut and sat down again. The *gurutigi* then offered the kola nuts to a representative of the lineage with whom he had a joking alliance. That man showed the kola nuts to the senior *karamoghou* lineage and continued to act as the agent of the deceased's lineage throughout the ceremony. He proceeded to distribute pages of *Dalā'il al-Khairāt* to everyone who could read Arabic. They then read in unison. The deceased's lineage then distributed the kola nuts to everyone present.

The *karamoghou* who "belonged" to the deceased's lineage then requested the other *karamoghou* lineages to offer prayers and blessings for the deceased. The ceremony ended with the recitation of the *Fatiha*, and the dead person's *gurutigi*, through his intermediary, then gave everyone permission to leave. Each man's role in this ceremony depended upon his lineage membership, the proper behavior for each lineage vis-à-vis the other lineages being historically determined.

The women played no part in the project of getting the deceased into heaven. Rather, they were active in the interpersonal, emotional, and domestic spheres. They took part in the visits of condolence that preceded the funeral. If the family of the deceased could afford it, they invited the community to a commemorative meal on the fortieth day after the death. In this case, the women labored to prepare the food that would be offered to the guests. In some cases the wives of a dead man observed a period of seclusion, during which they did not comb their hair or wash. These activities helped members of the community make a personal emotional adjustment to the loss.

The organization of the marriage ceremony followed the same broad division of labor. The men dealt with God, and the women ritualized the domestic changes. The marriage adjustments made it clear that marriage was first and foremost a contractual arrangement between two male heads of families. When he wished a girl's hand in marriage, a man asked the head of his family to send gifts to the head of the girl's family. If the gifts were accepted, the two families could begin to discuss the brideprice. The sum was usually paid in gold, cloth, kolas, cowries, and food. The preferred form of marriage was an exchange of women between two families of the same lineage; each family then paid much less.

On the afternoon of the wedding (usually a Thursday, the day before the Muslim day of prayer), male representatives of both families met in the mosque or in someone's courtyard to finalize the contract and to ask God's blessing for the union. The groom's family presented the remaining marriage gifts, and the appropriate *karamoghou* asked God's blessing and recited the *Fatiba*. Again, the role played by each person depended on the historical relationships between his own and the other lineages.

The women, meanwhile, had spent the week preparing food for the wedding festivities. They interspersed their work with dances and pounded grain in their mortars to the accompaniment of drums. In the evening, they danced in a circle, clapping their hands. Often, several weddings took place on the same day so that a number of households were making preparations, and all the women of the community participated.

Just after midnight of the wedding day, the brides walked weeping through the village accompanied by their female friends. After a while, male friends of the groom met the girls and dressed them in men's shoes and fancy headdresses. They joined together and danced, each bride carried on the shoulders of one of the young men. When one young man got tired, he tossed his burden back to the shoulders of another. The brides often carried a horse tail in each hand which they waved as they danced. The dancing ended just before dawn with the young men pouring perfume over the brides.

The following afternoon, while the men were in the mosque, the older married women replastered around the door of the house where the groom was to receive his bride, a gesture that symbolized replastering the whole house. They sang songs containing phrases from the Quran as they did so. The brides, meanwhile had run away and hidden outside of town. The grooms' friends went to find them and brought them back, dancing with the women on their shoulders, and handed them over to the older married women. The older women helped the brides to wash themselves, while all wept, grieving the loss of the brides to other lineages and fearing for their fates.

After the brides had washed, they dressed in white, prayed, and lay down in their new homes to await their husbands. An old woman waited all night in the anteroom of the house to receive the blood–spotted sheet that was proof both of the virility of the husband and the virginity of the wife.

Several days after the wedding night, the women gathered again to attend to the bride's coiffure and to give her advice on how to adjust to her new status. Drums and dancing accompanied this activity, and people gathered to dance in the evenings. The men participated in much of celebratory visiting, and the *karamoghou* often gave Quran readings.

The change in a girl's status and life conditions at marriage were much greater than those of a man. A man kept his residence in the same courtyard, although he might move from the unmarried men's sleeping house to a small house of his own. In any case, he was answerable to the same authorities and in the company of the same people, including his mother. The marriage rites included no preparation of the groom for his new role, suggesting that the change of status was less problematic for him than for the bride.

A woman, on the other hand, moved her residence, became answerable to the authority of her husband rather than her father and brothers, and often lost the company of women with whom she had been emotionally close. She was likely to be uncomfortably competitive with her co-wives and her mother-in-law for her husband's affections. For males, then, the social problem to be resolved in the marriage ceremony was the contract between two families that allowed them to transfer a woman from one to the other. For females, the social problem involved the personal adjustment to a new and not necessarily supportive interpersonal environment. Within this context, the men took the responsibility of asking God to look with favor upon their contract, while the women organized and carried out the ritual that eased the new bride's emotional adjustment.

The fast during the 28 days of Ramadan, commemorating God's revelation of the Quran to Muhammad, is one of the most taxing demands of Islam. The *karamoghou* saw fasting for themselves and their families as a way of winning God's favor and assuring themselves a place in heaven. The *sonangui*, on the other hand, did not fast with any degree of consistency, claiming that it interfered with their need for military preparedness. Women could fast only while they were not menstruating.

On nights before the 15th and the 27th of the month, the Dyula community spent the night awake, each group engaged in its own activity. The *karamoghou* men read the Quran aloud and translated it with commentary and admonitions to the audience about its implications for their behavior. One scholar provided the reading and the commentary, while others sang a type of chorus in between verses of the main reading and made exclamations of appreciation of the reader's words. The *karamoghou* and *sonangui* women and the *sonangui* men and children all danced and sang, often singing amusing satirical songs about community personalities and events. The men and boys danced separately from the women with their own music and songs. They drank a great deal of *dolo* and danced a vigorous, boisterous dance that became a test of endurance. The young unmarried women and women married for five years or more danced together. The former were scantily dressed, elaborately coiffed, and decked out in the finest gold jewelry the family could afford. The latter were dressed in their best clothes, without elaborate coiffures and jewelry. Older women stood on the sidelines and clapped their hands. The women of each lineage danced as a group. Planning and organizing the dancing provided leadership roles for the women within their lineages. Decorating and coiffing the girls was, for instance, a day's work in itself. After the 27th day, the women danced each day until the end of the month.

The night before the 27th day of Ramadan, *Lailat al-Qadri* or "the night of majesty," was the anniversary of the first revelation of the Quran to Muhammad. The Dyula believed that on this night, which they called Kurubi, the angels came to earth and distributed happiness for the coming year. One had to stay awake to receive one's share of good fortune. Each group kept itself awake by celebrating its own assets—the *karamoghou* men by reading the Quran, the *sonangui* men in boisterous, competitive, and physically demanding dancing, and the women in dances that displayed their physical beauty and their jewelry.

The day of the appearance of the new moon, the first day of Shawwal, everyone went to the mosque to pray and then home to feast and to dance. The dancing continued for seven days. Throughout the month of Ramadan, groups of boys and girls had been going around to each household dancing and playing music to obtain donations of food and money. This was used for their own celebration on the first of Shawwal (Quimby, 1972, pp. 45–48, 65–68, 72–75).

What, then, do these rites reveal about the relative positions of men and women, and what did each of these groups obtain through its participation? Men in this society were concerned with power and command. They excluded women both physically and ideologically from positions of power as much as possible. Legally, women were always dependent upon the male members of their families, and the male community excluded them from most public occasions for direct communication with God. The women seem to have put their energies into rites that helped them through difficult social transitions or that gave them scope for pleasurable self-expression and display.

The French conquest of Bobo-Dioulasso and concomitant changes in the economic structure of Dyula society not only destroyed the position of the *sonangui* warrior elite but put into question the whole structure of habitual relationships between social groups and the very definition of the groups themselves. Lineage solidarity weakened, the mutual association of *karamoghou* and *sonangui* altered its form, and the internal structure of the family changed. Children became less dependent upon, and respectful of, their elders. Men and women struggled with each other in the process of working out new patterns of interdependency. Religious doctrine and rites became weapons in the conflict over the proper constitution of sex roles and sexual behavior. These deep and complex social transformations whose roots go back to the colonial conquest and beyond were very much in evidence in Bobo-Dioulasso in 1969 and 1970.

When Bobo-Dioulasso surrendered to the French in 1897, the *sonangui* lineage descended from Seku Watara arranged an alliance with the conquerors. Seku's lineage was to rule in the name of the French and turn over a certain percentage of the tax revenues to the colonizers. As the years passed, the French grew increasingly disgusted with the *sonangui's* lack of effective control over their territory, and when the Bobo and other subject populations revolted in the period from 1915 to 1917, the French began systematically to remove the Watara from positions of authority in the colonial regime.

In addition to destroying *sonangui* public political power, the French introduced a series of laws and policies that changed Dyula family life. Slavery became illegal. Since many of the important households had contained substantial numbers of slaves who farmed, fought, engaged in commerce, and bore children on behalf of their masters, the dissolution of the institution of slavery weakened the social and economic position of these households. The power base of the *sonangui* male was eroded still further, when the French forbade the Dyula to beat each other. A man could no longer beat his wives or have his sons beaten to enforce his discipline. The colonizers also regulated the movements of individuals and of whole villages. When Bobo–Dioulasso became a colonial administrative center, the French required that the *gurutigi* of all the *sonangui* lineages live there (Fajawa Sanogho, March 21, 1970; Badawa Watara, Feb. 24, 1970; Basidiki Sanogho & Numutye Watara, April 21, 1970).

Colonial rule offered its own avenues to status and power that the Dyula evaluated and adopted selectively. The French tried to force the *gurutigi* to send their children to French schools. Most of the *gurutigi* refused, perceiving the schools as a way of alienating their young, and sent other children instead. As a result and much to their regret, very few Dyula born before 1950 were able to get positions in the government bureaucracy. French rule brought about the rapid expansion of Bobo-Dioulasso to contain a population of about 70,000 by 1960, and the building of roads and a railroad from Abidjan to Ouagadougou with the consequent growth of commercial opportunities (Al-Haff Muhammed Sanogho, Aug. 22, 1969; Dakar, National Archives, 15G 199, Registre 1899).

The growth of Bobo-Dioulasso as a commercial center brought increasing opportunities for women to make money as local traders. For a small but gradually increasing number of women whose parents had sent them to colonial schools, there were jobs as secretaries and clerks. The combination of colonial restrictions on the male use of physical force in domestic discipline with the increasing ability of women to develop economic independence challenged Dyula men to redefine and resubstantiate their sex role.

Bereft of their role as a warrior elite, and scornful, in many instances, of adopting the oppressor's culture, *sonangui* males sought a new socioeconomic position and a new identity. Many of them turned to farming. They also began to adopt parts of the *karamoghou's* life-style. Some *sonangui* became active long-distance traders or took up crafts like weaving and sewing. Most of them began to take the *karamoghou's* preachings more seriously and participated in the Ramadan fast, annual sacrifices, and daily prayers.

This Islamization of the *sonangui* developed its meaning in a context of social fragmentation and the secularization of many spheres of activity. The significance, if not the content, of religious ritual changed. Dyula rituals as carried out in the villages in precolonial days made certain statements and expressed certain feelings about community integration and the relationship of the community to God. As the community changed, so did the meaning of the rituals. A Dyula funeral in the nineteenth century expressed the actual, working interrelationship of Dyula lineages, or one aspect of it. A Dyula funeral carried out according to the same format in Bobo-Dioulasso in 1970 indicates something about people's feeling the need to preserve traditional forms in spite of changes in the social structure and its economic basis. The celebration of ritual takes time, energy, and money. People must have a motivation for investing the necessary resources, and this motivation is unlikely to be entirely the same in an urban environment as it was in a small village.

West African society in the twentieth century acquired new institutions that presented nonreligious alternatives to the services offered by the *karamoghou*. Among these were hospitals and French-trained doctors, schools with their own European intellectual tradition, courts of law, and a new legal code. Most people chose eclectically and pragmatically among the range of available options. When people turned to Islamic resources, it was either to look out for their interests in the hereafter or because they perceived those resources to have some advantages over available alternatives. That the Islamic institutions and the secular alternatives to them were based on different cosmological assumptions did not seem a problem to most of the Dyula who had no trouble assimilating the new technology to their old cosmology. The only apparent significant pressure for cultural consistency was more one of fashion—"modern people don't get involved in things like charms"—than one of perceived logical conflict.

With this in mind, one can examine the increasing size and seriousness of the Islamic community in Bobo-Dioulasso as a response to new opportunities, difficulties, and needs for self-definition. Among the new opportunities was the increasing ease of travel between West Africa and the Middle East. More and more Dyula made the pilgrimage to Mecca. The French shipped large numbers of pilgrims by sea and, later, by air in an effort to win the loyalty of Muslims. Even larger numbers of pilgrims went overland, usually on foot, earning a living by teaching, trading, and crafts as they went.

Within the city of Bobo-Dioulasso, Quran schools multiplied. Many *sonangui* learned at least the sounds associated with the Arabic letters and the proper prayers for various occasions. A small number pursued their studies and gained reputations as Muslim scholars. More members of the *karamoghou* lineages became literate and familiar with a certain body of classical Islamic literature. Many Dyula saw Quran school as a desirable alternative to the colonial educational system. Later in the colonial period, some scholars began modernizing the Muslim educational system with the creation of *medersas*. These used modern primary school texts from the Middle East to teach subjects like geography, mathematics, and science, in addition to religion. Where possible, they had students use desks, paper, and chalkboards, rather than the traditional mat on the floor and wooden writing board.

Islam, as the French were well aware, had a potential anticolonial spirit. The Quran identifies Christians as a people who have gone astray, and this for the Dyula defined their conquerors as religious inferiors and probably added to their tendency to emphasize the Islamic aspects of their identity. The French were nervous about their "politique musulmane." To the extent that they saw Muslim religious activity as safely apolitical, they supported it, but they kept files on all important Muslim leaders.

The *karamoghou* found new uses for their charms. Many of them were staunchly against acculturation to the colonial regime. They had a charm that they placed in the path going by a village to keep the French from noticing the area. Some of the traditional battle charms also found new use as protection against the French. Stories circulate about men who possessed magical powers strong enough to escape punishment by colonial officials (Bamori Watara, April 16, 1970; Al-Haff Muhammed Sanogho, June 9, 1969).

The solidarity of the lineage was disintegrating, proving more trouble to preserve than it was worth after the colonial reforms of the 1940s. Having served in the precolonial period as a structure for military organization, the lineage also helped the Dyula to deal with the exigencies of taxation, forced labor, and military conscription. Once these pressures disappeared, the utility of solidarity between brothers diminished, and the nuclear family took on greater importance. The Dyula began to follow Quranic laws of inheritance from parent to child, abandoning the inheritance rights of brothers and cousins.

As the *sonangui* lineages lost their cohesion, the relationship between them and the *karamoghou* became more individualized. No longer did a *sonangui gurutigi* support a whole entourage of *karamoghou*, and no longer did the *sonanrui* lineages contribute substantially to the support of "their" *karamoghou* lineages, or give them women as alms. In the city, the traditional corporate groups were becoming increasingly fragmented, and traditionally ascribed status was becoming far less important.

Slowly, there emerged a kind of ideal Muslim identity for Dyula males. Not hostile to French influence and modernization, it was carefully independent of it. The ideal Muslim male, by middle age when the pattern of his life had become clear, was the head of a large family and successful in his occupation, whether it be in government, commerce or scholarship. He listened carefully to the *karamoghou* and, if sufficiently educated, read for himself about the rules of proper conduct. He knew at least the sounds of the written Arabic letters so that he could read prayers aloud, though he might not understand their content. He prayed regularly five times each day and appeared, impressively dressed, at the mosque for the community prayers on Friday and at all the annual ceremonies. He gave alms on the appropriate occasions and had been on the pilgrimage, perhaps accompanied by one of his wives. He was as conscientious in his abstinence from alcohol as his *sonangui* ancestors had been enthusiastic in indulging.

He ruled his household kindly but firmly, dispensing money to his wives and children for food and clothing. Seeking the best of both worlds for his family, he sent some of his children to Quran school and some to government schools. When they came of age, he married them off. He was attractive and though never a "skirt-chaser," was likely to have as the last of his wives a very pretty young woman in her late teens who, in return for the status she gained as his wife, made her pregnancies proof of his continuing virility, while her youthful agility insured her care for him in his declining years. His wives and children all treated him with loving respect.

This male role required, of course, a complementary female role. The ideal wife in this family was pious, docile, and devoted to her husband. She bore and raised his children, supported him in all his activities, and treated him with the greatest respect. She showed no interest in other men, and if she earned money, she spent it on food for the family and clothing for herself and the children.

According to this male-defined modernization of the sex roles, the husband's financial position in the family reinforced his authority. This was a difficult, if not impossible, role for a man to insist upon when, as was often the case, his wife's financial resources were equal to, or better than, his own. Men worried about how to cope with this phenomenon.

Today, competition among men for women has intensified as women become economically more independent, as male solidarity within the lineage has weakened, and as changes in family life allow daughters more freedom to develop their own social lives. Men continually complain about this competition and about the untrustworthiness of women. Each sex suspects the other of using charms to manipulate and control relationships between them. The *karamoghou* are ever ready to sell such charms. The community's concern over this state of affairs finds expression in the *karamoghou's* repeated preaching that flirtation is sinful, that parents should marry off their children at a young age, and that women should respect their menfolk (Babakr Fofana, Aug. 26, 1969 & Sept. 5, 1969; Francis Watara, June 18, 1970).

Men use Islamic ritual and doctrine as a way of asserting their own superiority over women. They comment that according to Islamic law a woman is only half a person, that women make their best contribution to society as good housewives and should leave matters of religion to men. The husband is the religious authority in the home; it is his duty to warn his wife if she engages in sinful behavior. His responsibility, states the Quran, stops there, and God will not hold him accountable for his wife's behavior. Heaven, for men, promises an abundance of beautiful virgin handmaidens. There is no similar appeal to women; logic and domography indicate only that they become virgin upon entering heaven (Adam Sanogho, Nov. 6, 1969; Imam Kone, May 25, 1970; Basidiki Sanogho, Feb. 28, 1970; Al-Haff Babu Watara, Feb. 16, 1970).

The use of religious ritual to express the conflict between men's desire to control women and women's insistence on certain forms of self-determination came to a head in 1969 and 1970 in the dispute over the women's dances for the Kurubi festival. The men had already ceased their Kurubi dancing in the early 1960s, having decided that it was not important to them as modern, urban Muslims to dance in this manner. In the precolonial period, the *gurutigi* had commanded their lineages to dance, and none had refused. As the men born during the time when the *sonangui* warrior ethos was still viable became older, and as male prestige in the community derived more and more from other kinds of behavior, *sonangui* men increasingly opted for attendance at the *karamoghou's* Quran readings instead of their own dances.

The issue of whether or not the women should continue dancing was much more heated and elicited various analyses from different members of the community. One of the leaders of the movement to continue the women's dancing blamed the whole uproar on her ex-husband, a *karamoghou*. She had always led the dances in an open space in back of his house. After their divorce, it had upset him to have her doing that, and she claimed he had stirred up all the other young *karamoghou* to preach against the dancing as a means of retribution.

The Imam of the Dyula mosque in Bobo-Dioulasso let it be known that his religious texts said that drumming and dancing during Ramadan was not good Muslim behavior. The women dealt with the issue of religious authority by referring to *karamoghou* of previous generations whom, they claimed, had never forbidden the dancing. The *sonangui* men claimed that although *karamoghou* had tried to stop the dancing, the powerful warrior *gurutigi* had simply overridden them.

Most people agreed that the real issue was one of domestic authority. The dances were an opportunity for women to assert themselves and to display their wealth in the gold jewelry decorating their daughters and younger sisters. Furthermore, a husband at a Quran reading could never be sure, unless she was with him, whether his wife was really dancing or simply using that opportunity to spend time with a lover (Numutye Watara, Feb. 27, 1970; Basidiki Sanogho, Feb. 28, 1970; Drissa Cisse, Dec. 7, 1969; Makosarran Sanogho, Dec. 5, 1969; Imam Kone, Dec. 6, 1969; Kokasori Watara, Dec. 13, 1969; Badawa Watara, Nov. 16, 1969). In this context, the Kurubi dancing became, for the women who danced, an assertion of their social self–determination.

Religious ritual and ideology must be consonant with a community's deepest sense of its identity. Among the most basic questions of identity are the characteristics of masculine and feminine. In the late nineteenth century, when economic and political power was clearly in the hands of Dyula males, community religious rituals demonstrated and reaffirmed the articulation of the social structure, including the respective social roles of men and women. As the economic and political bases of male dominance disintegrated in the twentieth century, men continued to choose religious beliefs and patterns of behavior that expressed their ideas about appropriate sex roles. Many women, however, did not agree with the men's definition of social ideals. The modernized Islam espoused by the Dyula men held few rewards for them. They resisted this reassignment of ritual and, by continuing an old ritual in a new context, asserted their right to choose their own behavior.

CONCLUSIONS
The Arcadian Wish:
Toward a Theory
of Contemporary African Religion

Bennetta Jules–Rosette

Africa's new religions contain utopian ideals which, while they stress a crucial link to the past, are not synonymous with a return to it, for an uncalculated return is impossible.[1] Using ritual and doctrine, the members of these religious groups introduce a special form of community into contemporary life. Each study in this volume has been concerned with changing forms of symbolic expression revealed in ceremony and doctrine. The articles have emphasized that ritual reflects crucial aspects of the social organization of each group and is a barometer of change. The possibilities for change, stimulated by the absence of reliance on the rural economy and by a situation in which women engage in clearly defined forms of social participation, are suggested by the analysis of custom-linked movements in urban areas and by the rise of separatist urban and rural groups such as the Jamaa and the Upper Volta Islamic variations.

Much research on African religion makes too radical a dichotomy between traditional religions in rural areas and new religious movements on the urban scene.[2] Thus, the carryover between the two types, as well as the importance of religion as a transitional form of life, has not been stressed except in a small number of studies. At the same time, causal factors in the development of new religions have been dealt with too generally, both in regard to Africa and

[1]The false dichotomies often made between tradition and modernity are discussed by Gusfield (1973, pp. 1–33).
[2]Certain authors, however (Long, 1968; Murphree, 1971), have dealt with the influence of syncretic churches in the rural environment.

elsewhere.[3] While such groups have a definite ideological appeal for particular classes of individuals, it is necessary to examine their personal appeal, the overall religious organization, and the diverse social networks that become involved before comprehensive evidence can be brought to bear. The studies in this volume constitute a movement in the direction of that synthesis. They demonstrate that the meanings of ritual and symbol are a valuable definition of a group's social purpose and its relationship to the rest of the society. Similarly, the utopian visions of a changing society and the images of agents of change present themselves through investigating these religious associations. Why do leaders with a particular background and ascriptive characteristics emerge? What is the historical and customary background that lends weight to male versus female leadership and to the particular forms of symbolism and organizational interpretations that surround it? The question of changing gender-linked participation in the new religions is viewed here as an important case study in the structure of religious leadership and its relationship to social institutions in transition (see Wilson, 1970, 1973).

This volume emphasizes the importance of collaboration by researchers from several fields in the social sciences. An initial aim is to acquire familiarity with the study of ritual and symbolism in African religion through ethnographic materials, and to examine the universality of some of these modes of symbolic expression. Moreover, these forms of expression are linked to processes of change that are taking place within total societies and cross-culturally. They include the social reorganization accompanying urban migration and attendant conceptual adaptations that most of the authors emphasize develop from populations examined. This does not mean that the churches are exclusively urban products or that they are the only voluntary organizations that reinforce urban adjustment. The phenomenon of squatting (Stren, 1975; Turner & Starnes, 1976; Jules–Rosette, forthcoming) is often accompanied by the appearance of voluntary religious associations. They arise in most emerging nations and are not unknown in urban ghettos in the United States. Persons living in these areas carry cultural traditions with them and yet become susceptible to the forms of social organization generated by a marginal urban existence. These new urban churches share as characteristics not primarily that they are religions of the oppressed, but that they are expressions of hope and creativity. Fabian suggests a dialetical relationship in which the new religions both reflect, and are made possible by, much broader cultural transformations such as those found in popular art and music. These churches are new associations through which a means for survival in complex society is learned by social and economic cooperation, often at the price of some degree of isolation from the society at large. The case of women's

---

[3]Cf., for example, Needleman's (1973) causal explanation of dissatisfactions with the "demythologization" of American religion as a major factor in the rise of new religions in the United States.

participation and leadership in the churches may, therefore, be seen both as providing innovative relationships that may then be applied outside the group itself, and as allowing women's activities to be circumscribed by the restorative attempts that I have called traditionalism. The ambivalence expressed by and toward women in cultural change becomes a focus for the redefinition of custom and the modification of external influences.

There is a combination of the particular symbolism of custom and the expansiveness characteristic of cultural pluralism. The groups that use "world" religions or transplanted churches as a rubric for change stress that these religions form interethnic and transcultural associative networks. Christianity in Africa has most notably had this pluralizing effect (Fernandez, 1975, pp. 131–47). While some of the new Christian groups of Africa originate in ethnically homogenous areas, most emphasize the potential and even the necessity for cultural sharing through overarching symbols and doctrine. This does not mean that an external system is imposed upon, or destroys, old cultural forms (cf. Mannheim, 1952). Instead, aspects of modified systems encounter the previous cultural forms. The putative "purity" of ancient traditions is, therefore, called into direct question. Most of the well-known Lulua traditional music of Zaire today dates from the turn of the twentieth century, and includes references to Christianity within the context of traditional religious beliefs.[4] Cultural history is itself a social and historical construction. Through the processual study of a group's dominant symbols (as illustrated by Breidenbach and Fabian), the processes of diachronic change and preservation may be analyzed. In this way, the myth of an idyllic past emerges with respect to changes in contemporary belief systems. These processes of cultural combination and reconstruction allow members to gain a reflective stance toward immediate problems by comparison with a more distant cultural ideal. The types of religious responses to increased cultural options vary widely with respect to a group's attitudes toward tradition and to the degree of change considered possible. The traditionalistic, millenarian, revitalistic, and syncretic responses to present situations resolve ambiguities through a symbolic and conceptual balancing of competing claims to interpretation.

PROSPECTS FOR CROSS-CULTURAL RESEARCH

More than ever before, the present-day religions of Africa are an exercise in cultural encounter and mutual influence. In this regard, many scholars simply gloss the similarities in contemporary Afro-American and African religions. These similarities do not develop from a unidirectional cultural diffusion. Instead, similar processes of culture change and contact within the respective

---

[4]This may be expected given the long history of Christianity in the Zaire, which dates from the seventeenth century kingdom of the Kongo.

societies have taken place simultaneously, and the influence of New World black churches on the new African religions is also felt.[5] The parallel expressive forms in music, dance, and oratory represent creative combinations of indigenous cultural patterns with external media for representing them.

The thaumaturgical side of African "spirit-type" churches offers pragmatic answers to problems of illness and misfortune faced in an urban and secular situation (cf. Needleman, 1973). The operation of such a community relies on establishing a special type of social organization that parallels the functions of traditional life without entirely recreating it. It seems that both the traditional African religious associations in town and the new African churches provide a particular form of community for their members in response to the arcadian wish for an idyllic communal life. Through the rewards of community and a common social support structure, the African churches establish claims to loyalty. Culturally, they promise a religion that is not alien to the "masses." Yet, some of the contemporary groups emphasize the ultimate accomplishment of orthodox doctrines through a strict personal application of the Bible or the Quran. Part of this fundamentalism arises from efforts to return to the more explicit and self–contained aspects of traditional lore. These literalist interpretations develop a new fabric of ideas through which individuals attempt to create alternative types of social relationships.

Similar phenomena can also be found in the symbolic reinterpretations of the Afro-American cults of the Caribbean and Brazil. The Batuque cults, for example, began as preservations of West African religions in a Catholic idiom (Leacock & Leacock, 1975; Walker, 1972). Saints replaced ancestral gods and spirits, while possession continued in a similar form with some influence from surrounding Indian religions. Both Macumba and Candomblé illustrate mixtures of traditional content with a new cultural code influenced by Western religions. They are chiefly urban religions. The Leacocks (1975) located the *terreiro* or Batuque cult centers on the darkly lit streets of the Brazilian *favelas*. It is no coincidence that the cultural and social settings in which the world's contemporary religions appear foster conditions of plural culture contact on the margins of urbanizing areas. These religious groups encourage multilingual and multiethnic participation (Jules–Rosette, 1975a, pp. 99–127) and draw upon diverse cultural traditions. This does not mean that they *cause* multiethnic sharing or that the

---

[5]Cf. the transplantation of the (Afro-American) African Methodist Episcopal Church to South Africa in the late nineteenth century and the subsequent influence of this group upon South African Ethiopian churches. Although one may view both of these cases in terms of the "religions of the oppressed" thesis, one can also view them as creative adaptations and transformations of an indigenous culture. Herskovits (1937, 1948a, pp. 542–65, 1948b) finds such cultural "reinterpretations" to be a major factor in syncretic religion, marked by the retention of specific elements from traditional culture. Here I stress that since both the goals and manner of cultural expression may change, the resulting transformations may be more intensive than former discussions of syncretism have tended to assume.

process of urban migration necessarily results in voluntary associations of a religious nature.

Supernatural beings such as the *encantados* of Batuque are believed to be the causes of good and ill fortune (Leacock & Leacock, 1975, p. 55). Like the Shona shades shunned by the Apostolic groups, these spirits are considered causes of misfortune. In both cases, situations such as accidents, loss of employment, or failure in kinship support are explained by spiritual rather than mundane causes. Although the persistence of such personal logic cannot be analyzed solely in terms of social change, difficulties in a new social environment push individuals toward other comprehensive cognitive resolutions to these problems. The scientist faced with an array of empirical occurrences for an experimental problem seeks to resolve it through the logical reductions of theory. The syncretist seeks to resolve similar problems through an ontological reductionism. Competing explanations of reality are not discarded, but instead the implications of several alternatives are combined in the symbolic answer. Systems of belief resolution develop under specific situations of social and psychological ambiguity in which firm criteria for interpretation and reduction no longer exist. This social situation creates particular interpersonal responses. The regeneration of traditional beliefs and the rise of contemporary religions can be seen as responses to the decline of an overarching belief system as an explanatory device for diverse situations. A system containing multiple alternatives allows the group member to make pragmatic decisions in many cases of conflict.

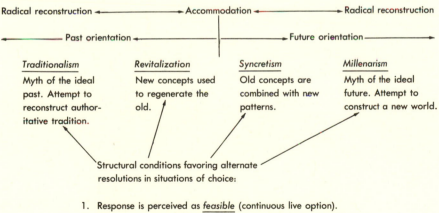

Figure 12.1 Structural conditions conducive to belief resolutions in contemporary religions and cult movements.

REGENERATION AND CHANGE: THE BROADER
IMPLICATIONS OF CONTEMPORARY RELIGIOUS
RESEARCH IN AFRICA

The cross-cultural implications of these studies must be seen with respect to the problem of cultural regeneration in Africa. While urbanization and its spinoff effects of industrialization and change are not unique to Africa, many of the social conditions under which these changes occur are. These conditions include the vast ethnic diversity of individual nations, and the maintenance of a large subsistence agricultural sector in most of subSaharan Africa. Several types of groupings coexist within limited geographical areas. In Ghana, for example, rural villages abut migrant hometowns and large cities (see Bartel, 1976). This proximity creates a direct link between custom, the remnants of colonial change, and the newer effects of urbanism. Migrants engaged in mining and other wage labor reside in hometowns. Although they were originally temporary in nature, these towns have become increasingly stable and are inhabited by large family and kin groups. The hometowns have intimate ties to rural villages to which migrants send cash and goods and to larger cities from which they obtain their livelihood. These residential forms are coterminous groupings in which individuals move from the unquestioned aspects of custom to more varied forms of social existence. While the Ghanaian example is more graphic than many others, it is merely representative of the interlocking of extremely different living conditions in urbanizing Africa. The rapid changes that have taken place across a single generation on the African continent and the resulting plethora of social alternatives have been reflected in the contrasts and diversity of the religious groups discussed here. When referring to the most viable, or at least the oldest, of Africa's contemporary churches, a period of thirty to, at most, sixty years is at issue (see Andersson, 1958, and Sundkler, 1961). The process of change may involve a shift in the purpose, as well as the performance, of traditional rituals over a very short time span. The nationalization of traditional African folkloric forms and dances for political use, which is termed political "animation" in francophone Africa, is an example of such a modification. The format and meaning of the dances retain only some evocative imagery, while the dominant symbols are transformed to communicate a political message.

Nevertheless, across such short periods of time, movements take on quite different configurations. Initial messianism settles into a highly institutionalized spirit church inspired by a founder whose powers remain legendary. The development of Kimbanguism from an anticolonial and ethnically insulated sect to one of the four major recognized religions of Zaire has already been emphasized. A traditionalistic revival may spread, becoming a major cultural trend so widely accepted that the elements it regenerates can no longer be separated from the "new." The changing images of women, whether they are oriented toward family life as described in the Jamaa article or toward a traditionalist retrenchment as described among the Dyula, are part of this process of regeneration and change.

Africa's new religions, together with the revival of custom, have provided a seedbed for innovative popular cultural images. Political persuasion may be framed in terms previously considered sacred as in the case of "animation." Here political leaders draw on customary assumptions of sacralized politics as well as the mass media and bureaucratic party organization. In addition, religious language and imagery, such as the Jamaa *mafundisho*, the Maranke preaching format, and the visual image of the mermaid, have now entered common parlance as essential aspects of popular urban culture.[6] They are utilized by secular leaders as means of creating and communicating with a mass society that has already been touched by religious transformations.

The more insulated religious movements still adamantly retain a radical separation from some aspects of the contemporary societies in which they appear. At the same time, their attitudes toward the role of women, toward work, and toward forms of expression (such as discourse and dress) permeate other sectors of social life that are entirely alien to their religious origin. From whatever perspective, the study of new African religions is, therefore, automatically an exploration of Africa's new expressive forms. Recent research in Zambia (Jules-Rosette, 1975b) has demonstrated that major administrative policies there are based on the self-help ethos established for doctrinal reasons by some of the indigenous churches. Taken from their original religious source, these beliefs have become the basis for motivating squatters toward community planning in a secular domain. Because religion involves a high concentration of innovative and restorative symbols, it is the wellspring from which these expressions are transmitted to a wider society, and is often the forerunner of new expressive forms that are eventually used in secular contexts.

The distinction between change and regeneration in the new religions is muted. When has the old ceased to function? Without a doubt, a revival of a tradition is never "the same" as its original form.[7] It is always revived with reference to the present. The activities of women as healers and spirit mediums among the Harrists and the Vapostori illustrate this active use of customary behavioral definitions in a new symbolic context. Similarly, the reemergence of the Kimbanguist movement took place with reference to the social and political conditions of that time. The rural healing movement forced underground in the 1920s became the urban expression of BaKongo revitalization and incipient political organization in the 1950s. Messianism and the promise of healing became secondary to the organization of the group around powerful intellectual and religious leaders whose spiritual goals were compatible with the political freedoms that they wanted.

[6]This problem influenced the history of Zairean popular art (Szombati-Fabian & Fabian, 1976).
[7]This type of process recurs in the plastic arts (see Fernandez in D'Azevedo, 1973).

The appearance of West African secret societies in town is another form of restoration that creates associations for mutual social and economic aid for women and secular political resources for men. Kenneth Little's (1965–66) analysis of the Poro Society among the Mende of Sierra Leone, deals largely with the group's functions as a voluntary association for urban Mende. The interesting fact that the religious aspects of the society can be invoked and reconstituted at will makes its transmutation even more adaptive simultaneously to both the urban and rural milieus. Little views ethnicity as one factor in Poro restoration. The possibility of social class and political antagonism toward Poro members would also make it an agent for the generation of prestige and self-esteem among oppressed males, as Fabian implies in his reference to the symbolic-sexual over-tones of political hierarchy. Further studies are needed to demonstrate how such groups react when urban members return to the rural milieu, and how new orientations affect the perpetuation of customary religious practices in town. One common reaction is extreme traditionalism, in which new members return in a calculated and researched manner to values and practices that have already been abandoned in the contemporary rural cult.

Three types of theories are generally used to summarize the attraction of contemporary religious groups and other voluntary associations. The first explanation, which has recently been criticized by Africanists of all disciplines, stresses the dislocation and "detribalization" undergone by urban migrants, their consequent loss of ethnic identity, and their need to establish a substitute identity in urban associations (Mitchell, 1969). A second explanation holds that the migrants' identity is reinforced through enclaves of ethnic identification (Fraenkel, 1964; Mayer, 1961; Pauw, 1963). This explanation intersects with Little's description of the Poro society as both an ethnically and religiously based association, at least in localized areas (Little, 1973). A third approach stresses the new amalgam of identities formed through urban social networks.

In contrast to these perspectives, this volume emphasizes that a cultural pluralization, not detribalization as such, is taking place across the African continent. Kashoki (1977) and others have emphasized this process in examining linguistic homogenization and innovative combinations as aspects of change in urbanizing Africa. This process is not contradictory to ethnic identification, which remains integral to both the cultural expressions and the organization of many voluntary associations. Each ethnic group is reinstated in concert with others. The new religious associations grow in an atmosphere of interethnic pluralism, meanwhile creating enclaves for ethnic reinforcement. Within these urban enclaves, former local identities become broadened. Loyalty to a town, village, or clan is transferred to an entire region, linguistic–cultural grouping, or nation. However, these local loyalties remain in "latent" form, and do not become salient unless they are specifically relevant.

Thus, for the resident in a pluralistic environment, a hierarchy of choices appears that shifts according to the social context in which the individual participates.[8] These alternative responses, which include work, ethnic, sexual, and religious identities, become relevant along a scale of intimacy and anonymity.[9] While voluntary associations work to reinstate a sense of community, they cannot provide the overlapping and flexible relationships necessary for urban survival. Again, this distinction becomes apparent in the contrast between the situation of women in customary cults and the specialization of their positions in urban voluntary associations, used for credit, marketeering, and community activities as well as general social reinforcement. Group membership both determines and figures in a series of putative identities. Frequently, it is necessary for the individual to manipulate multiple identities or affiliations at once in order to balance conflicting organizational claims. Contemporary religious associations act as a mediating force in this pluralization process.[10]

Every chapter in this volume allows an assessment of how members of cults and churches perceive religious experience and describe their own participation. The plans for further research in the field of contemporary African religion are outlined in this volume in three directions: (1) the detailed ethnographic study of regeneration in customary religions, (2) the study of newly emerging groups in terms of their belief structure and social worlds, and (3) a cross-cultural theoretical synthesis of the social and cultural conditions under which the groups arise and the types of changes to which they contribute. Studies emphasizing the changing images and roles of women crosscut all three of these emphases to provide a diachronic and comparative view of women in cultural change.

The present studies provide the empirical grounds for a theory of the psychological effects of religion on processes of social change. These remarks have been directed at providing the groundwork for a theoretical approach to contemporary religion based on cross-cultural data. The collection of these materials from various African societies has been an initial step. On the basis of these data, it is possible to develop further empirical generalizations about changing belief structures and the organizational similarities in contemporary religions, whether they are custom-linked or externally influenced.

[8]Schutz (1964) describes the stock of knowledge that the person has of his ordinary social world:

> To this stock of knowledge at hand belongs our knowledge that the world we live in is a world of more or less circumscribed objects with more or less definite qualities, objects among which we move, which resist us and upon which we may act. Yet none of these objects is perceived as insulated. From the outset it is an object within a horizon of familiarity and preacquaintanceship which is, as such, just taken for granted until further notice as the unquestioned, though at any time questionable stock of knowledge at hand. (p. 7)

[9]Schutz (1964, pp. 14–27) describes the social distribution of knowledge among members of society along a wide range of degrees of depth of expertise, familiarity, and preacquaintanceship.

[10]While a shift toward universalization may be observed in many of the African cases, it is important to distinguish the ways in which syncretism takes place within a single historical period, rather than letting the analysis rest at the positing of overall historical types of religions.

While many of the groups discussed here might simply be labeled "sectarian" (Troeltsch, 1912; Wilson, 1970 and 1973), this categorization is another way of referring to voluntary associations that wish to maintain particular ideological boundaries. The tendency not to recognize many contemporary African religious groups by their own self-appellation as churches and to prefer to view them primarily as social movements with political overtones ignores much about the internal organization of the groups and their self-conceptions. Both in customary lore and practice and in their local adaptation of world religions, these groups are not "sects" in the sense of doctrinal challenge. They are, however, "sectarian" in the sense of a shifting membership that struggles desperately to maintain a separate, often retreatist or isolationist, identity.[11]

In order to develop and sustain these boundaries, groups that appear to reject tradition periodically restore aspects of it. If, as Fabian suggests, the position of women is used as an indicator of change, the rise of churches is not always accompanied by an increasing liberalism in sex-role expectations. In fact, a contrasting process quite frequently occurs at least at a symbolic level, as in the indigenous, separatist, and Islamic groups discussed throughout this volume. Women become idealized as symbols of motherhood, family, unity, and of an idyllic past "as-it-should-be." Elsewhere (Jules-Rosette, 1978c) I have noted this nostalgic longing for the past as a symbolic expression in art as well as religion. Marris (1975) has also noted a conservative nostalgia and a conscious return to the past in the face of the radical disruption and change of the African continent. The bulk of the studies in this volume emphasize the significant effect that change, with both its nostalgic and adaptive reactions, has on women in religious groups.

A final reason why sectarianism is a less than useful term in the context of Africa's contemporary religions is the pervasiveness of these small enclaves of voluntary associations. Although one cannot say that they characterize *all* religious associations, their characteristics are so widespread that they may be considered to represent an overarching process of social grouping. The articles in this volume have offered an understanding of religion's place in culture change across societies. It has already been emphasized that comparative research in a new area has necessitated detailed first-hand studies as a data base. It is on the basis of these studies that a framework for symbolic and cultural transformations can be developed which acknowledges the realistic interplay between internal and external influences upon change. While there exists an expanding body of case studies on traditional African religions and indigenous churches, we have made a preliminary step in the direction of consolidating and bringing out the implications of these studies.

[11]Note that this is even the case in traditional secret societies. Gibbs (1965, pp. 210–15) notes that participation in the Poro is now not always expected of every adult Kpelle male.

Many geographical areas have not been covered, and adequate distinctions between rural and urban enclaves of the same group can be studied in greater detail.[12] Furthermore, there is still a need to emphasize and further develop studies of the ritual and symbolism of such groups that can furnish adequate detail to derive models of the cognitive structuring through which a group's members interpret their environment. It is on the basis of this analysis of symbolic form that a greater understanding of the relationship between social structure, perception, and cultural transformation in contemporary societies can be obtained. As the epitome of cultural expression, religion is a major vehicle through which these changes are reflected and can be readily examined. This volume opens the way for further ethnographic research and as such, develops a more comprehensive empirical and theoretical examination of comparative religion and social change. All of the contributors have approached these problems in an exploratory spirit. This synthesis of their work is meant to offer an emerging perspective rather than a conclusive analysis of religion and cultural transformation in Africa.

---

[12]This is particularly the case of studies on the Vapastori that have examined the group either in one environment or another, but never in both urban and rural settings.

Bibliography

African Daily News, June 7, 1962.

African Daily News, August 20, 1962.

Akrofi, C. A. *Twi Mmebus m, Twi Proverbs*. Accra, n.d.

Amos-Djoro, E. *Prophétisme et nationalisme Africains: Les Harristes en cote d'ivoire*. Paris: Ecole Pratique des Hautes Etudes, 1956.

Andersson, E. *Messianic popular movements in the lower Congo*. Uppsala: Almquist & Wiksells, 1958.

Aquina, Sr. M. Christianity in a Rhodesian tribal trust land. *African Social Research*, 1967, 1, 1–40. (a)

Aquina, Sr. M. The people of the spirit: An independent church in Rhodesia. *Africa*, 37, 1967, 203–219. (b)

Aquina, Sr. M. Zionists in Rhodesia. *Africa*, 1969, 39, 2.

Ardener, E. Belief and the problem of women. In *The interpretation of ritual*. London: Tavistock, 1972.

Baëta, C. G. *Prophetism in Ghana: A study of some spiritual churches*. London: SCM Press, 1962.

Baëta, C. G. *Christianity in tropical Africa*. London: International African Institute, 1968.

Balandier, G. Messianism and nationalism in Black Africa. In P. Van Den Berghe (Ed.), *Africa: Social problems of change and conflict*. San Francisco: Chandler, 1965.

Balandier, G. *La sociologie actuelle de l'Afrique noire*. Paris: Presses Universitaires de France, 1971.

Bamunoba, K. and Welbourn, F. B. *The Uganda journal*, 1965, 29, 1, 13–25.

Banda-Mwaka, J. Le kimbanguisme en tant que mouvement prepolitique chez les Kongo. *Bulletin trimestriel du CEPSI: Problèmes sociaux Zairois*, Nos. 92–93, 1970.

Banton, M. *West African city: A study of tribal life in Freetown*. London: Oxford Univ. Press, 1957.

Barber, B. Acculturation and messianic movements. *American Sociological Review*, 1941, 6, 663–69.

Barrett, D. B. *Schism and renewal in Africa: An analysis of six thousand contemporary religious movements*. Nairobi: Oxford Univ. Press, 1968.

Barrett, D. B. (Ed.). *African initiatives in religion*. Nairobi: East Africa Publishing House, 1971.

Bartel, P. Conjugal roles and fertility in old country Ghana. Paper presented at the XVth International Seminar on Family Research, Lomé, Togo, January, 1976.

Beidelman, T. O. Swazi royal ritual. *Africa*, 1966, 36, 373–405.

Bellman, B. L. The hermeneutics of Fala Kpelle secret society rituals. Paper presented at the Third Triennial Symposium on Traditional African Art, Columbia University, April, 1974.

Bellman, B. L. *Village of curers and assassins: On the production of Fala Kpelle cosmological categories*. The Hague: Mouton, 1975.

Bellman, B. L. Ethnohermeneutics: On the interpretation of intended meaning among the Kpelle of Liberia. In W. McCormack and S. A. Würm (Eds.), *Language and thought*. The Hague: Mouton, 1976.

Bellman, B. L. & Jules-Rosette, B. *A paradigm for looking: Cross-cultural research with visual media*. Norwood, N.J.: Ablex, 1977.

Berger, I. Living theater: Women as spirit mediums in Eastern Africa. Paper presented at UCLA Colloquium on Women and Change in Africa, 1870–1970, April, 1974.

Bessell, M. J. Nyabingi. *The Uganda journal*, 1938, 6, 2, 73–86.

Binger, L. G. *Du Niger au Golfe de Guinee*. 2 vols. Paris: Sevil, 1892.

Biebuyck, D. La société kumu face au Kitawala. *Zaire: Revue Congolaise*, 11, 1, 1957, 7–40.

Bittner, E. Radicalism and the organization of radical movements. *American Sociological Review*, 1963, 28, 928–40.

Bowen, E. S. *Return to laughter*. Garden City, N.Y.: Doubleday, 1954.

Breidenbach, P. S. Sunsum Edumwa, the spiritual work: Forms of symbolic action and communication in a Ghanaian movement. Doctoral dissertation. Northwestern University, 1973.

Buell, R. L. *The native problem in Africa*, Vol. 1. New York: Macmillan, 1928.

Burke, K. *A rhetoric of motives*. Englewood Cliffs, N.J.: Prentice-Hall, 1950.

Burke, K. *A grammar of motives*. Englewood Cliffs, N.J.: Prentice-Hall, 1954.

Capron, J. & Kohler, J. M. Pouvoir et pratique matrimoniale dans la société mossi. Paper presented at the XVth International Seminar on Family Research, Lomé, Togo, January, 1976.

Cartwright, J. R. *Politics in Sierra Leone 1947–1967*. Toronto: Univ. of Toronto Press, 1970.

Casagrande, J. B. (Ed.). *In the company of man*. New York: Harper, 1960.

Castaneda, C. *The teachings of Don Juan: A Yaqui way of knowledge*. New York: Ballantine, 1968.

Castaneda, C. *A separate reality: Further conversations with Don Juan*. New York: Simon & Schuster, 1971.

Castaneda, C. *A journey to Ixtlan*. New York: Simon & Schuster, 1972.

Castaneda, C. *Tales of power*. New York: Simon & Schuster, 1974.

Chomé, J. *La passion de Simon Kimbangu*. Brussels: Les Amis de Présence Africaine, 1959.

Cicourel, A. V. *Method and measurement in sociology*. New York: Free Press, 1964.

Cisse, Driss, personal communication, December 7, 1969.

Colle, P. *Les Baluba*. Brussels: Institut International de Bibliographie, 1913.

Colson, E. Spirit possession among the Tonga of Zambia. In J. Beattie & J. Middleton (Eds.), *Spirit mediumship and society in Africa*. New York: Africana Publishing Corp., 1969.

Curtin, P. D. Jihad in West Africa: Early phases and interrelations in Mauritania and Sénégal. *Journal of African history*, 1971, 12, 1, 11–24.

Dahl, R. *Who governs?* New Haven: Yale Univ. Press, 1961.

Dakar, Sénégal, National Archives, Registre 15G 199, 1899.

Dalby, D. The Mel languages: A reclassification of southern West Atlantic. *African Language Studies*, 1965, 6, 1–17.

Daneel, M. L. *The God of the Matopo Hills*. Leiden: Africa Study Center, 1970.

Daneel, M. L. *Old and new in southern Shona independent churches*. The Hague: Mouton, 1971.

D'Azevedo, W. L. Mask-makers and myth in western Liberia. In A. Forge (Ed.), *Primitive art and society*. London: Oxford Univ. Press, 1973.

De Craemer, W. *Analyse sociologique de la Jamaa*. Léopoldville (Kinshasa): Centre de recherches sociologiques, mimeographed, 1965.

De Craemer, W. Jamaa and Ecclesia: A charismatic movement in the Congolese Catholic Church. Doctoral dissertation, Harvard University, 1973.

Denzin, N. *The research act*. Chicago: Aldine, 1970.

Des Forges, Alison, personal communication, 1970.

Dieterlen, G. *Essai sur la religion Bambara*. Paris: Presses Universitaires de France, 1951.

District Tour Book, Kinkizi entry, Kigezi District Archives, April 1, 1938.

District Tour Book, entries of the Deputy Commissioner, Kigezi District Archives, Kagunga, Ruzhumbura, August 8, 1945.

District Tour Book, entires of the Deputy Commissioner, Kigezi District Archives, Kebisoni, Ruzhumbura, September 19, 1946.

Douglas, M. *The Lele of the Kasai*. London: International African Institute, 1963.

Douglas, M. The Lele of Kasai. In D. Forde (Ed.), *African worlds*. London: International African Institute, 1965.

Douglas, M. *Purity and danger: An analysis of the concepts of pollution and taboo*. New York: Praeger, 1966.

Douglas, M. *Natural symbols: Explorations in cosmology*. New York: Pantheon, 1970.

Dupire, M. Women in pastoral society. In D. Paulme (Ed.), *Women in tropical Africa*. Berkeley: Univ. of California Press, 1963.

Durkheim, E. *The elementary forms of the religious life*. New York: Free Press, 1965.

Edel, M. M. *The Chiga of western Uganda*. London: International African Institute, 1957.

Elam, Y. *The social and sexual roles of Hima women*. Manchester, England: Manchester Univ. Press, 1973.

Erchak, G. The position of women among the Kpelle of Liberia. *American Anthropologist*, 1974, 76, 2, 344–45.

Evans-Pritchard, E. E. *Witchcraft, oracles and magic among the Azande*. Oxford: Clarendon Press, 1937.

Evans-Pritchard, E. E. *Nuer religion*. London: Oxford Univ. Press, 1956.

Fabian, J. *Philosophie bantoue: Placide Tempels et son oeuvre vus dans une perspective historique*. Brussels: Etudes Africaines du CRISP, 1940.

Fabian, J. *Jamaa: A charismatic movement in Katanga*. Evanston, Ill.: Northwestern Univ. Press, 1971.

Fabian, J. Genres in an emerging tradition: An anthropological approach to religious communication. In A. W. Eister (Ed.), *Changing perspectives in the scientific study of religion*. New York: Wiley, 1974.

Fernandez, J. W. African religious movements: Types and dynamics. *Journal of modern African studies*, 1964, 2, 531–549.

Fernandez, J. W. The ethnic communion: Inter-ethnic recruitment in African religious movements. *Journal of African studies*, 1975, 2, 131–77.

Festinger, L. *A theory of cognitive dissonance*. New York: Row, Peterson, 1957.

Field, M. J. *Religion and medicine among the Ga paople*. London: Oxford University Press, 1937.

Fitzgerald, D. K. Prophetic speech in Ga spirit mediumship. Working paper No. 36, Language-Behavior Research Laboratory, Univ. of Berkeley, California, 1970.

Fofana, Babakr, personal communication, August 26, 1969 and September 5, 1969.

Fortes, M. Kinship and marriage among the Ashanti. In A. R. Radcliffe-Brown & D. Forde (Eds.), *African systems of kinship and marriage*. London: International African Institute, 1950.

Fortes, M. Religious premises and logical techniques in divinatory ritual. *Philosophical transactions of the royal society of London*, 1966, B, 251, 409–22.

Fortes, M. & G. Dieterlin (Eds.). *African systems of thought*. London: International African Institute, 1965.

Fox, R. C., De Craemer, W. & Ribeaucourt, J. M. The second independence: A case study of the Kwilu rebellion of the Congo. *Comparative studies in society and history*, 1965, 8, 78–110.

Fraenkel, M. *Tribe and class in Monrovia*. London: International African Institute, 1964.

Frisch, R. E. & McArthur, J, W, Menstrual cycles: Fatness as a determinant of weight necessary for their maintenance or onset. *Science*, 1974, 185, 949–51.

Fry, P. *Spirits of protest: Spirit mediums and the articulation of consensus amongst the Zezuru of southern Rhodesia (Zimbabwe)*. London: Cambridge Univ. Press, 1976.

Fyfe, H. *A history of Sierra Leone*. London: Oxford Univ. Press, 1962.

Fyfe, C. *Sierra Leone inheritance*. London: Oxford Univ. Press, 1964.

Garbett, G. K. Prestige, status, and power in a modern valley Korekore chiefdom, Rhodesia. *Africa*, 1967, 33, 207–25.

Garfinkel, H. *Studies in ethnomethodology*. Englewood Cliffs, N.J.: Prentice-Hall, 1967.

Garfinkel, H. & Sacks, H. On formal structures of practical actions. In E. Tiryakian & J. McKinney (Eds.), *Theoretical sociology*. New York: Appleton-Century-Crofts, 1970.

Ghana National Archives, January 9, 1918.

Ghana National Archives, Report of A. Q. Kyiamah to District Commissioner, Sekondi, February 6, 1940.

Gibbs, J. L. The Kpelle of Liberia. In J. L. Gibbs (Ed.), *Peoples of Africa*. New York: Holt, Rinehart & Winston, 1965.

Gluckman, M. *Custom and conflict in Africa*. New York: Free Press, 1956.

Gluckman, M. *The ideas in Barotse jurisprudence*. New Haven: Yale Univ. Press, 1969.

Golde, P. (Ed.). *Women in the field: Anthropological experiences*. Chicago: Aldine, 1970.

Goodale, J. C. *Tiwi wives*. Seattle: Univ. of Washington Press, 1971.

Greenberg, J. *The languages of Africa*. The Hague: Mouton, 1966.

Gurwitsch, A. *The field of consciousness*. Pittsburgh, Pa.: Duquesne Univ. Press, 1964.

Gusfield, J. R. *Utopian myths and movements in modern societies*. Morristown, N.J.: General Learning Corp., 1973.

Haliburton, G. MacK. *The prophet Harris*. London: Longman, 1971.

Harley, G. W. *Native African medicines*. Cambridge, England: Cambridge Univ. Press, 1941.

Hayford, J. E. Casley. *William Waddy Harris: the West African reformer*. London: Phillips, 1915.

Hayward, P. B. Displays of membership: Participation and change in Lusaka's indigenous churches. Doctoral dissertation, University of California, San Diego, 1977.

Hayward, P. B. Masculine identity and work performance: The case of ritual expression. Paper presented at the Annual Meetings of the Pacific Sociological Association, Spokane, April, 1978.

Hébert, G. and M. Guilhem. Notion et culte de Dieu chez les Toussian. *Anthropos*, 1967, 42, 1–2, 139–64.

Herskovits, M. J. African gods and Catholic saints in new world religious belief. *American Anthropologist*, 1937, 39, 635–43.

Herskovits, M. J. *Man and his works: The science of cultural anthropology*. New York: Knopf, 1948. (a)

Herskovits, M. J. The contribution of Afroamerican studies to Africanist research. *American anthropologist*, 1948, 50, 1–10. (b)

Hewitt, G. *The problem of success: A history of the church missionary society 1910–1942*. London: SCM Press, 1971.

Hoffer, C. P. MacC. *Acquisition and exercise of political power by a woman paramount chief of the Sherbro people*. Ann Arbor, Mich.: Xerox Univ. Microfilms, 1971.

Hoffer, C. P. MacC. Mende and Sherbro women in high office. *Canadian journal of African studies*, 1972, 6, 151–64.

Hoffer, C. P. MacC. Madam Yoko: Ruler of the Kpa Mende confederacy. In M. Z. Rosaldo & L. Lamphere (Eds.), *Woman, culture, and society*. Stanford: Stanford Univ. Press, 1974.

Holas, B. *Le separatisme religieux en Afrique noire*. Paris: Presses Universitaires de France, 1965.

Holleman, J. F. *Shona customary law*. Manchester, England: Manchester Univ. Press, 1952.

Holleman, J. F. Some Shona tribes in southern Rhodesia. In E. Colson & M. Gluckman (Eds.), *Seven tribes of British Central Africa*. Manchester, England: Manchester Univ. Press, 1961.

Hopkins, E. The Nyabingi cult of southwestern Uganda. In R. I. Rotherg and A. Mazuri (Eds.), *Protest and power in Black Africa*. New York: Oxford Univ. Press, 1970.

Horton, R. *Kalabari sculpture*. Lagos, Nigeria: Dept. of Antiquities, Federal Rep. of Nigeria, 1965.

Horton, R. African traditional thought and Western science. *Africa*, 1967, 38, 50–71, 155–87.

Horton, R. African conversion. *Africa*, 1971, 41, 1, 85–108.

Horton, R. On the rationality of conversion, Part One. *Africa*, 1975, 45, 3, 219–235.

Huber, H. A diviner's apprenticeship among the Bayaka. *Man*, 1965, 65, 46–48.

Ifeka-Moller, C. Female militancy and colonial revolt: The women's war of 1929, Eastern Nigeria. In E. Ardener (Ed.), *Perceiving women*. London: Malaby Press, 1975.

Jules-Rosette, B. Ritual contexts and social action: A study of the Apostolic Church of John Marangue. Doctoral dissertation, Harvard University, 1973.

Jules-Rosette, B. Ceremony and leadership: The influence of women in African independent churches. Paper presented at the UCLA African Studies Center Symposium Women and Change in Africa, 1870–1970, April, 1974. (a)

Jules-Rosette, B. Reflexive ethnography, part I: Instructions as data: The Apostolic case. Paper presented at the UCLA Ethnomethodology Colloquium, Los Angeles, May, 1974. (b)

Jules-Rosette, B. Some everyday uses of prophecy and curing among the Bapostolo. Paper presented at the 73rd Annual Meetings of the American Anthropological Association, Mexico City, 1974. (c)

Jules-Rosette, B. *African Apostles: Ritual and conversion in the church of John Maranke*. Ithaca: Cornell Univ. Press, 1975. (a)

Jules-Rosette, B. Marrapodi: An independent religious community in transition. *African studies review*, 1975, 18, 2. (b)

Jules-Rosette, B. Song and spirit: The use of song in the management of ritual settings. *Africa*, 1975, 45, 2, 150–65. (c)

Jules-Rosette, B. The conversion experience. *Journal of religion in Africa*, 1976, 7, 132–64. (a)

Jules-Rosette, B. Family and ceremonial authority. Paper presented at the XVth International Seminar on Family Research, Lomé, Togo, January, 1976. (b)

Jules-Rosette, B. The mushecho: A girls' purity rite. Companion to the edited videotape, "The Mushecho," first presented at the Seventh Annual Conference on Visual Anthropology, Temple University, Philadelphia, March, 1976. (c)

Jules-Rosette, B. Grass-roots ecumenism: Religious and social cooperation in two urban African churches. *African social research*, 1977, 23, 185–216.

Jules-Rosette, B. Art and ideology: The communicative significance of some urban art forms in Africa. *Semiotica*, spring, 1978. (a)

Jules-Rosette, B. From art to manufacture: Some aspects of contemporary art production in urban Africa. Paper presented at the Annual Meetings of the Northeastern Association, Middletown, Connecticut, 1978. (b)

Jules-Rosette, B. Prophecy and leadership in an African church: A case study in continuity and change. In G. Bond, S. Walker, & W. Johnson (Eds.), *Prophets and sects in black Africa*, 1978, forthcoming. (c)

Jules-Rosette, B. *Symbols of change: Urban transition in a Zambian community*. Completed manuscript, 1978.

Karugire, S. R. *A history of the kingdom of Nkore in western Nganda to 1896*. Oxford: Clarendon Press, 1971.

Kashoki, M. E. Between-language communication in Zambia. *Lingua*, 1977, 41, 145–68.

Kigezi District Annual Report, 1942, Kigezi District Archives.

Kileff, C. & Pendleton, W. (Eds.). *Urban man in Southern Africa*. Gwelo Country, Rhodesia: Mambo Press, 1975.

Kileff, M. The Apostolic Sabbath Church of God: Organization, ritual and belief. Unpublished manuscript, Univ. of Tennessee, Chattanooga, 1973.

Kilson, M. Libation in Ga ritual. *Journal of religion in Africa*, 1969, 161–78. (a)

Kilson, M. Taxonomy and form in Ga ritual. *Journal of religion in Africa*, 1969, 3, 45–60. (b)

Kilson, M. *Kpele Lala: Ga religious songs and symbols*. Cambridge, Mass.: Harvard Univ. Press, 1971. (a)

Kilson, M. Ambivalence and power: Mediums in Ga traditional religion. *Journal of religion in Africa*, 1971, 4, 171–77. (b)

Kilson, M. Twin beliefs and ceremony in Ga culture. *Journal of religion in Africa*, 1973, 5, 171–97.

Kilson, M. *African urban kinsmen: The Ga of Central Africa*. London: Hurst, 1974.

Kone, Iman, personal communication, December 6, 1969 and May 25, 1970.

Kuhn, T. *The structure of scientific revolutions*. Chicago: Univ. of Chicago Press, 1962.

Kyiamah, A. Q. Formal report, District Commissioner's Office at Sekondi on Activities of Water Carriers, February 4, National Archives, Cape Coast, 1940.

Lantenari, V. *Religions of the oppressed*. New York: Mentor, 1963.

Lanzas, A. & Bernard, G. Les fidèles d'une novelle église au Congo. *Genève-Afrique: Acta Africana*, 1966, 5, 189–216.

Leacock, S. & Leacock, M. *Spirits of the deep: A study of an Afro-Brazilian cult*. Garden City, N.Y.: Anchor Books, 1975.

Lee, R. B. What hunters do for a living. In R. B. Lee & I. De Vore (Eds.), *Man the hunter*. Chicago: Aldine, 1968.

Lewis, I. M. *Ecstatic religion: An anthropological study of spirit-possession and shamanism*. Harmondsworth, England: Penguin, 1971.

Linton, R. Nativistic movements. *American anthropologist*, 1943, 45, 230–240.

Little, K. *The Mende of Sierra Leone: An African people in transition*. London: Routledge & Kegan Paul, 1951.

Little, K. *West African urbanization: A study of voluntary associations in social change*. Cambridge, England: Cambridge Univ. Press, 1965–1966.

Little, K. The political function of the Poro. *Africa*, 1965, 35, 349–65; 1966, 36, 62–71.

Little, K. *African women in towns*. Cambridge, England: Cambridge Univ. Press, 1973.

Little, K. *Urbanization as a social process*. London: Routledge & Kegan Paul, 1974.

Long, N. *Social change and the individual*. Manchester: Manchester University Press, 1968.

MacCormack, C. P. Wono: Institutionalized dependency in Sherbro descent groups. In S. Miers & I. Kopytoff (Eds.), *Slavery in Africa: Historical and anthropological perspectives*. Madison [Wisc.]: Univ. of Wisconsin Press, 1977. (a)

MacCormack, C. P. Biological events and cultural control. *Signs*, 1977, 3, 93–100. (b)

Magubane, B. A critical look at indices used in the study of social change in colonial Africa. *Current Anthropology*, 1971, 12, Intro. 22, 415–45.

Mannah-Kpaka, J. K. Memoirs of the 1898 rising. *Sierra Leone Studies*, 1953, n.s., 1, 28–39.

Mannheim, K. *Essays on the sociology of knowledge*. London: Routledge & Kegan Paul, 1952.

Maranke, J. *The new witness of the Apostles*. Bocha, Rhodesia: Mimeographed, 1953.

Margai, M. A. S. Welfare work in a secret society. *African Affairs*, 1948, 47, 227–30.

Marris, P. *Loss and change*. Garden City, N.Y.: Anchor Books, 1975.

Martin, M-L. The Mai Chaza Church in Rhodesia. In D. B. Barrett (Ed.), *African initiatives in religion*. Nairobi, Kenya: East Africa Publishing House, 1971.

Marwick, M. The Bwanali-Mpulumutsi anti-witchcraft movement. In M. Marwick (Ed.), *Witchcraft and sorcery: Selected readings*. London: Penguin, 1950, 1970.

Mathieu, N-C. Homme-culture et femme-nature? *L'Homme*, 1973, 13, 101–13.

Mayer, P. *Townsmen or tribesmen*. Cape Town, South Africa: Oxford Univ. Press, 1961.

Mayoyo, R. Bimanye-Mane: Le liberateur du monde. Kananga, Zaire: Mimeographed, September, 1971.

Mbiti, J. S. *African religions and philosophy*. Garden City, N.Y.: Anchor Books, 1970.

Mendonsa, E. L. Divination among the Sisala of Northern Ghana. Doctoral dissertation, Cambridge University, 1973. (a)

Mendonsa, E., Sisala marriage. *Lambda Alpha Journal of Man*, 1973, 5, 2, 39–73. (b)

Mendonsa, E. Traditional and imposed political systems among the Sisala of Northern Ghana. *Savanna*, 1975, 4, 2, 103–15. (a)

Mendonsa, E. Characteristics of Sisala diviners. In A. Bharati (Ed.), *The realm of extrahuman agents and audiences*, No. 56 in Vol. 96, *World anthropology*. The Hague: Mouton, 1975. (b)

Mendonsa, E. Elders, office-holders and ancestors among the Sisala of Northern Ghana. *Africa*, 1976, 46, 57–65. (a)

Mendonsa, E. The value of children in Sisala society: Implications for demographic change. Paper presented at XVth International Seminar on Family Research, Lomé, Togo, January, 1976. (b)

Mendonsa, E. Aspects of Sisala marriage prestations. *Research Review*, 1976, 9, 3. (c)

Millett, K. *Sexual politics*. Garden City, N.Y.: Doubleday, 1970.

Mitchell, C. The meaning of misfortune for urban Africans. In M. Fortes & G. Dieterlin (Eds.), *African systems of thought*. London: International African Institute, 1965.

Mitchell, C. (Ed.). *Social networks in urban situations*. Manchester, England: Manchester Univ. Press, 1969.

Mlambo, E. *Rhodesia: The struggle for a birthright*. London, n.d.

Monfouga-Nicolas, J. *Ambivalence et culte de possession*. Paris: Editions Anthropos, 1972.

Morris, C. *The end of the missionary? A short account of the political consequences of missions in Northern Rhodesia*. London: Cargate, Methodist Missionary Society, 1962.

Murphree, M. W. *Christianity and the Shona*. London: Athlone Press, 1969.

Murphree, M. W. Religious interdependency among the Budjga Vapostori. In D. B. Barrett (Ed.), *African initiatives in religion*. Nairobi: East African Publishing House, 1971.

Nackabah, J. Bye-laws of the Twelve Apostles Mission Gold Coast Colony, November 7 (jointly signed with Madame Tani's mark). Essowa, Ghana: Church Archives, 1944.

Native Commissioner's File for the Rusape Chiefdom, S1542-M8B, National Archives of Rhodesia, Salisbury.

Needleman, J. *The new religions: The teachings of the East—their special meaning for young Americans*. New York: Pocket Books, 1973.

Niane, D. T. *Sundiata: An epic of old Mali*. London: Longmans, 1965.

Norbeck, E. *Religion in primitive society*. New York: Harper & Row, 1961.

O'Dea, T. F. *The sociology of religion*. Englewood Cliffs, N.J.: Prentice-Hall, 1966.

Oosthuizen, G. C. *Post-Christianity in Africa: A theological and anthropological study*. London: Hurst, 1968.

Parsons, T. *Sociological theory and modern society*. New York: Free Press, 1967.

Paulme, D. Une religion synchrétique on Côte d'Ivoire: le culte déima. *Cahiers des Études Africaines*, 1962, 3, 1, 5–90.

Pauwels, M. Le culte de Nyabingi (Ruanda). *Anthropos*, 1951, 46, 3–4, 337–57.

Pauw, B. A. *The second generation*. Cape Town, South Africa: Oxford Univ. Press, 1963.

Peaden, W. R. *Missionary attitudes to Shona culture 1890–1923*. Salisbury, Rhodesia: Central Africa Historical Pamphlet No. 27, 1970.

Peel, J. D. Y. *Aladura: A religious movement among the Yoruba*. London: Oxford University Press, 1968.

Peeraer, S. Toespraken tot jonggehuwden bij de Baluba (Katanga). *Kongo-Overzee*, 1939, 5, 241–76; 1943, 9, 1–59.

Perrin-Jassy, M-F. *La communauté de base dans les églises Africaines*. Bandundu, Zaire: Centre des Études Ethnologiques, Serie 2, 3, 1971.

Phillipps, J. E. T. The Nyabingi. *Congo* (Brussels), 9, Tome 1, 3, 1928, 310–21.

Pitt-Rivers, J. *The people of the Sierra*. Chicago: Univ. of Chicago Press, 1971.

Platt, G. & F. Weinstein. *The wish to be free*. New York: Free Press, 1969.

Powdermaker, H. *Stranger and friend: The way of an anthropologist*. New York: Norton, 1966.

Quimby, L. G. *Transformations of beliefs: Islam among the Dyula of Kongbougou from 1880–1970*. Doctoral dissertation. University of Wisconsin, 1972.

Ranger, T. The early history of independency in Southern Rhodesia. In W. M. Watt (Ed.), *Religion in Africa*. Univ. of Edinburgh, Centre of African Studies, mimeographed, 1964.

Ranger, T. The nineteenth century in Southern Rhodesia. In T. Ranger (Ed.), *Aspects of Central African history*. Evanston, Ill.: Northwestern Univ. Press, 1969.

Ranger, T. *The African voice in Southern Rhodesia.* Evanston, Ill.: Northwestern Univ. Press, 1970.

Ranger, T. *Dance and society in Eastern Africa, 1890–1970: The Beni Ngoma.* London: Heinemann, 1975.

Ranson, B. H. A. *A sociological study of Moyamba Town, Sierra Leone.* Zaria, Nigeria: Ahmadu Bello Univ. Press, 1968.

Rattray, R. S. *Ashanti.* London: Oxford Univ. Press, 1923.

Report to A. Q. Kyiamah to District Commissioner, Sekondi, Ghana National Archives, February 6, 1940.

Rhodesian National Archives, Salisbury, Rhodesia, File S1542 M8B, 1933.

Richards, Audrey I. *Chisungu: A girl's initiation ceremony among the Bemba of Northern Rhodesia.* London: Faber & Faber, 1956.

Rigby, P. Some Gogo rituals of purification: An essay on social and moral categories. In E. R. Leach (Ed.), *Dialectic in practical religion.* Cambridge, England: Cambridge Univ. Press, 1968.

Rigby, P. *Cattle and kinship among the Gogo.* Ithaca, N.Y.: Cornell Univ. Press, 1969.

Robins, C. E. *Tukutendereza:* A study of social change and withdrawal in the *Balokole* revival of Uganda. Doctoral Dissertation, Columbia University, 1975.

Roscoe, J. *The Bakitara or Banyoro: The first part of the report of the Machie ethnological expedition to Central Africa.* Cambridge, England: Cambridge Univ. Press, 1923.

Ross, A. G., District Commissioner, Ghana National Archives, January, 1918.

Sacks, H. Lecture notes, University of California, Irvine, mimeographed, 1966.

Sacks, H. On the analyzability of stories by children. In D. Hymes & J. J. Gumperz (Eds.), *Directions in sociolinguistics.* New York: Holt, Rinehart & Winston, 1972.

Sacks, H., Jefferson, G. & Schegloff, E. A simplest systematics for the organization of turn-taking in conversation. *Language,* 1975, 64, 696–735.

Sangree, W. H. The dynamics of separatist churches. Seminar paper, *Changing Africa and the Christian dynamic,* Center for the Study of the Christian World Mission, The Federated Theological Faculty, Univ. of Chicago, mimeographed, 1960.

Sanogho, Adam, personal communication, November 6, 1969.

Sanogho, Al-Haff Muhammed, personal communications, June 9, 1969, August 22, 1969, and May 26, 1969.

Sanogho, Basidiki, personal communication, February 28, 1970.

Sanogho, Bastikidi and Numutye Watara, personal communication, April 21, 1970.

Sanogho, Fajawa, personal communication, March 21, 1970.

Sanogho, Makosarran, personal communication, December 5, 1969.

Schutz, A. *Collected papers,* Vol. I. The Hague: Martinus Nijhoff, 1964.

Schwartz, T. The cargo cult: A Melanesian type response to change. In G. A. De Vos (Ed.), *Responses to change: Society, culture and personality.* New York: D. Van Nostrand, 1976.

Segall, M., Campbell, D. & Herskovitz, M. J. *The influence of culture on visual perception.* Indianapolis: Bobbs-Merrill, 1966.

Shepperson, G. *Independent African.* Edinburgh: Edinburgh Univ. Press, 1958.

Shepperson, G. Nyasaland and the millennium. In S. Thrupp (Ed.), *Millennial dreams in action. Comparative studies in society and history,* Suppl. 2. The Hague: Mouton, 1962.

Shepperson, G. Church and sect in central Africa. *Rhodes-Livingstone Journal,* 1963, 33, 82–93.

Sithole, N. The interaction of Christianity and African political development. Leverhulme History Conference, Salisbury, mimeographed, 1960.

Sierra Leone Government. *Report of the commission of enquiry into the conduct of certain chiefs and the government statement thereon.* London: Her Majesty's Stationery Office, 1957.

Smoker, D. E. W. Decision-making in East African revival movement groups. In D. B. Barret (Ed.), *African initiatives in religion. Twenty-one studies from east and central Africa.* Nairobi: East African Publishing House, 1971, 96–108.

Stenning, D. J. *Preliminary observations on the Balokole movement particularly among the Baluma in Ankole district.* Kampala, Uganda: East African Institute of Social Research, mimeographed, 1958.

Stenning, D. J. Communication to B. K. Taylor, *The Western Lacustrine Bantu* (ethnographic survey of Africa), 1962.

Stenning, D. J. Salvation in Ankole. In M. Fortes and G. Dieterlen (Eds.), *African systems of thought.* London: Oxford Univ. Press, 1965, 258–75.

Stren, R. E. *Urban inequality and housing policy in Tanzania.* Research Series No. 24, Berkeley, California, Institute of International Studies, 1975.

Sundkler, B. G. M. The concept of Christianity in the African independent churches. Seminar paper, University of Natal, Institute of Social Research, 1958.

Sundkler, B. G. M. *Bantu prophets in South Africa.* London: International African Institute, 1961.

Szombati-Fabian, Fabian, I. & Fabian, J. Art, History, and society: Popular art in Shaba, Zaire. *Studies in the Anthropology of Visual Communication,* 1976, 2, 2.

Tabate, Bassar, personal communication, July 29, 1970.

Taylor, J. V. *The growth of the church in Buganda.* London: SCM Press, 1958.

Taylor, J. V. & Lehmann, D. *Christians of the copperbelt.* London: SCM Press, 1961.

Tempels, P. Le mariage indigène et la loi. *Kongo-Overzee,* 10–11, 265–82, 1944–1945.

Tempels, P. *La philosophie bantoue.* Paris: Présence Africaine, 1945.

Tempels, P. *Bantu philosophy.* Paris: Présence Africaine, 1969.

Tempels, P. *Notre rencontre.* Leopoldville (Kinshasa): Orientales pastorales, 1962.

Thomas, H. B. & Scott, R. *Uganda.* London: Oxford Univ. Press, 1935.

Thrupp, S. (Ed.). *Millennial dreams in action. Comparative studies in society and history,* Suppl. 2. The Hague: Mouton, 1962.

Tiger, L. *Men in groups.* New York: Vintage, 1969.

Troeltsch, E. *Protestantism and progress* (W. Montgomery, trans). London: Williams and Norgale, 1912.

Tshiaba, D. with Gibson, Z. Église Apostolique par le Prophète John Marangue: Instructions Apostoliques. Kananga, mimeographed, 1970.

Turner, V. W. *Schism and continuity in an African society.* Manchester, England: Manchester Univ. Press, 1957.

Turner, V. W. *The forest of symbols: Aspects of Ndembu ritual.* Ithaca, N.Y.: Cornell Univ. Press, 1967.

Turner, V. W. *The drums of affliction.* London: Oxford Univ. Press, 1968.

Turner, V. W. *The ritual process: Structure and anti-structure.* Ithaca, N.Y.: Cornell Univ. Press, 1969.

Turner, J. H. & Starnes, C. E. *Inequality: Privilege and poverty in America.* Pacific Palisades, CA: Goodyear Publishing Co., 1976.

Twelve Apostles Church of Ghana, Church's earliest existing by-laws, meeting at Akobra (mouth), November 7, 1944.

Van Allen, J. Sitting on a man: Colonialism and the lost political institutions of Igbo women. *Canadian Journal of African Studies,* 1972, 6, 165–82.

Van Avermaet, E. & Mbuya, B. *Dictionnaire Kiluba-Francais.* Tervuren: Musée Royal, 1954.

Van Gennep, A. *The rites of passage.* Chicago: Univ. of Chicago Press, 1960.

Vansina, J. *Kingdoms of the Savanna.* Madison, Wisc.: Univ. of Wisconsin Press, 1968.

Vansina, J. Ndop: Royal statues among the Kuba. In D. Fraser & H. M. Cole (Eds.), *African art and leadership.* Madison, Wisc.: Univ. of Wisconsin Press, 1972.

Walker, S. S. *Ceremonial spirit possession in Africa and Afro-America.* Leiden: Brill, 1972.

Walker, S. S. Christianity African style: The Harrist Church of the Ivory Coast. Doctoral dissertation, Univ. of Chicago, 1975. (a)

Walker, S. S. The medium as the message: Harrist Churches in the Ivory Coast. Unpublished manuscript, University of California, Berkeley, 1975. (b)

Wallace, A. F. C. Revitalization movements. *American Anthropologist,* 1956, 58, 264–81.

Warren, M. A. C. *Revival: An inquiry.* London: SCM Press, 1954.

Watara, Al-Haff Babu, personal communication, February 16, 1970.

Watara, Badawa, personal communications, November 16, 1969 and February 24, 1970.

Watara, Bamori, personal communications, March 25, 1970, April 16, 1970, May 10, 1970, and May 16, 1970.

Watara, Francis, personal communication, June 18, 1970.

Watara, Kokasori, personal communications, December 13, 1969 and July 6, 1970.

Watara, Ladji Babu, personal communication, March 16, 1970.

Watara, Numutye, personal communication, February 27, 1970 and July 6, 1970.

Weber, M. *The theory of social and economic organization* (T. Parsons, trans.). New York: Free Press, 1947.

Weber, M. *The Protestant ethic and the spirit of capitalism.* New York: Scribner, 1958.

Weber, M. *The sociology of religion* (E. Fischoff, trans.). Boston: Beacon Press, 1964.

Welmers, W. E. Secret medicines, magic, and rites of the Kpelle tribe in Liberia. *Southwestern Journal of Anthropology,* 1949, 5, 208–43.

West, M. African churches in Soweto, Johannesburg. In C. Kileff & W. Pendleton (Eds.), *Urban man in Southern Africa.* Gwelo, Rhodesia: Mambo Press, 1975.

Whitaker, R. *The language of film.* Englewood Cliffs, N.J.: Prentice-Hall, 1970.

Wilks, I. The transmission of Islamic learning in the Western Sudan. *Literacy in traditional societies,* 1968, 161–97.

Wilson, B. R. *Religious sects.* London: World University Library, 1970.

Wilson, B. R. *Magic and the millenium: A sociological study of religious movements of protest among tribal and Third World peoples.* London: Heinemann, 1973.

Worsley, P. *The trumpet shall sound.* New York: Schocken Books, 1968.

Young, C. *Politics in the Congo: Decolonization and independence.* Princeton, N.J.: Princeton Univ. Press, 1965.

Anon. Court Brief: Accusation of fetish worship against John Nackabah, Church Archives, Essowa, January 8, 1918.

Author Index

Page numbers in *italics* indicate where complete references are listed.

Subject Index